8.95

Corvina Books

Graham Petrie

History Must Answer to Man

The Contemporary Hungarian Cinema

Corvina Kiadó

Cover by István Murányi
Design by Zsuzsa Mező
Photographs by courtesy of Hungarofilm, Budapest

ISBN 963 13 0485 X
Printed in Hungary, 1978
Kner Printing House, Gyoma

Contents

Preface

The organization of a book of this kind, which is intended to introduce to English-speaking audiences a tradition of film that is still almost completely unknown to them, presents considerable problems. Most serious film-goers, for example, will probably know something about Miklós Jancsó, though—despite the valiant efforts of the Academy Cinema in London, and the New York Film Festival—they may not have had much opportunity to see very many of his films. And though individual films by Gaál, Szabó, Makk and others have been highly praised and quite widely shown, these tend to appear, for American and British viewers, almost literally out of a vacuum: there is not the sense of a personal and historical context in which to place them that is taken for granted with even second-rank French and Italian directors.

I have also wanted to avoid an arrangement that simply provides brief descriptions of dozens, or hundreds of films, most of them probably unknown to the reader. The method I have chosen, therefore, is selective, concentrating on those directors I consider to be most significant, and providing a thorough consideration of their work. The final chapter is not intended to be all-inclusive but provides, again, a selective overview of significant tendencies and works in the past decade.

I have felt obliged, under these circumstances, to provide a good deal of description of the content of most of the works discussed, though I have always attempted to do this in such a way that something of the *feel* of the film—its mood, style, and outlook, and not just its plot—is conveyed to the reader. The exception is the chapter on Jancsó, which takes up approximately half the book: here, working on the assumption that something at least is already known about the films, I have felt free to carry out a more detailed and thorough critical analysis that I hope will contribute to a better understanding of the way in which his work has developed over the past fifteen years. A more modest hope is that this book might encourage distributors to take a chance on making more Hungarian films available to the English-speaking public: in terms of quality alone, they deserve the opportunity.

I would like to express thanks to the following, whose encouragement and practical assistance proved invaluable in the conception and writing of this book: Miklós and Tünde Vajda, Lia Somogyi, Vera Surányi, Márta Ozorai, and István Gaál. Also to Hungarofilm (Budapest), Faroun Films (Montreal), McMaster University (Hamilton, Ontario), and the Hungarian Institute of Cultural Relations (Budapest). for generous financial assistance in enabling me to travel to view the films, or for making the films themselves available to me. Photographs are reproduced by courtesy of Hungarofilm.

Chapter One

The Soil Under Your Feet

In its seventy-five year history, Hungarian cinema has enjoyed two major periods of widespread international recognition. The first, from 1955 to 1958, saw the appearance of such films as *Merry-Go-Round, Professor Hannibal, A Sunday Romance* and *The House Under the Rocks*, the first three of which in particular are still respectfully mentioned in any standard history of the cinema. These films were backed up by such works as *Spring Comes to Budapest* and *Abyss* which, though less well known abroad, testify to the overall strength of the Hungarian cinema of this period. The second, which can be dated from 1963 or 1964, with the first major works of Miklós Jancsó, István Gaál and István Szabó, reached its peak in the early 1970s (in terms of international acclaim at least), but can legitimately be seen as continuing in major works by each of these figures and in the existence of a new generation of very talented directors to support them.

Despite the fact, however, that Hungarian cinema of the past decade has long been acknowledged as the most consistently interesting in Eastern Europe and one of the more significant features in European cinema as a whole, much of the best work has been seen only intermittently in the English-speaking world and, when seen, it has often been misunderstood or misinterpreted. Part of this can be attributed to the notorious cultural laziness, or blindness, or arrogance, of Anglo-Saxon society: it has long been taken for granted that, outside Britain and America themselves, the only cultural traditions worth taking seriously are those of France, Italy, Germany, Spain and Russia. The occasional Norwegian playwright, Swedish film director or Polish composer may break through this barrier, but there is rarely much interest in examining in any depth the artistic or social heritage from which his works derive.

Where Hungary is concerned, the problem is compounded by an extremely difficult (and, to a foreigner, almost unpronounceable) language, and by the fact that many of the best Hungarian films take their starting-point in historical events that are only vaguely known to, or comprehended by, outsiders. Linked to this is the question of the political content or intention of the movies: to some in the West they are merely Socialist propaganda, and therefore bad; to others they are Socialist propaganda, and therefore good. For both sides, the question of artistic merit is almost wholly irrelevant.

It must be admitted that, occasionally, these barriers are insurmountable, and that there are a few Hungarian films whose meaning is opaque or incomprehensible to even the best-intentioned foreigner. Usually, however, despite the unfamiliar settings, costumes, and behaviour, the films are dealing with emotions and ideas to which anyone can relate: love, hate, fear, forgiveness, betrayal, on the personal level; responsibility, guilt, self-respect, integrity, loyalty, in the social or political sphere. These topics may suggest a certain sombreness of tone, and it is true that Hungarian films are rarely particularly light-hearted. There are very few good film comedies, for example: although Károly Makk's *Liliomfi* and Zoltán Fábri's *The Tót Family* are highly admired within Hungary, both strike me as heavy-handed in their effects and lethargic in their pacing. The country's tragic history during this century may provide a clue as to why Hungarians, by nature extremely convivial and warm-hearted people, should find it difficult to transfer these characteristics into their art.

Hungary has a long tradition of making films designed to reveal and explore social conflicts and even before the nationalization of the film industry in 1948, the best Hungarian films had almost always chosen to tackle rather than ignore social and political problems. The period up to 1918 shows much the same characteristics as in other countries: the films of the Lumière Brothers were being exhibited in Budapest soon after 1896, and a native film industry developed shortly afterwards.[1] Hungary was apparently unusual in deriving almost all its films from literary sources; nevertheless by 1918 a high artistic standard had been achieved and two of the most prominent figures, Mihály Kertész and Sándor Korda, were later to gain international recognition as Michael Curtis and Alexander Korda respectively. Most of these

[1] Much of my factual information on the pre-1930 period is obtained from: István Nemeskürty, *Word and Image: History of the Hungarian Cinema* (Corvina Press: Budapest, 1968).

films were essentially commercial in their orientation, though one of the few films by Kertész that survives, *My Brother's Return*, displays a strong revolutionary fervour.

During the brief period of the Republic of Councils in 1919, the film industry was nationalized (even before that of the USSR), and thirty-one feature films were made. Only one of these, *Yesterday*, still exists: touchingly clumsy in its execution, it is a story of class warfare, a factory strike, and bourgeois decadence.[2] With the repression of the Republic of Councils and the White Terror that followed, film as an art virtually ceased to exist in Hungary, and when the industry was fully re-established in the 1930's it was once more in the hands of private enterprise and geared primarily towards entertainment. Yet even in these conditions traces of a social conscience remain: the most successful Hungarian film of this decade, *Hyppolit the Butler* (1931)—a work whose popularity has persisted through a series of revivals, the most recent only two or three years ago—is a satire on middle-class pretentiousness and social climbing; and *Spring Shower* (1932), directed by Paul Fejős,[3] is a powerful indictment of bourgeois hypocrisy and exploitation and of the narrow-minded intolerance of village life. The serving-maid in a middle-class household is seduced

[2] Not all the films made or planned in this period displayed such a strong Socialist orientation, though a significantly high proportion of them did.

[3] Paul Fejős (1897–1963) made films in Hungary, the United States France, Austria, Denmark and the Far East. His two "Hungarian periods" were from 1920 to 1923 and in 1932, when he made two films. His best-known American films are *Lonesome* (1928) and *Broadway* (1929).

by the suitor of the daughter of the family, and becomes pregnant. She is brusquely and humiliatingly dismissed and rejected by all the respectable inhabitants of her village. She finds her way to a town where she is befriended by the Madam of a brothel and allowed to live there until the child is born. A group of local women decide, however, that it is immoral for a child to be brought up in these circumstances, and forcibly remove it to an orphanage. The distraught girl returns to her village where she is once more harried and mistreated until, on her death, she is seen ascending to Heaven accompanied by an angelic choir. This facile religiosity is redeemed to some extent by a tongue-in-cheek conclusion that shows her emptying out a bowl of water from her household chores in Heaven, thus causing a "spring shower" that drives indoors her daughter who is on the point of succumbing to the same fate as herself. Though the plot is rather tritely melodramatic, Fejős creates some very powerful scenes, notably one in the brothel where the clients sit around in silent, nervous suspense as the birth takes place upstairs, then break out into exultant rejoicing when the safe delivery is announced. The use of music in this and other scenes is particularly striking.

In the midst of the turmoil of the Second World War, a film was produced that both sums up the finest elements in earlier Hungarian cinema and points the way to the most interesting developments of the next two decades. Directed by István Szőts, *People on the Alps* (1942) possesses the strong feeling for landscape and setting, the sense of taking place in an unforgettably real and concrete environment that characterises Hungarian film art at its best. The story is one of class conflict: it details the exploitation of a community of forestry workers by the local landowner and their growing sense of solidarity as they come to understand the nature of their situation more clearly, instead of passively accepting it as divinely ordained. The finest parts of the film come at its beginning and its end: it opens with a series of beautiful sequences in which a woodcutter and his wife baptise their baby with frozen holy water brought home in his pocket by the father, the priest being unable to come to them through the snowstorm; later they take the child on an expedition through the forest, introducing him to the trees, birds, animals and fish among whom he will live, and receiving spontaneously offered gifts from their neighbours. Towards the end, when the wife has died as a result of the landlord's ill-treatment, her impoverished husband is forced to resort to deception to bring her body home for burial: he takes her on to the train, pretending that she is ill; gradually the other passengers and even the conductor guess the truth but they keep silent. He carries her body back through the familiar Transylvanian landscape, darkly silhouetted against the mist and trees; after her burial he kills the landlord and is arrested. His fellow foresters get the date of his trial wrong and arrive to plead in his defence after he has been found guilty; they offer in vain to serve his sentence instead or share it between them. They make themselves responsible for his child, however, and the film ends with their performance for him of a Nativity play they have created for themselves.

The quality of the film comes largely from the sobriety

of its treatment, its rejection of melodrama or overt pathos, its steady concentration on facts rather than emotions, and the manner in which it conveys that none of this is exceptional and is merely what is to be expected as part of a corrupt and unjust social system. Szőts made one other film, of almost equal quality, before vanishing from the Hungarian film scene (he now lives in Vienna). *Song of the Cornfields* (1947) is more fatalistic in its implications than *People on the Alps* and concentrates almost exclusively on the personal tragedy at its centre, though it places this in a firmly realised background of poverty, back-breaking toil, and superstition. The images throughout convey a strong sense of darkness and oppressiveness, achieved largely through the consistent use of heavy shadows and low-angle shots, most notably in the scenes that show the half-crazed wife deluded into acting as a "holy woman" so that the local fortune-teller can better exploit the superstitious peasants.

In 1947 also appeared one of the most remarkable of all Hungarian films, *Somewhere in Europe* (directed by Géza Radványi)—a film that deserves to be much better known than it is and at least to rank alongside such Italian neo-realist works as *Open City* and *Bicycle Thieves*. A group of children, ranging in age from 5 to 17 or 18, orphaned by the war or separated from their parents, band together to keep alive by raiding untended farms and fields. The first half of the film chronicles, quietly and absolutely without sentimentality, the process by which they become steadily more hardened and anarchic: they take the boots from the bodies of men hanged by the wayside, they are chased and shot at by indignant farmers, they come to accept death and deprivation as their normal lot in life. Finally they discover an old musician living alone in a half ruined castle: they over-power him and tie him up and, in an extraordinary sequence, begin an orgy of singing, dancing and drinking, at the end of which some of the ten year olds are on the point of putting their prisoner to death and are restrained only by the intervention of the oldest member of the group.

Gradually the old man wins their trust, however; he provides food and shelter for them, and with the help of the older boys, begins to lead them back to some kind of normal existence. They start to co-operate with each other instead of fighting for every scrap of food, they help the musician repair parts of the castle, they achieve, under his guidance, a sense of community, identity, and responsibility. But the local villagers learn that they are living in the castle and resolve to root them out and put them where they belong—in prison. An armed attack on the castle in the old man's absence is repulsed, but the smallest child is gravely wounded. The others decide to take him *en masse* to find a doctor, knowing perfectly well what their subsequent fate will be. The revengeful villagers hastily put them on trial, but the old man re-turns and, in an impassioned and moving speech, shames them into an awareness of the hypocrisy and brutality of their behaviour: the adults who have created the cir-cumstances in which the children find themselves have no right to punish them for doing what they can to stay alive. Not a word or an image in the film rings false, the acting is superlative throughout, and the humanity and

People on te Alps: much of later Hungarian cinema is implicit in this image: a barren landscape, a solitary fugitive, a gendarme with a feathered hat

People on the Alps: the woodcutter and his wife admire their baby

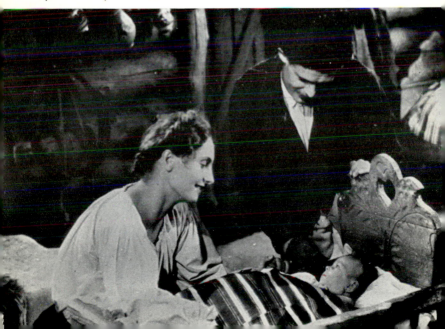

Géza Radványi

Somewhere in Europe: the children make themselves at home in the ruined ▶
castle where the old musician lives

Somewhere in Europe: the children overpower the musician (Arthur ▶
Somlay) and threaten to kill him

Merry-Go-Round: the peasant woman sadly advises her daughter to resign herself to fate and marry the rich suitor chosen for her by her father

◀ Zoltán Fábri

Merry-Go-Roud: Mari Töröcsik and Imre Soós as the young lovers

Professor Hannibal: the isolated, lonely teacher (Ernő Szabó) is abused, denounced, stoned, chased and beaten...

The Unfinished Sentence: Lőrinc (András Bálint) discovers the body of the murdered worker

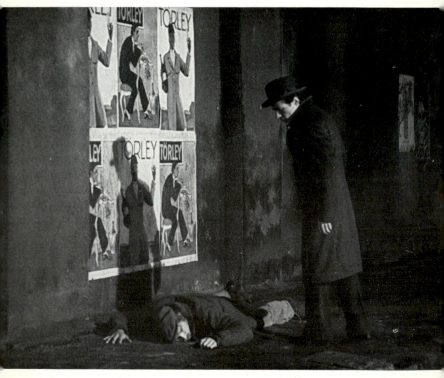

compassion that permeate it speak just as clearly today as they did thirty years ago.

The nationalization of the Hungarian film industry in 1948 brought not so much a change of direction then, as a firmer ideological standpoint from which films came to be made. Frigyes Bán's *The Soil Under Your Feet* (1948) takes up themes from the work of Szőts in particular and handles them with almost equal effectiveness.[4] Once again the basic problem is class conflict: a young girl forced into marriage with a rich suitor runs away on her wedding night with her former lover. The rejected groom offers to allow a divorce if the couple can pay back all the wedding expenses incurred by his family. In his attempt to earn the money the young man is cheated by his boss and then fired when he protests the latter's attempt to rape his wife. Finally he and a friend start an irrigation project of their own but are forced by drought to divert water from the landowner's illegally maintained dam in order to survive. The landlord arrives, protected by gendarmes, to defend his property; the friend is shot and the young man kills the landowner in the ensuing scuffle. An epilogue indicates that injustice of this type will no longer exist after 1945. The film is made with considerable visual power and the sequence of the water-stealing is edited with a vitality comparable to the irrigation scenes of Vidor's *Our Daily Bread*: ideology and artistic skill co-exist happily together.

This state of affairs, unfortunately, lasted for little more than a couple of years and, under the Rákosi

---

[4] Szőts was in fact originally scheduled to direct the film.

regime, the legitimate concern with social justice hardened into ever cruder and more rigid propaganda. Even quite talented directors and otherwise quite interesting films were blemished to a greater or lesser extent by this process. Félix Máriássy in *Anna Szabó* (1949) handles with some degree of interest a standard theme of the period: a conscientious factory supervisor instils a sense of responsibility into the frivolous or lazy women in her charge, and also finds times to shame her admirer into a realization that his private and working lives must both meet the same high standards; but certain elements within the film have little artistic justification. Near the end, for example, the workers emerge from the factory counting their productivity bonuses, and in the upper left-hand corner of the frame a slogan in praise of Rákosi is visible: the moral is clearly that Rákosi is responsible for their prosperity. Another quite interesting film, *The Birth of Menyhért Simon* (1954), that clearly derives from *People on the Alps* in its story of how the neighbours of a couple trapped by a blizzard in the mountains co-operate to bring a doctor to the pregnant wife, suffers from its over-insistence on the fact that it is the local Communist Party official who is responsible for getting the rescue operation under way and inducing the initially recalcitrant town-dwellers to take part. This film was directed by Zoltán Várkonyi, who is still a prolific and active figure on the Hungarian film scene.

A less dogmatic tone began to make itself felt in the mid-1950's and Hungarian cinema found itself able to return to a more relaxed, though no less committed standpoint. Máriássy's *Spring Comes to Budapest* (1955), with its vivid reconstruction of the last days of the German occupation in 1944, had pointed the way: the film concentrates on the basic humanity of the characters rather than on their ideological position, and such anomalies as the Countess who sets up her own table and china amid the general disorder of the air-raid shelter are treated as subjects for wry humour rather than denunciation. Nevertheless sequences like the mass shooting of Jews on the banks of the Danube, or the defeated Fascists using civilians as hostages against the advancing Russians, give the film a horrifying immediacy.

It was the work of Zoltán Fábri, however, which first brought Hungarian cinema back into international recognition. In *Merry-Go-Round* (1955) he set a convincingly created love story against a background of social conflict and succeeded in making the two elements interrelate and give force one to the other. Despite some unfortunate over-acting near the beginning, the film still holds up well today and certain sequences are especially memorable: a peasant woman of 38 (who looks more like 60) mechanically shells corn as she sadly advises her daughter to resign herself to fate and marry the rich suitor chosen for her by her father; a clock ticks monotonously in the background and a tap drips water, emphasising the empty routine that is behind the one woman and awaits the other. Later in the film we are shown a peasant wedding in which the girl (as a guest) dances with her true lover, making their relationship obvious to all: the hypnotic whirling of the dancers, the unceasing frenzy of the music, the ever increasing pace of the cutting, all combine to make the audience share the young couple's sense of existing on their own, outside space and time.

In *Professor Hannibal* (1956) Fábri details the mindless persecution of a shy, retiring schoolteacher who finds himself used as a pawn in the political in-fighting that attended the birth of Hungarian Fascism in the late 1920's. The world around him becomes steadily more nightmarish and beyond his comprehension, his most innocent statements and actions are twisted out of all recognition and turned against him, the friend who had promised to help him rehabilitate himself becomes his chief accuser and denounces him as a traitor at a mass rally. The most successful scene takes place at a swimming bath with artificial waves in which the teacher tries desperately to keep his footing while he explains his problems to his "friend"; the latter, while sympathising with him, can't resist the temptation of knocking him off balance and almost drowning him—just as a joke. The intention behind the climactic final sequence of the Fascist rally is admirable—the isolated, lonely teacher is abused, denounced, stoned, chased and beaten, till, to save his life, he recants, uttering a stream of absurdities that the crowd delightedly greets as divine wisdom—but the filming is often crudely over-emphatic, weakening rather than reinforcing the horror of the situation. During these scenes his pupils look on, trying to understand how the man who spoke to them so nobly of ideals could come to betray them; ironically, his recantation does not even save his life, for he later falls to his death from the steps of the amphitheatre.

Imre Fehér's *A Sunday Romance* (1957) tells the story

of a love affair destroyed by class barriers: during the First World War an upper class young man whose profession is journalism but who is in the army reserve and required to wear his uniform on Sunday, picks up a servant girl one Sunday in the park. She assumes that he is of her social class and they begin to meet once a week, the young man rather enjoying the knowledge that the girl works for the family of the young lady with whom he has an "understanding". Finally he forces a confrontation on her by accepting an invitation to dine with this family; the result is that she loses her job but also firmly rejects his belated attempt at reconciliation. The film still possesses considerable freshness and insight: the young man's selfishness and thoughtlessness are well conveyed, as is his sudden repentance; the petty bullying of the girl by her employers and their sublime unawareness that she might actually be human are convincing in themselves and make the dinner party revelation even more shocking for them; and the background of war, death, and mutilation is kept unobtrusively in view throughout the film.

The work of László Ranódy has never gained the international acclaim awarded to these films but, at its best, it possesses considerable interest. In *Abyss* (1956) a schoolteacher returns to work in his native village and is shocked by the poverty and misery that he finds there. He determines to work for improvement through harmony and persuasion; meanwhile the rapacity of the local landowner, whose daughter the teacher is courting, is shown to be the chief cause of the people's problems. Waking at last to this fact, the teacher realises that social justice must be fought for if it is to be more than a pious hope, even though this recognition leads for him to the loss of his fiancée. Ranódy's *For Whom the Larks Sing* (1959) also has a pre-1945 setting and presents a rather subtler version of social conflict. Here the "oppressor" (a slightly richer than average farmer) is almost as much of a victim as those who are forced by poverty to work for him: his own sense of being caught in a trap is the cause of much of the brutality and hostility he displays towards others. The bleak setting of the whitewashed farmhouse on the empty plain; the pathetic furnishings and ornaments with which the wife has attempted to give it some warmth; the series of 360 degree pans that follow the pregnant servant girl as she wheels a barrow round and round the yard in a vain attempt to induce an abortion; the young couple's wedding day, with its highlights of a visit to the man's mother as she slaves over the washing tub and the purchase, with most of their savings, of a couple of lollipops—all these give the film a memorable authenticity.

Despite the undoubted quality of almost all the films discussed, it has to be pointed out that none of the really significant works produced between 1945 and 1960 (not even *Somewhere in Europe*) is set at a date that corresponds *exactly* to the time at which the film was made: there is always a gap of at least two or three years, and most usually twenty or thirty. Much of this can be attributed to the political conditions and tensions of the 1950's, which allowed considerable freedom in the discussion of the mistakes and injustices of the past, but left much less scope for honest analysis of the problems of the present. The appearance of Károly Makk's *The Fanatics* in 1961 is therefore something of a landmark, even if the film seems nowadays somewhat simplistic and schematic. Makk had begun his career in film-making at the age of 19 and had worked on *Somewhere in Europe*; he was still under 30 when he directed his own first feature, *Liliomfi*. He later gained considerable acclaim for *The House Under the Rocks* (1958), a morbid and gloomy story of the thwarted love of a hunchbacked woman for her brother-in-law that fails to escape being ludicrous in its most solemn and melodramatic moments.

Though it is based on an actual event, *The Fanatics* borrows heavily from *The Soil Under Your Feet* in its story of how two engineers back their hunch that an underground sea can be used to irrigate a section of barren and infertile landscape; they resist bureaucratic indifference that turns to hostility and persecution when they refuse to back down, but their project is ensured success only when an influential Cabinet Minister throws his weight behind it. The film's open criticism of official rigidity and narrow-mindedness (even though this is limited to one specific, clearly defined instance and tempered by the intervention of a more tolerant official) and its firm backing of the judgement of a qualified individual, heralded a change of atmosphere that was to lead to the great flowering of Hungarian cinema over the next few years.

By 1960, then, firm foundations had been laid on which a generation of newer directors was able to build: a thematic orientation and even an iconography had been established that were carried over almost intact into works that were in other ways very different from the films of the 1950's. Personal and even enigmatic as Jancsó's films often are, for example, they contain a whole pattern of visual imagery to which Hungarian audiences had become accustomed from *The Soil Under Your Feet* onwards, but which Western audiences tend to see as bizarrely remote and exotic. The menacing soldiers with their rifles and plumed hats; the peasants in their dark suits, with their weatherbeaten, impassive faces; the isolated, whitewashed farmhouses set in the middle of a barren plain — these and other images, though used with an intensity and subtlety that surpass Jancsó's predecessors, are part of a common heritage that he shares with Gaál, Kósa and others and that each has reworked for his own way and for his own purposes.

Although one can definitely talk about a "new generation" of film-makers that came into prominence in the early 1960's, the situation is not really comparable to a phenomenon like the French *Nouvelle Vague* of roughly the same period. Whereas the young French directors saw themselves as consciously rejecting a once rich cinematic tradition that had (with a few cherished exceptions) become stale and shallow, their Hungarian equivalents were content to base themselves on the achievements of the past and continued to take it for granted that their task as film artists was to explore and analyse their society and the forces that had brought it into being. Moreover, some of the older directors, [5] like Fábri with

[5] The term "old" is a relative one here. Makk, who was born in 1925, began making films in the early 1950's, at the same time as the rather older Fábri and Ranódy. In turn he is only a few years older than such members of the "younger" generation as Pál Gábor and Zoltán Huszárik who made their first features around 1970.

Twenty Hours (1964) and Makk with *The Fanatics* and *Love* (1970), showed that they were capable of expanding their range and even of opening up new avenues of theme and subject matter for their younger contemporaries to explore.

The renaissance of Hungarian film-making that made itself felt around 1963 coincides with the first features made by a group of directors who had graduated from the Academy for Theatre and Cinematography in the late 1950s, many of them afterwards working together at the Béla Balázs studio that had been created in 1958 to allow the production of experimental low-budget films, free from the bureaucratic pressure that accompanied "serious" film-making. Apart from their own innate and varied abilities, these people had the confidence that comes from a sound training in their craft, together with the satisfaction of knowing that their aspirations and aims as artists were shared by a body of like-minded people of their own age. The relatively small scale of film-making in Hungary (an average of twenty films a year, some half-dozen of which have serious artistic pretensions) ensures that all the major directors know each other well and often collaborate on each other's films, as scriptwriters or cameramen. Another source of inspiration was certainly a growing familiarity with the best work being produced elsewhere in Europe, and the influence of Bergman, Truffaut, Godard, Fellini and Resnais is particularly noticeable.

Although there are regular complaints that not enough younger directors are being given a chance to make features, the Hungarian system seems to ensure that newcomers move into feature film-making in their early

or mid-thirties[6] (a few, like István Szabó, even earlier)—
a pattern that compares favourably with most other film
industries—and that directors of all ages, from thirty to
seventy, are working under the same conditions and in
much the same atmosphere. All budding film-makers
must, of course, graduate from the Academy for Theatre
and Cinematography, where they receive a thorough
professional training in all aspects of film-making, en-
suring that each director is normally also a competent
scriptwriter, cameraman, and film editor.

On graduation, a director becomes an employee of the
state and is paid a basic monthly salary with bonuses
when he is working on a film and further remuneration
according to the film's ranking in the annual classifica-
tions for artistic merit. When he wishes to make a film,
he may offer the script to either of four studios and may
obtain financing from the studio, the Ministry of Culture,
and one or two other recognised sources. The completed
script must be approved by the Ministry of Culture and
the film itself must also be submitted before release. In
practice, few films nowadays are significantly altered or
withheld from distribution.

Hungarian audiences, like audiences everywhere, prefer films that entertain to those that challenge or puzzle
them, yet some of the finest of the new Hungarian films
have also been very successful at the box-office. In an
attempt to improve the level of sophistication of the

---

[6] Here are some of the ages, for example, at which directors made
their first feature films: Judit Elek, 32; István Gaál, 30; Ferenc Kardos,
28; Zsolt Kézdi-Kovács, 34; Ferenc Kósa, 28; Márta Mészáros, 37;
János Rózsa, 28; Pál Sándor, 28; István Szabó, 26.

film-going public, most Hungarian schools now offer a systematic, if somewhat sketchy, programme of film study in the last four years of high school. This involves the viewing of some Hungarian classics (Gaál's *Current*, Ranódy's *Skylark*, Jancsó's *The Round-Up*) as well as such foreign works as Fellini's *La Strada* and Richardson's *Loneliness of the Long-Distance Runner*.

The high quality of Hungarian film in the past decade, then, is not the result of accident: it stems from a combination of individual talent, a well-established and respected film tradition, and an official policy which, if sometimes guilty of excess and blindnesses, has been generally positive and enlightened. It is now time to examine what resulted from the coming together of these elements.

Chapter Two

Somewhere in Europe: Miklós Jancsó

Despite the overall unity of Hungarian cinema already noted, there have been several periods of total or relative stagnation in the country's film history. One of these occurred between 1958 and 1962, when only a handful of films of any real interest was produced and even the best of these (Makk's *The Fanatics*, Ranódy's *For Whom the Larks Sing*, and *Land of the Angels* by György Révész) display a heavy-handedness that contrasts sharply with the more open, sceptical, and subtle work that was soon to appear from the younger generation of directors. *Land of the Angels* (1962), for example, which has as its subject the gradual growth of working class solidarity in a slum area in response to the harassment of landlords and factory bosses, persistently overstates and over-emphasises its case, though some scenes, especially those that show a young girl forced by poverty to work as an automaton in a routine at a sleazy fairground, have a weird, almost expressionistic power.

During this period there appeared the first feature film by a director already in his late thirties who had been turning out a series of documentaries since 1954. *The Bells Have Gone to Rome* (1958) is a laboured, dogmatic piece of work that in no way rises above the general mediocrity that surrounded it, and it gives no sign whatever that its creator was later to be recognised as one of the most original film stylists in the contemporary cinema. It was four years before Miklós Jancsó made another feature film and though *Cantata* (1963) still gives few hints of his unique outlook and abilities, it is an altogether more accomplished and sensitive achievement, and can be seen, along with such works as István Gaál's *The Green Years* (1965) and Zoltán Fábri's *Twenty Hours* (1964), as inaugurating a new period of outspoken and often controversial investigation into the traumatic events of the 1950's.

The hero of *Cantata* is a rising young doctor who makes his first visit in many years to his peasant father and meets a former friend, just as talented as himself, who had been expelled from medical school because her father was too rich. He is forced to face up to the realization of just how much he has taken his own good fortune for granted and to confront his own moral cowardice in acquiescing in and profiting from this kind of injustice. Stylistically the film is conventionally shot and edited and many of the scenes owe an obvious debt to the French *Nouvelle Vague* and the young Polish school of the late 1950's—parties, intellectual discussions, and the use of a surrealist short film made by one of the hero's friends. With the benefit of hindsight, it is possible to detect flashes of the "true" Jancsó here and there, however: in the farmhouse and its setting on the barren *puszta*, or in the ambiguous scene in which the hero's father gently and lovingly calls his oxen to him—then sends them off to be slaughtered.

It was not until the semi-autobiographical *My Way Home* (1964 — and thus in his tenth year of film-making) that Jancsó came fully to terms with the themes and settings that have dominated his work ever since. In the dying days of the Second World War, a sixteen year old Hungarian conscript who has deserted from the army and is attempting to make his way back home, finds himself the victim of each of the conflicting national or political groups in his country: he is attacked, beaten, imprisoned or threatened by Hungarian partisans, the advancing Russian army, Cossacks who appear to be a law to themselves, and retreating Hungarian Fascists. In the central section of the film he finds himself assigned to help a young Russian soldier look after a herd of cattle; the two strike up a wary but unspoken friendship (neither knowing the other's language) and when the Russian dies of the after-effects of an earlier war wound, Jóska finds himself nominally free but in fact just as much the victim of chance and random violence as before as he sets off once more on his journey.

Though it is still relatively straightforward in form, the film contains the seeds of all Jancsó's later work: the study of power and the links that bind prisoner and guard; the interchange of roles between them; the casual and almost abstract violence that usually takes place just off-screen or towards the edges of the frame; the barren landscapes that fill the screen, reducing humans to scarcely visible pinpoints; an elliptical narrative style in which dialogue is purely functional (consisting mainly of orders) and is rarely used to define personality or motive; the use of music[1] to punctuate the narrative and impose a particular rhythm on it; a visual style that obtains its effects through movement of camera and actors rather than editing; an understanding of the role of clothes, uniforms, and nakedness in defining the degree of power one character may hope to obtain over another; and an impassivity of countenance and overall lack of response on the part of the actors that (deliberately) keeps the audience at one remove from them and inhibits identification or overt sympathy.

Though the camera is almost constantly on the move throughout *My Way Home*, subtly altering our perspective on the characters and their relationship to each other, there are few particularly long takes and the total number of shots in the film is probably close to the average for a work of its length. Yet the opening and closing shots indicate clearly the future direction that Jancsó's camera style was to take: to begin with, the camera follows a group of some half dozen characters as they wander in and out of the frame in an apparently random manner while, nevertheless, a sense of the relationships and tensions between them is being created. At the very end of the film Jóska,

[1] The music of *Cantata,* in contrast, is the weakest element in the film and is consistently obtrusive and over-emphatic. It is worth noting that, though it is Jancsó's camera style that has drawn most critical attention, he is also a master of the sound track. His characteristic blending and alternations of dialogue, music, sound effects, and silence is fully evident already in *My Way Home;* his typical camera style took rather longer to evolve. Dialogue and sound effects are now always postrecorded, partly because Jancsó likes to give instructions to his actors while shooting, and partly so that last-minute changes can be made to the dialogue in the dubbing.

having left the farm after the death of his Russian guard, is seen approaching a railway station (in an interesting anticipation of Jancsó's later handling of time and space, we are given no indication of how far or how long he has travelled to reach there). Some young men strumming guitars appear and wander past; gradually the platform fills up, with Jóska and other characters moving in and out of the frame; finally an already crowded train arrives. Jóska, wearing the Russian soldier's uniform, scrambles on top of one of the carriages, but is recognised by a group of his own countrymen whom he had earlier tried to force to assist the dying Kolya; they drag him down from the train and, watched by the camera in impassive high-angle long-shot, they begin to beat him. The train starts to move away, the camera travelling with it, and the men break off and climb on board.

All this has been presented in a handful of quite long takes; now Jancsó cuts to a helicopter shot of the tiny, isolated Jóska struggling to his feet and beginning to run blindly off along the road. He enters a wood and the camera swoops high over it, picking him up as he emerges on the other side; it follows him again as he moves off along a road totally indistinguishable from the one we had seen him travelling at the opening of the film, no further forward than before and no closer to his goal. There is a cut to a close-up of him from behind, then he turns to face the camera and stares at us impassively as a piano plays a few notes of Bartók on the soundtrack. In this film, as in *The Red and the White* and *Silence and Cry*, Jancsó uses András Kozák, who plays Jóska, as his representative of humanity and conscience in a world

Miklós Jancsó

Cantata: a young Zoltán Latinovits is on the right in an image that few would immediately associate with a film by Miklós Jancsó...

My Way Home: ...while this, one year later, could come from no one ▶
else. Jóska (András Kozák) begins the first of his many captivities

My Way Home: the anxious Russian soldier (Sergei Nikonenko) ▶
examines himself for overt signs of illness

The Round-Up: nudity, uniforms, anonymity, power, humiliation are all present in this image, as is the formality of composition characteristic of Jancsó

The Round-Up: the rain and the sombre tones of the image heighten the atmosphere of despair and helplessness

The Round-Up: father, son and informer are all chained together. The composition is perfectly balanced (a prisoner and a soldier on each side of the central figure) and all are trapped and held together by the curve of the archway

The Round-Up: one of the few high-angle shots in all of Jancsó's work, this allows us to view an image of almost abstract formality

The Red and the White: Whites capture Reds near the beginning of the film and issue the ritualistic order: "Take off your clothes"

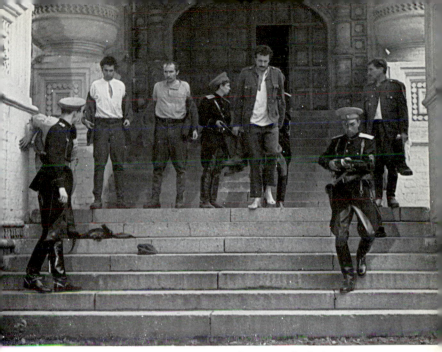

The Red and the White: the uniform makes the man as the Red prisoners are marched off to their fate

Silence and Cry: the farmer (József Madaras) undergoes his daily ordeal that serves little purpose other than to satisfy his guard's desire to experience a feeling of total power. A characteristic circling movement is in progress here

Silence and Cry: Now the camera too begins to circle endlessly, accompanying the oppressors as they prowl around their prey, probing for weak spots and assessing their vulnerability

Silence and Cry: the four people are held together within the frame, yet each inhabits his or her mental world and scarcely even looks at the others. From left to right: Zoltán Latinovits, Mari Törőcsik, András Kozák, and Andrea Drahota

Agnus Dei: an ambiguous and erotic image that heralds a shift in Jancsó's presentation of female nudity: from vulnerability to aggression

◄ *Agnus Dei:* the Whites commit some of their worst brutalities to the accompaniment of a violin. Daniel Olbrychsky as the soldier

Agnus Dei: a naked girl is made to listen as a woman reads out the detailed method of torture by which she is to die. The young priest who will eventually refuse to collaborate in such atrocities is seen on the right

Confrontation: soldiers and students form part of the chain of solidarity; for a brief moment, everyone can be part of the dance

Confrontation: but here the linking is used to encircle and intimidate; to separate rather than to include

Elektreia: the straight lines formed by the characters symbolise the control Aegisthos possesses over them; Electra is ostensibly free to move where she wishes, yet here she can go in only one direction

◀ *Red Psalm:* the disciplined music of the soldiers intrudes into the spontaneous rejoicing of the peasants; the contrasts are visual as well as aural

◀ *Red Psalm:* nakedness is still ambiguous here; the doves suggest peace and reconciliation, but during the film these women will use their bodies as weapons

Elektreia: Electra (Mari Törőcsik) and Aegisthos (József Madaras) against a typically strange background

otherwise almost totally devoid of these attributes: in all three films he is left facing us, the audience, at the end, in mute accusation or challenge.

This sequence demonstrates Jancsó's characteristic handling of violence which, in its refusal to dwell on the intimate details of pain, suffering, and bloodshed paradoxically becomes far more disturbing than the fashionable contemporary gruesomeness that tends to leave us asking, "How did they achieve that effect?" rather than feeling any involvement with the supposed victim. It is strange that so many people attack Jancsó for presenting violence and cruelty as being cold, inhumane, and horrible; this is surely a far more responsible and honest position than to suggest that violence is liberating, glamorous, or exciting, as so many other directors tend to do. Only a sadist could enjoy the violence in Jancsó's films, whereas even such superb film-makers as Kubrick, Penn, and Peckinpah can provoke an extremely ambiguous response among their audiences, whatever their own opinions or intentions may be.

The opening scenes of the film also present us with examples of casual, impersonal killing, as the Hungarian deserters, a group of partisans, some Cossacks, and then the Russian army quickly replace each other as the wielders of power and authority. In an anticipation of *The Red and the White*, oppressors and victims exchange roles with bewildering rapidity; men are forced to strip and thus made more vulnerable and defenceless, both physically and psychologically; prisoners are disposed of off-screen, the sound of gunfire our only signal of their fate, in such a way that we, as audience, are forced to make the moral protest to which the characters them-selves seem oblivious and insist that it is *people* who are being treated in this way. Jancsó's coldness and detach-ment as a film-maker are not a symptom of his own moral indifference: he is simply presenting, with ruthless honesty, the consequences of a particular political and social situation, but in such a way that it is the audience that is forced to supply an *overt* moral dimension to the film.

Other aspects of *My Way Home* are appropriate to this overall atmosphere. Questions of life and death are decided in a chance, almost arbitrary manner: charac-ters are selected at random from groups, perhaps for execution, perhaps merely to carry out some task. Jóska obtains a brief period of freedom at one point because a Russian guard can't count very well and doesn't realise that five prisoners and one guard returning from an expedition to fetch water are the equivalent of the five people he was told to watch out for: he therefore tells Jóska, as the man standing nearest to him, to go away again. Characters appear and disappear without any warning or explanation; we are not told where they come from or where they go to; they play their appointed role in events and then disappear. Most of the dialogue consists of orders or warnings that are never explained or justified, and many stages of the growing relationship of trust between Jóska and Kolya are conveyed, not merely through gesture and action, which is appropriate enough when neither speaks the other's language, but through visual signals that only an alert spectator will interpret correctly. On the morning after Jóska's arrival at the farm, for example, he wakes up to find that Kolya has gone outside. The camera pans slowly round the walls of their little cottage, passing, *but not pausing on,* Kolya's rifle hanging there. The boy's trustfulness, and perhaps his naivety, are conveyed by this, and also a reminder that, even if Jóska does escape from here, there are few places where he can safely go.

There are no fences enclosing Jóska, though there is a minefield that blocks off movement in one direction at least: paradoxically it is the very openness of the landscape that provides the main barrier to escape. This point is made clear earlier in the film when Jóska and a group of other prisoners are drawing water from a well: one of them attempts to escape and runs off frantically across the barren plain where there is nowhere to hide and no destination except the endless horizon. The solitary guard pursues him, catches up with him and drags him back; meanwhile Jóska and the other prisoners calmly continue with their work, aware that there is no point in their trying to take advantage of the moment of illusory freedom offered to them. Jancsó shoots the whole scene in long shot, emphasising the lack of tension, the futility of the attempt, the inevitability of recapture.

A similar incident occurs later on when Jóska and Kolya come across a group of young women bathing in a nearby reservoir (typically, there is no indication of who the women are, or where they have come from). More out of high spirits than for any other reason, they start to chase the women as they scramble out of the water and run naked across the smoothly rolling hills that surround the farm. Jancsó films the pursuit in a helicopter shot that emphasises movement, space, an impression of freedom, exhilaration, and activity. Suddenly, from nowhere, appears a small aeroplane that has been seen at earlier stages of the film; it makes several low swooping passes at the boys, finally forcing them to abandon the pursuit. The total arbitrariness of the plane's arrival stresses the point that Jancsó is making: confinement and enclosure are all-pervasive and inescapable. Throughout the film the landscape is filmed from such an angle that horizons are either nonexistent or squeezed so high in the top of the frame that a mere strip of sky is visible; almost the only shot that conveys a sense of the beauty of nature is one that shows Jóska and some other prisoners being escorted through a field of head-high grain by a troop of horsemen; but even here the image is ambiguous, for the grain encloses and dwarfs the human figures.

Within this almost claustrophobic framework, however, and in this world ruled by chance, and random violence, Jancsó allows more scope than in any of his later films for ordinary human sympathy and understanding. The moral centre of the film is the growing trust and friendship between the two boys whose uniforms classify them as enemies: they discover how difficult it is to kill, or even to hate, someone whom you have come to recognise as an individual, and thus provide a strong counterpoint to the anonymous and impersonal mass killing that goes on all around them. There are moments too of bizarre humour as Jancsó unobtrusively reminds us throughout of how young both these boys are: Kolya's self-importance as he struts around doing his exercises, his childish joy in romping with a dog brought by some visitors to the farm, the trusting way in which he allows Jóska to play with his pistol and pretend to threaten him with it.

Though few critics would claim *My Way Home* as Jancsó's best film, there are many for whom it is his most attractive and humane work and one of the main critical problems in assessing his subsequent development is to decide whether the prodigious stylistic and technical achievement of films like *Red Psalm* and *Elektreia* is not matched by a corresponding abstraction and coldness in Jancsó's treatment of human beings—to such an extent that for many critics these are merely empty displays of stylistic virtuosity with no human significance whatso-ever. Jancsó's own response to this charge[2] would prob-ably be that, despite their very real stylistic changes, the subject matter of his films has remained constant and that his work has been concerned throughout with the struggle to establish a just and humane society, to recog-nise the rights of the poor and the oppressed, and to pro-test against a cynical and arbitrary exercise of power: to contribute, in short, in their tiny way, towards changing the world.

All Jancsó's major films centre round political con-flicts of some kind, usually in a Hungarian setting, though his growing international prestige has led to his being invited to make several co-productions that display a slightly different orientation. Whether the film is set in

[2] Jancsó's own comments on his work can be found in the various interviews listed in the Bibliography.

Hungary, Russia, Italy or North Africa, however, Jancsó's basic method remains the same: from an overall theme of great national importance (the repression of Hungarian nationalism in the 1860's, the peasant movements at the end of the nineteenth century, the attempt to establish a Communist regime in Hungary at the end of the First World War, the confusions in the Roman Empire following the death of Julius Caesar) he deliberately isolates a peripheral and complex episode (often giving no other explanation or background than a mere date) and works this through to a rigorously logical conclusion. In isolation, the problem, without losing its specific local relevance, becomes more abstract, allowing the inner realities of power, oppression, violence, cruelty, and dehumanisation inherent in any similar historical situation to come to the forefront.

In *The Round-Up* (1965)[3] a group of peasants suspected of having fought with Sándor Rózsa in the Hungarian War of Independence of 1848 are kept under constant surveillance and interrogation by the pro-Austrian authorities, who attempt to extract information, not by physical torture (though force is used at judicious intervals, and on obviously innocent victims, as an additional means of persuasion), but by destroying the solidarity and trust among the prisoners, setting the peasants against the "outlaws" and encouraging the latter to betray each other. The members of Sándor's group are finally tricked into revealing themselves and thus sealing their own fate.

[3] Also known in English as *The Hopeless Ones*.

The Red and the White (1967) is set in Russia in 1918, near the beginning of the Civil War, in some undefined and minor area of the battlefront. Groups of Red and White soldiers conduct a series of skirmishes in which first one and then the other gains and loses the upper hand. Each momentary victory becomes the signal for the massacre or systematic humiliation of prisoners; often the business has hardly started before the situation has reversed itself and the potential victims have become the executioners. The film ends with the survivors of a group of Hungarian Red volunteers marching to certain death against a numerically superior White force. *Silence and Cry* (1968) is set a few years later, this time in Hungary, in the aftermath of the suppression of the Republic of Councils in 1919. A young Red soldier has taken refuge at a farm owned by a man already under police supervision. The local White commander knows of his presence but, for reasons of his own, tolerates it and even helps to conceal him during routine searches. The soldier discovers that the farmer's wife and her sister are slowly poisoning the farmer, whom they consider a weak and worthless burden to them; he reports this to the police, identifying himself as a fugitive in the process and thus virtually committing suicide.

Confrontation (1968) signals a radical change in Jancsó's style but, like *My Way Home,* it is semi-autobiographical, dealing with the attempts made in 1947 by student revolutionaries to remould the whole educational system, a process in which Jancsó was himself involved. The film is centred round a running debate as to the morality of using violence to achieve revolutionary ends, together with the question of whether confrontation between, or reconciliation of, opposing viewpoints is in the best interests of society. The question of leadership, which is also a major issue in *Confrontation,* is taken up again in *Winter Wind* (1969), a Franco-Hungarian co-production which examines a small group of Croat nationalist terrorists in the 1930's as they lay plans for the assassination of King Alexander II of Yugoslavia. Informed by the Hungarian government that they will continue to receive shelter and support only if they dispose of their over-idealistic leader, the others kill him, then cynically use him as a martyr-figure to justify their cause.

Agnus Dei (1970), perhaps the most enigmatic and obscure of all Jancsó's films, is again set in the period following the defeat of the Republic of Councils. In what can be seen as the logical culmination of Jancsó's development to this point, plot virtually vanishes as an organising factor in the film and is replaced by a series of variations on some of Jancsó's favourite themes: power, oppression, leadership, and violence. *Red Psalm* (1971), to my mind his finest film so far[4], combines the techniques and themes of *Confrontation* and *Agnus Dei* into a dazzling meditation on the nature and meaning of revolution, taking as its starting point the peasant movements of the late nineteenth century and their suppression by an alliance of landowners, army, and Church.

---

[4] I have not seen his Italian production *La Pacifista* (1970).

In *Rome Wants Another Caesar* (1974), the setting is North Africa and the time period that immediately following the assassination of Julius Caesar, but the central issues remain the same: should Octavius respond to the call to return to Rome and become another Caesar, but a "just" one this time, or will the very fact of his accepting power automatically corrupt and destroy him? And with *Elektreia* (1974), Jancsó's most recent film at the time of writing, the examination of tyranny and the relationship between ruler and ruled is carried out by means of an updating of the Greek legend to a setting both universal and timeless. Here, for the first time in Jancsó's films, the representatives of freedom and revolution appear to be unequivocally victorious.

Although some critics complain that the thematic consistency revealed by a summary of this kind merely proves that Jancsó is compulsively making the same film over and over again, most people would probably agree that this is essentially what many other artists have done throughout history and that repetition in itself is not a defect, provided that some shift of viewpoint or perspective is discernible from time to time. A more serious charge is that Jancsó's themes have remained static because he has steadily lost interest in both ideas and human beings and has become caught up instead in a sterile display of stylistic virtuosity, most aptly represented by his use of the endlessly moving camera and an apparently obsessive desire to reduce the number of shots in his films to the minimum possible with current technology—the record being shared at the moment by

Winter Wind and *Elektreia,* with twelve shots apiece over a running time of some eighty minutes each.[5]

The surface naturalism of *My Way Home* had already co-existed with a certain degree of stylisation and even mannerism, but it is in *The Round-Up* and *The Red and the White* that Jancsó's characteristic formal preoccupations become most evident. Every composition is carefully and exactly framed and even the moving camera seems to pass through a series of tableaux into which nothing arbitrary or accidental has been permitted to intrude. The movement of the actors within, into, and out of the frame is carefully choreographed and the characters are constantly being drawn up into highly formalised patterns of diagonals, horizontals, or circles that match either the shape of the Cinemascope screen or the contours of the landscape (the most striking example of this comes in the last few scenes of *The Red and the White*). Along with this goes a steady reduction of the number of shots required in each film, so that as early as *Silence and Cry* the total is well under forty.

With *Confrontation,* new elements are introduced, most notably colour and the use of folk songs, revolutionary songs, and dances to structure the film and convey many of the ideas and the emotions and feelings of the characters. It might be possible to justify this on a naturalistic level as being an appropriate representation of the exuberance and high spirits of the youthful revol-

[5] The average ninety-minute feature film, by contrast, contains around 500 shots.

utionaries, but this flimsy pretext would have to be abandoned with *Red Psalm* where every image has symbolic rather than realistic connotations and the abandonment of naturalism is complete, with characters dying and then coming to life again later in the film. *Elektreia* pushes the elements of ritual and symbol to an extreme, with the ideological argument being expressed almost entirely through the imagery, and the characters moving through a series of choreographic patterns that have the precision and beauty of an intricate ballet.

Jancsó's working methods have changed to correspond with the new directions taken by his formal style. Like most great directors he has assembled a team of collaborators who work with him from film to film and so come to understand his intentions and his methods of achieving these. Tamás Somló was his cameraman from *Cantata* to *The Red and the White*, while János Kende has photographed all the subsequent films except *Confrontation* and *La Pacifista*. Gyula Hernádi has been his regular scriptwriter on all the Hungarian-based films since *My Way Home* and also on *Winter Wind*. And, as with Bergman, there is a regular company of actors who appear from film to film, sometimes in major roles, sometimes in relatively minor ones—András Kozák, Zoltán Latinovits, József Madaras, Mari Törőcsik, Andrea Drahota, and many others.

Jancsó's most recent films are to a large extent improvised on location and the shooting script generally runs to no more than a few pages containing the basic outlines of the dialogue and action.[6] Each shot is rehearsed again and again during the day, miles of tracks are laid down to accommodate the camera, the movement and positioning of the actors is carefully prepared, and the scene is finally filmed just at the end of the day. Usually only one or two takes are necessary and the conditions of filming require that dialogue and sound effects be dubbed in later. Editing, naturally, is an easy enough process, with Jancsó requiring only to choose the best takes of each shot and then supervise the sound mixing.

The question still remains, however, as to whether these scrupulously worked-out procedures exist largely for their own sake, or whether they continue to be fused with the political and humanistic concerns that most critics agree predominate in Jancsó's earlier work. As the significance of any Jancsó film is rarely to be found in its plot and as the basic thematic material remains consistent from film to film, it might be best to approach this question through an investigation of certain recurring motifs, images, and techniques throughout his work as a whole.

[6] A useful first-hand account of Jancsó's shooting methods is given by Gideon Bachmann in: "Jancsó Plain", *Sight and Sound* 43 (Autumn, 1974), pp. 217–221. Bachmann describes the making of *Elektreia* but, for some reason, insists that the finished film contains only eight shots. Additional information can be found in the interview with Jancsó published in *Cahiers du Cinéma* 212 (mai 1969), pp. 16–30.

Power/leadership/violence/revolution

The three films that followed *My Way Home* contain
Jancsó's most detailed examination of the nature of power. In *The Round-Up* and *Silence and Cry* the situation is
essentially that of one group having unlimited control
over the lives and destinies of another group and the
individuals within it. In *The Red and the White* the absolute nature of power remains, but its exercise fluctuates
between the two groups, first one and then the other
briefly gaining the upper hand.

The credit sequence of *The Round-Up* presents us
with a collection of the symbols of power: detailed
drawings of uniforms, weapons, chains, whips, and man-
acles, all to the strains of "Gott erhalte!". The opening
scenes show the exercise of this power as an accomplished
fact, as a band of horsemen circle and herd along three
groups of peasants, and we are then taken inside a stockade where those peasants suspected of sympathy with
the revolutionary forces are confined. An officer approaches one of these men and silently orders him to
follow him. The man is left standing in front of a row of
cells; he tries the doors, one swings open, he enters and
the door closes behind him. He walks through a labyrinth of passages and suddenly is in the open air again.
The officer takes him to the nearby house that serves as
a headquarters and where an old woman is identifying
bodies of those who have been murdered for collaborating with the authorities. The man is told that he can go.
Uneasily he sets off across the bare, exposed farmyard,

glancing nervously around him as he goes. A shot rings out; he falls to the ground.

The effect of this sequence is deeply disturbing, less because of the violence that concludes it, than in its enigmatic, almost somnambulistic nature. No words are spoken, no one tells us, or even any of the participants, why these actions are being performed; the victim makes no resistance or objection to his fate and seems almost to co-operate in bringing it about; his death is random and arbitrary, for it could have occurred at any stage and he has done no more to justify it at the end of the sequence than he had at the beginning.

Though these features are to become the trademarks of Jancsó's handling of the nature of authority, there are several variations of the theme within *The Round-Up* itself. Much of the film is centred around one of the peasants, Gajdor, who is made to confess his guilt and then assured that he will be pardoned if he can find someone who has committed more killings than himself. The authorities, who have forced his confession by the gruesome expedient of telling him to place a noose around his neck and then shutting him up in a room with the bodies of his victims, make use of his ever more frantic series of betrayals, not merely to identify a few "outlaws" (who, given the desperation with which Gajdor is attempting to save his own skin, may or may not be guilty), but, more importantly, to create an atmosphere of fear, mistrust, and hostility among the peasants. Once their solidarity and the sense of uniting against a common enemy has been destroyed, it will be much easier for the authorities to suppress whatever resistance remains.

It is therefore not particularly important *who* Gajdor identifies, and some of the subsequent scenes deliberately border on the grotesque: he accompanies an already condemned comrade to the foot of the gallows, desperately begging him to provide him with the names of all his victims. But before the list is complete, the execution is carried out. One of the officers is punished for misconduct by being stripped of his insignia and thrust into the compound with the prisoners; Gajdor immediately begins to harass and accuse him, but the man is taken away again before he can achieve his purpose. Meanwhile, the authorities make no attempt to hide the fact that they have found an informer, or even to conceal his identity: Gajdor is led openly among the men both by day and by night to select his victims, and the fact that he can claim to recognize as a member of Sándor's band a man with a hood over his head causes his captors no qualms at all. His most vicious betrayal, however, and the one that leads to the most horrifying scene in the whole film, is that of one of the young women who bring food and clothing each day to the prisoners. She is forced to strip and then made to run the gauntlet of two lines of soldiers who beat her with whips until she dies.

The remaining prisoners have been assembled to watch this punishment and three of them hurl themselves to their deaths from the wall of the stockade, perhaps in vain protest, perhaps in an attempt to distract attention and to save the woman's life. Gajdor has by now both served his purpose and outlived his usefulness; when the enraged prisoners finally turn on him and beat him, the guards rescue him and lock him in a cell for protection;

that night, however, they deliberately leave the doors of two nearby cells unlocked and Gajdor is found strangled in the morning.

Now a new aspect of the game begins. The two cells are occupied by a father and son; they are interrogated, both separately and together, as to who committed the crime. Each is told that he can save the other's life by confessing. The son offers to identify Sándor himself: he picks, obviously at random, a man from a line of hooded figures, and the guards tell him that, unless he and his father really co-operate, they will have to choose themselves which one of them is to die. The father too selects one of the hooded figures; the man spits contemptuously at his feet and the three are taken away and chained to posts outside the stockade.

Once again there is a change of tactics. The remaining prisoners are ordered to put on military uniforms; they join the regular troops in marches and manoeuvers. The three men are unchained and the father and the suspect are ordered to fight a duel on horseback, with whips. The suspect wins and is told that, as a reward, he can form a semi-autonomous troop within the army, made up of members of Sándor's band and under his leadership. He agrees and picks out all his former comrades from among the prisoners. One of the officers then reads a proclamation announcing full pardon for Sándor; the delighted men start to cheer and to sing one of their revolutionary songs. The officer continues: the pardon is for Sándor only; all his followers are condemned to death. Soldiers surround the men who have been tricked into identifying themselves, throw hoods over their heads, and hustle them off to execution.

Perhaps what is most disturbing about the film, even more than the awareness of the absolute control exercised by one group over another, is the almost aesthetic refinement displayed by the interrogators as they carry out their manœuvres. It is not enough simply to be able to eliminate another person, or even to break his will: he must co-operate and assist in his own destruction, either through turning traitor or unwittingly revealing his true identity. The oppressor may actually see his own position as a paradoxical or even tragic one, for his power can continue to exist only to the extent that it is never fully exercised: once it has been taken to the logical conclusion of the death of the victim, it ceases, by definition, to have any meaning. This is no doubt why Jancsó's characters prefer to postpone this culmination as long as possible, and, wherever they can, use death selectively, as a means of instilling confusion or fear in the survivors.

This element is clearest in *Silence and Cry,* where the scale is narrowed down to the interplay between half a dozen characters, one of them a fugitive, another a White officer who refuses to make use of his powers of arrest until the young man himself forces him to do so. For much of the film, the officer's motives remain obscure, but, as we see him conduct searches of the farm where István is hiding and order the arrest and execution of other suspects, he cannot be refraining for humanitarian reasons. Aware at one point that István is concealed in a wagon of hay that is about to be searched by soldiers, the officer whispers to him to lie still and manages to divert attention away from him. Shortly after this, Kémeri visits the farm, orders the inhabitants to give him a meal, and invites István to join him. The latter refuses, and in the dialogue that follows, we gather that the two had known each other earlier and that Kémeri harbours a secret admiration for István's stubborn adherence to principle, at the risk of his life, in contrast to Kémeri's choice of alliance with the winning side. No doubt Kémeri also expects some expression of gratitude from István for the "favours" he is doing him, but, ironically, István maintains an attitude of studied disdain throughout. Towards the end of the film István, disgusted by his discovery that the farmer is being slowly poisoned by his wife and sister-in-law, goes to report this to Kémeri. The officer warns him to keep silent but, when he persists, Kémeri conducts an interrogation in which he ends up by answering the relevant questions about István's activities himself, thus confirming the long association between them. He sends the prisoner off for further interrogation in the town, a euphemism for the summary execution which is in store for him on the journey; but later changes his mind and gives István the alternative of killing himself with Kémeri's gun. As he has no doubt expected, István uses the one bullet to shoot him instead.

Silence and Cry thus deals with the paradox of the oppressor's situation: it is the victim who is morally superior and rouses a reluctant envy that to a large extent negates any satisfaction which the mere exercise of power itself might provide. Yet there is a strong "cat and mouse" element in the relationship too, and Kémeri can perhaps comfort himself with the thought that Ist-ván's life is wholly within his hands and he has only to choose the moment at which to spring. Like the inter-rogators of *The Round-Up* he delays this moment as long as possible, knowing that with the death of his victim his whole *raison d'être* disappears and his own death too becomes inevitable.

At first glance, *The Red and the White* seems less subtle and more schematic in its handling of these themes than either of these two films. First one group, then the other, wields absolute power; each reversal is followed by a systematic humiliation of the victims, that usually involves forcing them to strip, and then either a mass or a selective killing begins. The choice of individual victims is often a random one and executioner and prisoner display an equal degree of impassivity and indifference— each perhaps realising that it will not be too long before the tables are turned once more. Though neither side seems actively to enjoy the killings, they are carried out with a certain degree of refined cruelty: at one point the Whites give their half-naked, unarmed prisoners fifteen minutes to escape from the grounds of an old monastery; all exits are blocked off, however, and the respite is nothing more than a fraud. Earlier in this sequence, individual Red prisoners have been literally used for target practice by the Whites, and, later in the film, several men are killed by being stabbed with boat-hooks and held under water.

If the film consisted of nothing more than this cata-logue of atrocities, it would perhaps deserve the condem-nation it has received from several critics. But Jancsó is once again conducting a moral inquiry and, the more the film is examined, the less clear-cut the issues appear. The exigencies of warfare rule out the possibility of delaying the gratification of power, as in the other films: prisoners have to be eliminated before they have a chance to participate in the always imminent reversal of the situation. Although it is the Whites who are shown carrying out the cruellest killings, the potential for the same kind of mindless violence exists on the Red side too and is only with difficulty restrained: the character played by András Kozák refuses to begin a massacre of prisoners ordered by his superior officer, saying that "it is possible to fight and still be human", and later in the film a Red officer has to be prevented from carrying out the execution of a randomly selected group of his own men for alleged cowardice.

The moral ambiguities deepen as the scale narrows to the acts and treatment of individuals. A Cossack officer who allows his men to rape a peasant woman is given a summary court-martial by a superior officer and shot: he meets his death bravely and with apparent nonchalance. This same White officer is later responsible for some of the most appalling cruelties in the film. Towards the end of the film, as the Reds enjoy their final moment of superiority, they execute this officer and also a nurse who is accused of collaboration with the Whites by helping them to identify for subsequent execution the Reds among the wounded soldiers.

On the surface this reprisal, however horrible, appears justified, and the nurse's behaviour contrasts unfavourably with that of her superior at the field hospital, who had earlier refused to carry out this task and stated: "There are no Reds or Whites here, only patients." Yet it is this nurse who has been responsible for the temporary victory of the Reds by allowing a messenger to escape from the hospital and inform them of the whereabouts and strength of the Whites; she has also shown affection for another Red prisoner and attempted to assist him to escape. When ordered to identify the prisoners, she at first refuses; a wounded man is selected at random and killed, and she is told this will happen to all of them unless she co-operates. Faced with responsibility for the death of all the wounded, or merely a few of them, she can hardly be blamed for acting as she does and it is impossible easily to condone her execution.

One of the most disturbing illustrations of power and helplessness in the film, and also of the paradoxical co-operation of the victims with their oppressors, is also the only major sequence utterly devoid of violence. The White officers select a dozen of the prettiest nurses and drive off with them into a wood. The remaining soldiers run after them, uttering whoops of joy. We expect some kind of mass rape or overt humiliation to follow; instead the officers, with the utmost courtesy, invite the women to change into elegant dresses and then make them dance with one another, to the music of a military band. In some ways, this scene is, in its forest setting and in the graceful movements of the dancing women, extraordinarily beautiful; in others, if we remember what the officers *could* do if they chose, it is chilling and terrifying. Meanwhile two of the women, forgetting these implications for a moment, begin to enjoy the situation; they dance with skill and fluid grace.[7]

Though the film ends on a heroic note, with the defiant march of the surviving Reds and the knowledge that the ultimate victory was to be theirs, it seems clear that the key statements of the film are those of the head nurse and László (András Kozák) already mentioned. The dominant impression left by the film is that of the waste and senselessness of warfare and in *Confrontation,* made a year later, Jancsó begins a systematic exploration of the morality of violence and whether good ends can ever justify the use of inhuman means to achieve them.

The film is structured round a conflict between fanatical idealism on one side and pragmatic, and even unscrupulous, expediency on the other, with the representatives of compromise and reconciliation caught helplessly in the middle. Two central debates take place: one, within the group of revolutionary students, as to tactics and ideology; the other, between this group and the students and teachers at a seminary that they intend to reform. As usual with Jancsó, this peripheral situation becomes a microcosm of the struggle for power, leadership, and control in any political situation, and it is saved from aridity by the way in which ideas are worked out in terms of concrete actions, in movement, song, and

[7] There is a scene in *Silence and Cry* which, in a similar manner, provides a microcosm of one of the aspects of power treated in that film: a soldier who had previously been ordered by Kémeri to "rabbit-jump" (hopping round the courtyard with his rifle held above his head) as punishment for molesting one of the women, later attempts to inflict the same humiliation on the farmer.

dance; yet it remains, even after several viewings, a puzzling work, because Jancsó seems unable to make up his mind which viewpoint he really supports.

In the early scenes at the seminary, the organised, disciplined students have things all their own way to begin with: in gestures and movements that symbolise their solidarity, they link arms and rush at or encircle the confused, bewildered pupils, scattering or isolating them at will. They incite them to debate with them and meet no response; they emphasize their own freedom and unity in their songs and dances. At last one of the pupils (played by András Bálint) takes up their challenge: he tells Laci, the students' leader, that he hates terrorism. Laci agrees with him and for a time some kind of understanding begins to emerge between the students and a few of the pupils; Laci meanwhile defends his tactics to his own group by arguing for openness and reasonableness. Jutka (Andrea Drahota) objects to this; she attempts to insult and intimidate the spokesman for the pupils, but he responds with a provocative coolness, half contemptuous and half amused. Reconciliation seems to win out for the moment and pupils and students mingle and dance together.

A new factor is introduced with the arrival of a young police officer (András Kozák) with a warrant for the arrest of five of the pupils. Laci attempts to argue with him, saying that this will ruin the harmony they have just established; the officer brushes him aside, but when he tries to make the arrests he is thwarted by an unexpected resistance from the pupils. Laci again tries to intervene and tells the officer (a friend of his) that he is beginning to be frightened of the changes in him; he is told that he and his fellows are mere romantics with no grasp of political realities.

The students move off to discuss the situation and Jutka demands that Laci, who has proved himself weak and indecisive, must be dismissed as leader. She browbeats a majority of them into supporting her and returns with them to the seminary. In a significant gesture, she has herself raised on to the shoulders of two of the men and begins to harangue the pupils. "There can be no democracy for the enemies of democracy," she tells them. "He who is not with us, is against us." In a scene reminiscent of the random, impersonal selections of *The Round-Up* and *The Red and the White,* she has her companions pick out some of the pupils from the crowd, and makes them take off their shirts. She is dissuaded from ordering that their heads be shaved by a whispered reminder that this is exactly what the Nazis did to their victims; she chooses another form of humiliation and makes them parade in dunce's caps instead.

She next turns her attention to the priests and tells them they can continue to teach only if they renounce their allegiance to the Church. One young priest does this, but the rest refuse and the head priest makes an attempt to defend the historic values that the students seem determined to destroy.[8] He is ignored, however,

---

[8] Jancsó himself has, in several interviews, confessed to being torn between a desire to see a totally new society, free of all the debris of the past, and an emotional and intellectual attachment to the architecture, literature, music, and painting that would have to be destroyed to make the new society possible.

and the students start to carry books into the courtyard and pile them up for burning. The police officer reappears and demands an explanation; Jutka argues for a policy of terror, and he tells her that evil means can destroy the best of causes. In another significant scene, two of the students force one of the pupils to try to hit them, then accuse him of "provocation". The students now start to break the windows of the seminary as they chant slogans against reactionaries.

A group of party officials appear in the midst of this and ask Laci what has been happening. He says that he is no longer in control, and they call a meeting of the students. They tell them they have gone too far and that Jutka and her closest associates must be dismissed; Laci protests that policy changes should not happen so rapidly, and in such an arbitrary and cynical way. An official replies that the main object at the moment is to retain power at all costs; he then offers to make a gesture of reconciliation and says that he will annul the decision to expel Jutka.

Up to this point, it is possible to find a coherent pattern in these complex events and to see Jancsó as warning both against excesses committed in the name of a good cause, and against a cynical pragmatism that subordinates ideals to expediency. Jutka's actions when she gains power can hardly be condoned: they are too reminiscent of the behaviour of the authoritarian figures in Jancsó's other films and, in the proposals for shaving heads and burning books, are explicitly paralleled to Fascism. Laci's "middle road" would thus seem to be the acceptable position, and the images of dancing, reconciliation, and harmony are certainly the most attractive in the film.

The comments of the police officer and the actions of the party officials introduce a disturbing element, however. It now seems that the students have merely been playing at power, on suffrance of those who wield the real authority; paradoxically, this brings about a sudden reversal of sympathies and Jutka is now presented as a victim whose idealism, however misguided, at least has a purity and strength that rises above the grubby compromises of her superiors. In the first really intimate close-up of the whole film, Jancsó shows her rejecting the official's concession and telling him he is disgusting; she moves away, accompanied by a few of the students who remain loyal to her. The final scenes show this little group dancing and singing on their own; a potential conflict with the other students is avoided, and the police officer tells her not to worry: things are rarely as bad as they seem. The film ends with a close-up of her face and thus with a strong expression of sympathy for her revolutionary fervour.

The ambiguities which remain unresolved in *Confrontation* are explored further in *Winter Wind,* where once again a small fanatical group indulges in debates, dissension, and tests of loyalty, ignoring for the most part the fact that its very existence is dependent on the tolerance of a higher authority—in this case the right-wing Hungarian government of the early 1930's. But whereas in *Confrontation* the debates were mostly verbal ones, in *Winter Wind* the characters indulge in an endless series of rituals that are designed to test or to express their loyalty.

One of the most conspicuous of these is performed with pistols: the characters often group together and advance or circle in unison firing their guns in the air; at one point they form a circle and dance, tossing a gun from hand to hand; and in one of the most sinister scenes of the film, we see some small children being initiated into the mystique of the gun and being trained in target practice.

The strongest impression left by the film, however, is one of futility. Marko, the leader of the group, constantly chafes under the restrictions placed on their freedom of action by the Hungarian government in return for protection against the Yugoslav government whose king they intend to assassinate. He appears almost insanely suspicious at times, insisting on interrogating every stranger who appears, and yet events seem to show that his mistrust is based on solid foundations. Frustrated by their enforced inactivity, the terrorists seem to have little better to do than to question one another's loyalty: in one scene they insist, somewhat against Marko's will, on reaffirming their oath of allegiance to him; as they sing a patriotic song together, the one dissenter who has refused to take part in this ritual is almost casually shot as he stands patiently outside the window.

Later an outsider (played by András Kozák) appears and claims that he wants to join them. This initiates a veritable orgy of interrogations and loyalty tests: he is first given a gun and told to shoot a dog belonging to one of the group; when he hesitates he is given an inanimate target to shoot at instead. His aim proves so good that this rouses a new set of suspicions; he is questioned further and accused of being a spy sent to assassinate

Marko. When he denies this, he is ordered to lie on his face in the snow for a time; he is then allowed to stand up and is given a flask of wine to hold. One of the group, twirling his guns with cowboy bravado, then shoots at the flask, failing to hit it, though the suspect never flinches. He is shown some photographs and told to identify the persons represented in them; after a good deal of prompting, he admits that he is himself one of them. He is then shot. Marko orders the man who killed him to be searched and beaten. This man is then shot in his turn. Shortly after this, Marko tells all of them to leave: he can no longer trust them, and he turns to the more pliable children instead.

At the end of the film, Marko is suddenly told by the rest of the group that the Hungarian government threatens to expel them unless they dispose of him. In the final shot, after they have killed him, they begin the process of myth-making, exploiting him as a martyr for the cause. The endless rituals start again: banners bearing Marko's name, his death-mask reverently borne before them, patriotic songs, an oath of loyalty taken in Marko's name, pistols fired in the air...

The enigmatic and highly ritualistic qualities of this film, and of *Agnus Dei,* which followed it, have proved profoundly irritating to many critics, and it is around this stage of Jancsó's career that the charges of "mannerism", "self-parody", and "empty formalism" begin to gather momentum. Yet it should be clear from the account of the films given above that Jancsó cannot be accused of repeating himself on a thematic level: each film picks up on ideas presented in its predecessor, examines them in a different context and from a different viewpoint, and in turn introduces some new concepts that provide the starting-point for the next film. The earlier films centre round the subject of power—its effect on both victim and oppressor, the need of the oppressor for his victim's co-operation, the degradation and corruption that the oppressor, as well as the victim, experiences. In *Confrontation, Winter Wind,* and *Agnus Dei,* the focus shifts to the question of leadership and, after some hesitation, a quite unequivocal scepticism about the motives, behaviour, and effectiveness of political leaders emerges. Questions of the morality of violence and the nature of revolution, which have been undercurrents in all these films, then emerge as the major topic of *Red Psalm, Rome Wants Another Caesar,* and *Elektreia.*

Agnus Dei, which is set in the period following the defeat of the Republic of Councils in 1919, seems at first to pick up from *The Red and the White* in its chronicling of a series of shifting power relationships between two opposing groups and the numerous atrocities that accompany this. But the film is even more stylised and abstract and many of the scenes have to be interpreted in a symbolic rather than a realistic manner, while the use of rituals and of songs and dances to counterpoint and even accompany scenes of murder and torture, and the emphasis on the motifs of fire, water, blood, and nudity, all make the *experience* of the film a very different one.

Though the exercise of power is as transitory as in *The Red and the White,* it is not held in quite as absolute and unquestioned a fashion as in the earlier film. The Reds, who are trying to win the allegiance of a group of superstitious peasants, are forced to tolerate the behaviour of an elderly priest who heaps curses and invective on them, for to suppress or kill him would be to alienate the peasants completely. When the Whites take over, they are under fewer restrictions, and the priest, in an anticipation of a basic theme of *Red Psalm,* lends them his full support, even in their killings.

As in *Confrontation,* an attempt is made to rationalise the system of terror and reprisals that both sides adopt:

"Violence must be met with violence," proclaims one of the Red officers at one point. Yet the nature of the killings and tortures, the cruel and cynical paradoxes and refinements with which they abound, can only disgust us. In one of the most horrifying scenes in all Jancsó's work, a naked girl, who can hardly be more than twelve years old, is made to listen as an older woman reads out the detailed method of torture by which she is to die, a method that will prolong and intensify her suffering while being guaranteed to keep her alive and conscious as long as possible. Later, during one of the periods of White domination, the priest performs a marriage ceremony for two couples among the prisoners; when it is over, the two men are ordered to start running and are shot down; the priest then tenderly baptizes a child belonging to one of the couples. One of the women agrees to join the Whites; the other is killed later on.

As the film proceeds, the deaths become more ritualistic and are woven into a framework of songs, dancing, and celebration that accentuates, by contrast, the sense of indifference and callousness with which human life is disposed of. Occasionally a protest is raised against this: a young White soldier who shows sympathy for one of the victims and tears down one of the religious banners is beaten by his fellows. A young priest finally objects to the atrocities carried out by the Whites and is shot by the older priest. As in some of the earlier films, it seems that non-involvement and indifference are necessary if one is even to hope to survive in such circumstances, and yet we are grateful that the protests are made, however futile and ineffectual they may be.

The young White officer who has been responsible for most of the events in the second half of the film can be seen as performing an important role in Jancsó's continuing study of the corruption and ambiguities of leadership. His last gesture in the film, as he leaves by train the typically confined and enclosed area in which the action has taken place, is to shoot the elderly priest whose actions have contributed so much to the White success but who, like so many other figures in previous films, has now outlived his usefulness.

Whereas *Confrontation* is confusing mainly because no clear resolution is reached between the various viewpoints presented, *Agnus Dei* is often bewildering because the narrative structure leaves so many essential questions unanswered, and perhaps too because the film contains several different types of stylisation within it that tend to lie side by side rather than merging into a unity. Nevertheless it remains one of the most haunting and memorable of all Jancsó's films and its very obscurity may be an important factor in the nagging, hallucinatory impact that it achieves. *Red Psalm* combines crucial elements from both these films, but molds them into something that is far more coherent, both on an ideological and a stylistic plane.

The debate as to the morality of violence continues, but the tone of the argument is stronger and more consistent, though never simplistic. The film begins with a young woman (Andrea Drahota) holding a dove, symbol of peace; it ends with the same woman holding aloft a gun circled with a wreath of red cloth, symbol of revolution. Jancsó charts the process by which the initially peaceful group of peasants is goaded and forced into violence, not simply to achieve its ends of social justice but in sheer self-defence against the systematic terror employed by the ruling classes. For much of the film, they try to argue with the landowners and the soldiers that the former have called on to support them, and at many stages of the film some kind of reconciliation and understanding does seem possible; each time, however, some action on the part of the authorities shatters the fragile truce that has been achieved.

Near the beginning of the film the peasants present their basic demands for a decent standard of living to the bailiff, who rejects them, and then orders the soldiers to set fire to the stocks of grain gathered by the peasants. In the extremely ambiguous scene that follows, the peasants retaliate by seizing the bailiff and, apparently, throwing him on to the burning pyre.[9] The peasant

---

[9] The presentation of this scene will be examined in more detail later in this chapter.

women shame the soldiers into remaining neutral at this point, and when the soldiers revert to their normal allegiance, the men try, unsuccessfully, to debate with them. As in *Agnus Dei,* however, one of the younger officers seems more open-minded and ready to listen to an opposing viewpoint: he joins tentatively in one of the peasant dances and, when he is driven away by his fellow soldiers, he throws away his pistol in a symbolic gesture of disgust. A superior officer picks up the pistol and shoots one of the peasant women in the hand; the cadet attempts to comfort her and is himself killed as a result. He is brought back to life again, however, by the women, and the oscillation between retribution and passivity, reprisal and conciliation, continues for a time.

The landowner appears: he is a well-intentioned but vacillating figure who is ready to support the peasants in principle but lacks the strength of will to put his promises into effect. He too dies, in a manner that symbolises his inner conflict and almost as though the opposing forces within him have fought themselves to a standstill and made him incapable of functioning any longer. With the arrival of his fiancée,[10] the rulers return to a policy of overt repression, harassing and browbeating the peasants.

Again the peasants retaliate, as one of them, brandishing a whip, drives away the horsemen; but now dissensions within the oppressed group itself make themselves felt. Some are still under the influence of the Church and support the argument put forward by a priest that rebel-

[10] I assume for some reason that she is his fiancée: she could equally well be his wife or even his sister.

lion against established authority is sinful. Others, on a secular level, argue along the lines of Laci in *Confrontation* that true socialism involves peaceful protest and respect for the opinion of others. The supporters of direct action seize the initiative, however: they barricade the priest within his church and set fire to the building, while, in a later scene, one of the main proponents of the pacifist approach commits suicide. The change in mood and the hardening of position are further signalled when another of the advocates of peaceful resistance puts on a shirt bearing a symbolic red rosette.

Yet the next major scene of the film returns to the possibility of reconciliation and even fraternisation, as, after an episode in which an army deserter is inducted into the ranks of the peasants, soldiers and peasants mingle and dance together to the strains of a military band. The music is suddenly interrupted by the call of a bugle: the soldiers immediately withdraw, form ranks and shoot down those with whom they were dancing a moment before. The offer of reconciliation does not seem to have been a trap, as it was in *The Round-Up;* rather Jancsó appears to be suggesting that, in a crisis, class allegiance, the habit of obedience, the rigidity of behaviour and self-image that accompany the wearing of a uniform, will always prove the decisive factors.

This scene is, of course, symbolic rather than real, and a moment later we see the same situation from a different, and slightly contradictory viewpoint, with the alliance of landowners, military, and Church celebrating its victory and the defeated peasants divided into two groups: those who are willing to recant, and the inflexible revolutionaries who have been condemned to death.[11] The young cadet wanders away from the festivities and comes to a stream which, as he watches it, begins to flow red with blood. He walks into the water and kneels, accepting his guilt and his complicity.

One of the renegades among the peasants tries to convince the others to join him: he speaks of "necessary compromise" and the uselessness of further struggle. He is stabbed by the guitar player who has performed the role of Chorus throughout the film (a significant act of involvement), but who is in turn shot by an officer. The condemned peasants take farewell of one another and are reassured by one of their number that, despite their temporary defeat, they have sown the seeds of victory in the future; all now wear the red rosette of revolution. The closing shot of the film shows their bloodstained bodies and then the officers complacently drinking toasts to one another; the avenging figure of the woman played by Andrea Drahota, dressed in a red shift, rises to shoot them down.

It is significant that there is no one leader among the peasants: several of them, both men and women, take turns to exhort and inspire them, but decisions are reached and acted upon by common agreement. The power relationships are much more straightforward and clearcut than in a film like *The Round-Up*; certainly there are some changes of allegiance, either physical or moral,

[11] The effect of the juxtaposition of these two scenes could be compared to that of a Cubist painting in which different and, to conventional perception, contradictory aspects of an object, overlap with one another.

but in general the dividing line between victim and oppressor remains stable and unambiguous. The doubts about the morality of revolutionary violence that plagued Jancsó in *Confrontation,* are finally swept away—perhaps because soldiers carrying rifles are so much more obvious and real a threat than a bunch of confused schoolboys. The brilliance of the film, nevertheless, lies not so much in the conclusions that it reaches, as in its recreation of the painful process by which the decision is arrived at: for those to whom the gun at the end appears too crude and easy a solution, there is always the haunting image of the moment when reconciliation appears a reality and the opposing forces join together in a carefree dance—a moment broken into by the harsh call of the bugle.

Rome Wants Another Caesar transfers the basic arguments of the Hungarian-made films into the setting of the Roman colony of Numidia at the time of the assassination of Julius Caesar. Of Jancsó's recent films, it seems to be the one that most justifies the charges of creative exhaustion and which (apart from a change of landscape) provides little in the way of a fresh perspective on his basic themes. It is probably symptomatic that, whereas *Red Psalm* presents complex political and social ideas in terms of concrete, immediately accessible imagery, *Rome Wants Another Caesar* is much more verbal than most of Jancsó's films and most of the ideas are presented, in crude and explicit form, through the dialogue. Octavius, who has been plotting a revolution against the Roman colonial government, finds that he has been nominated as successor to the dead Caesar.

He decides to accept, arguing that, once in a position of power, he can implement the ideals of justice and equality for which, as an adversary, he has just been struggling. His colleague Claudius warns that he will inevitably be corrupted by power, no matter how generous and noble his original intention may have been. Claudius emerges as the successor to Jutka in *Confrontation,* an intransigent opponent to any kind of compromise, a zealot and a purist who comes dangerously close to emulating the behaviour of his opponents in his desire to overthrow them. But little of this is particularly new and much of the film appears half-hearted and perfunctory in its treatment;[12] it is also rendered excessively tedious at times by the introduction of a sage given to uttering gnomic banalities.

While *Elektreia* does not entirely avoid some of the pitfalls into which the previous film falls, it represents a return to the more fruitful methods of *Red Psalm* with, once again, a significant advance on these. Jancsó's free adaptation of László Gyurkó's play, which is in turn based of course on the Greek legend, takes as its prime concern the nature and overthrow of tyranny. The subject is raised in the very first shot, where Electra talks of the need to resist tyranny, and much of the film deals with her attempts to rouse a cowardly and apathetic population against an Aegisthos who treats her efforts, for

[12] It may be significant that, when Jancsó was asked, after the screening of this film at the 1974 New York Film Festival, to explain the symbolic significance of the smoke flares brandished by the characters, he replied that they were used to cover up the fact that he had no money to pay extras.

the most part, with amused and tolerant contempt. He argues that his subjects are happier under an authoritarian regime that makes all the important decisions for them and so removes the burdens of both responsibility and freedom of choice. Though the threat of force is always present, and Aegisthos can call on his soldiers in any emergency, he prefers to use as his instruments of repression his subjects' own worst instincts, their sloth and apathy and their reluctance to exchange a stultifying, but reasonably secure present existence for the risk and challenge of a more open future.

For much of the film, Aegisthos' analysis appears to be correct and Electra's exhortations have little impact on the populace as a whole. When Aegisthos proclaims a "Feast of Truth" during which his subjects can freely voice any complaints or criticisms of his rule, without fear of reprisal, they respond with a chorus of sycophantic praise, thanking their benefactor for all his gifts, in a litany whose elements become progressively more absurd. He is given credit for the food they eat, the wine they drink, the success of the harvest, the fertility of their wives: "salt was never so salty; sugar never so sweet", and all is the work of Aegisthos. No doubt a healthy awareness that they would be walking into a trap by voicing their true opinions combines with lethargy and self-interest in producing this response; later, however, when Electra walks among them and accuses them of these faults, they clasp their hands over their ears and refuse to listen to her.

Despite his elaborate façade of indifference, Aegisthos is well aware that Electra, simply by her very existence and her determination to destroy, not just him but the whole system he represents, poses a potential threat to the stability of his rule: he attempts to humiliate and discredit her by forcing her to undergo a mock marriage with a dwarf and, when she stabs a messenger who brings her the news that Orestes, on whose support she was relying, is dead, he seizes the opportunity to order her execution. As in *Red Psalm,* events develop in a symbolic rather than a realistic manner, following the logic of the film's ideas rather than that of everyday fact. The messenger, therefore, who is of course Orestes himself, comes back to life, for "the destined liberator cannot be killed"; almost single-handedly he deposes Aegisthos who, with his two closest confederates, is put under arrest. Electra demands more concrete revenge than this and Aegisthos is turned over to his former subjects who torment and mock him for a time; meanwhile Orestes kills the tyrant's right-hand man. When Aegisthos attempts to escape, he is contemptuously allowed to pass at first by Orestes, and then he is shot. These events are, in their cold-blooded detachment, more than a little disquieting, and it is hard to avoid the conclusion that Jancsó has become increasingly rigid in his thinking in his most recent films, and that a black-and-white conflict has come to replace the various shades of gray that predominated earlier.

In its best moments, nevertheless, *Elektreia* remains subtle and ambiguous, whether it is charting the relationship between ruler and ruled or allowing Aegisthos to meditate on the fear that dominates every moment of his existence—fear of outside enemies, fear of his subjects, fear of himself. The ending of the film, which seems to express some of Jancsó's deepest convictions about justice, equality, freedom, and mutual love and respect, is marred, unfortunately, by an over-facile method of presentation. Electra and Orestes, restored to life after a mutual suicide in which Electra has asked, "Do we have the strength for daily death?", are carried away in a red helicopter which circles, scattering leaflets, as Electra's voice on the soundtrack meditates on the future society that will follow once the world has been cleansed by revolution. The helicopter (which is not in itself an anachronism in a film whose setting and props are timeless) is clearly associated with the "bird of happiness" that Electra also speaks of, which tires and dies each day at the end of its East-West journey but (like Orestes and Electra) rises again each morning to continue its struggle. However worthy the sentiments may be, they tend, like much of the dialogue of *Rome Wants Another Caesar,* to remain divorced from the images, platitudes rather than experiences that are given dynamic shape and tension by their visual presentation.

Although Jancsó's themes have, in one sense, remained constant in the ten years between *My Way Home* and *Elektreia,* they have shifted quite radically in emphasis and orientation. The earlier films study the mechanics of oppression, present the annihilation of the victims, and allow us the satisfaction only of a sense of indignation and the knowledge that the victory and the defeat are merely temporary. In recent years Jancsó has shown himself more concerned with charting the successful struggle of the revolution and, after a good deal of debate (in which light *Confrontation* emerges as a key film) decides that too many scruples, too much soul-searching and too ardent a desire to see all sides of the question, can have a paralysing and numbing effect on the will. If the revolution is ever to succeed, it must be prepared to seize its opportunity and to act decisively and even brutally when it comes. Whether one agrees with this analysis or not, it at least has the merit of posing, over a series of films, all the unavoidable—yet too often avoided—questions and examining them from different and credible perspectives before reaching a conclusion.

Enigmas/impassivity/landscape/women

Jancsó's films tend to be enigmatic on two levels: within the film itself characters rarely deign to explain the reasons for their actions, to justify or defend them, or even to protest against the indignities to which they are forced to submit. We are thus often left at a loss to account for much of their behaviour, or rather we are forced to supply the explanations for ourselves by piecing together those few clues that we receive in the course of the film. On a more general level, and, though this is a problem for foreign audiences in particular, it has been known to cause difficulties for Hungarian viewers too, Jancsó rarely fills in much of the background detail, or gives much explanation of the setting within which the action is played out. Either it is assumed that the (Hungarian) audience can pick up enough information from such clues as clothing, or the specific situation is regarded as being of less significance than the eternal mechanisms at work inside it.

This process is seen at its purest in *Silence and Cry,* which represents an almost systematic series of frustrations of the viewer's normal narrative expectations. Mysteriously, events occur, and the explanations for them are given, if at all, almost incidentally towards the middle, or even the end of the film. The film opens with a soldier and a prisoner walking among some sand dunes; the soldier orders the other man to pick a particular flower for him and, as he scrambles about following instructions, the soldier casually unslings his rifle and shoots him. It is only in almost the last scene of the film that we understand the reason for this, and discover that the sand dunes are regularly used by the authorities as a place of summary execution for political suspects; but, by that stage, questions of cause and effect have ceased to play any significant role in our understanding of the film. We never learn who this particular prisoner was or what his "crime" may have been and, in terms of plot, the scene contributes nothing whatever to the film. But it is of crucial importance in introducing us to a world of random and casual violence, where death seems hardly to matter to those who inflict or order it, and in establishing the mood of questioning and constant anxiety that the audience is forced to share with the characters themselves.

Other major scenes follow the same pattern: Kémeri, the commandant, arrives at the farm with his soldiers, asks a few enigmatic questions of one of the men and orders a soldier to beat one of the women. It is only later that we understand why this farm is kept under supervision and why the characters submit to these humiliations. When we see the farmer's wife administering doses of poison to her mother-in-law, she appears at first simply to be giving her some medicine; when she and her sister later begin to poison the husband too, we are given a choice of explanations, all of which are equally valid. The husband and the old woman are "weaklings" who no longer deserve to live; the husband stands in the way of a liaison between one or both of the women and István, the Red fugitive; they might even be acting out of kindness in putting an end to lives based on ceaseless misery and humiliation.

Kémeri's reasons for protecting rather than arresting István, and the degree and length of his knowledge of him, are likewise questions that are left hanging until the very end of the film and, even then, are not fully or unambiguously resolved; the same is true of Kémeri's gesture in handing his gun to István in the final scene. In a normal film, this refusal to explain basic, and apparently essential, aspects of plot and character motivation would be a flaw; here it is a virtue, forcing us to participate in the tension, the unease, the fear, the frustration, the mystery that are the true subjects of the film.

The pattern of *Silence and Cry* holds for almost all the films between *The Round-Up* and *Agnus Dei,* and it would serve little purpose to give an account of each particular instance. In each case, we are introduced to an already fully developed situation and are left to put together the details, and assemble the overall context, as the film proceeds. Shifts of time and place are often arbitrary and apparently unmotivated: at one point in *Winter Wind,* for example, the two female characters are shown approaching the Hungarian frontier; they are challenged by two border guards, one of whom attempts to rape Ilona; Marko appears from nowhere to turn the tables and Maria, the other woman, then kills the soldiers. In the next scene, they are all shown back at their base, with no reason ever being advanced as to why the women attempted to cross the frontier in the first place and, why, with the guards out of the way, they all then returned to the farm. One consequence of this method is that time and space in the films become very flexible; with few clues ever being given as to how much time has elapsed between scenes, the action could extend over a period of several days or even weeks, or perhaps only a few hours.

A constant atmosphere of tension and suspicion is maintained in these films by the lack of explanation or overt motives. Characters prowl round each other in endless circular patterns, waiting for the right moment to pounce. Men are ordered to perform actions without being told the reasons or the possible consequences. Sometimes the actions are bizarre and frightening; usually they seem commonplace: "Walk!", "Run!", "Go over there!", but all too often they lead to death, to a bullet in the back. People are picked out of groups at random, their fate uncertain, the purpose unexplained. The total effect is dreamlike, hallucinatory, and the characters perform their allotted roles with resigned and even fatalistic acceptance.

A variation of this method is seen in *The Red and the*

White, contributing strongly to the see-saw like effect of the film, as power tilts first to one group and then to the other. We rarely see the build-up to any of these reversals, and our first clue is usually provided by the reactions of the people on the screen as they suddenly become aware of what has happened. Early in the film, as the Reds are in control of the monastery, we see one of their officers walking along a corridor towards the camera; abruptly he stops and raises his hands, and only then do his White captors move into frame. Later on, as the Whites are carrying out their massacre of the wounded Red prisoners, one of their officers becomes aware of some activity on the far bank of the river; he turns to investigate it and, as he looks back again, is shot down by the Red troops who have just arrived on the scene from the opposite direction. One of the few exceptions to this pattern comes while the Cossack officer is permitting the rape of the peasant woman and we see a line of soldiers approaching from the background; ironically they are White troops too, yet their arrival is to lead immediately to the Cossack's death.

In more recent films this enigmatic element in the narrative structure tends to give way to a more explicit avowal of motivation on the part of the characters *(Confrontation, Elektreia)* or to the ballad-like, symbolic form of *Red Psalm* where cause and effect no longer have any real importance. In these films too, the long tracking shots force Jancsó to deal in terms of "real time", with the events on the screen corresponding exactly to the time taken to film them. Each of these works seems to take place within a twenty-four hour period, *Confronta-*

tion over a single day, and *Red Psalm* and *Elektreia* over a day and a night. Here there is also a more Brechtian structure of debate, argument, polemic, and quotation from political or historical texts that replaces the pattern of arbitrary question-and-order of the earlier films.

Jancsó's handling of actors intensifies the laconic treatment of action and motive within the narrative. He demands of them something of the same impassivity of countenance as Robert Bresson, but whereas Bresson insists on using non-actors in his films, Jancsó has consistently worked with some of the best actors in Hungary, as well as with Monica Vitti for *La Pacifista* and Daniel Olbrychski in *Agnus Dei* and *Rome Wants Another Caesar*. This is not mere perversity on his part, however, for it is not that the performers are being requested *not* to act, as with Bresson; rather they are required to work within an overall style in which meaning is conveyed obliquely, through implication and inference, instead of overtly and on the surface.

Whether asking or answering questions, whether they are about to order or to suffer execution, whether they are reacting to the seizure or the loss of power, Jancsó's characters rarely offer any clues to their feelings through their facial expressions. There are few smiles and few outbursts of anger, few displays of fear or of triumph, yet there are often signs that the characters are attempting to reach out to one another, or are reacting with sympathy or indignation to the plight of others. Usually this is expressed in touch or gesture, or in a cautious exchange of glances that is rarely more than half completed before one of the participants turns away. There is no doubt, for example, that Kémeri in *Silence and Cry* wants to come to some understanding with István, and that it is the latter who consistently rejects the officer's advances. The personal tensions at work in *Confrontation,* both within the student group and in their conflict with the seminarians, are also strongly evident. Overall though, it is true to say that Jancsó uses actors as one factor among many—and not necessarily the most important one—in the total pattern of his films and that the audience is constantly forced to interact with the film by supplying the emotions that the characters themselves so conspicuously refuse to provide.

The landscape, for example, is as prominent and important a feature in most of the films as the characters who prowl and circle, hunt and attempt escape, across it. Mostly, of course, we are in the flat and barren Hungarian *puszta,* though *Rome Wants Another Caesar* takes us to the sand dunes and the ocean of North Africa, and *Winter Wind* is situated mostly in a snow-covered, forest setting. Usually there is little sense of a total context: the action, whether the scene changes during the course of the film or not, is typically confined to a building or group of buildings surrounded by an anonymous and hostile environment. The characters rarely stray far into this external landscape, and, when they do, they generally return—or are forced to return—very quickly. Limitless as the landscape seems, it usually contains its own built-in barriers or boundaries, such as rivers at which fugitives are caught or within which they flounder helplessly before being cut down; or else the camera angle constantly presents a stiflingly high horizon, with only the merest, almost inaccessible strip of sky at the top of the frame to suggest the possibility of escape.

The apparent openness of the landscape, then, is merely an illusion; in fact the more open and spacious the countryside appears, the more of a trap or cage it proves in reality. In *The Round-Up,* when Gajdor identifies a suspect among the women bringing food to the prisoners, she and her companions turn and begin to run across the plain. For a brief and—to the audience—puzzling moment, the soldiers merely stand and watch them, making no effort to pursue or call them back. The reason becomes clear as a troop of horsemen sweep into the frame and, in a matter of moments, overtake the fugitives. When Jancsó shows horsemen thundering across the plain in *The Red and the White,* they are not filmed *à la* John Ford as heroic silhouettes upon the skyline; instead they are seen from a helicopter, flattened into and almost dwarfed by the immensity of their surroundings. In *Silence and Cry,* István is paradoxically safer within the confined space of the farm than he is in the apparent openness of the countryside; this becomes clear when he goes to ask for work from a neighbour and is sent away again. On the way home the wagon he is hiding in is searched and it is only Kémeri's intervention that saves him from discovery. It is also out of doors, among the sand dunes, that the executions in the film take place. In *Red Psalm* and *Elektreia,* the characters rarely even make the effort to move away from the confined space in which most of the action occurs, as though aware in advance of the futility of the attempt; the familiar pattern occurs, however, when Aegisthos attempts to flee on horseback after his downfall: Orestes steps aside to let him pass and a moment later a group of horsemen recapture him.

The constant movement of the camera in the later films can deceive us as to how limited the overall space is within which the characters operate. *Confrontation,* for example, which gives a strong visual impression of fluid and open movement, takes place entirely within the confines of a large courtyard, the interior of the seminary, a flight of steps outside the seminary walls, and a stretch of river bank a few yards away. In *Winter Wind,* where a landscape other than the *puszta* is also used, the camera appears to have more freedom within the farmhouse, where it weaves quite extraordinary arabesques and at times appears to abolish the distinction between indoors and outdoors, than it does in the bleak, cold landscape outside. Here a tension is set up visually that matches the illusory freedom of the conspirators, whose sphere of action really extends no further than the boundary of the farm.

Another feature of the landscape, which is most evident in those films like *The Round-Up, The Red and the White,* and *Silence and Cry* that are shot in Cinemascope, is that it encourages the tendency towards visual abstraction that becomes such a prominent feature of Jancsó's art. Whenever groups of characters appear, they are systematically drawn up into horizontal, vertical, or diagonal lines, or into patterns of circles, squares, and triangles. The two most striking examples, partly because they involve the largest number of characters, are *The Round-Up* and *The Red and the White,* where lines of men are constantly shown extending across the width of the Cinemascope screen, or forming diagonals that intersect with the boundaries of the frame to create complex visual effects. Though many of these compositions are quite breathtaking in their own right, the effect is rarely purely gratuitous: normally, by their very formality, they accentuate the elements of coldness and inhumanity inherent in the actions taking place. When two lines of soldiers form diagonal lines in *The Round-Up* and monotonously whip to death a woman forced to run back and forward between them; or prisoners are executed in *The Red and the White* against a wall that, once again, extends diagonally across most of the screen, the horror of the events is intensified by the abstraction of the representation.

Towards the end of *The Red and the White,* when trapped Red soldiers are marching to certain death against the massed White forces, Jancsó presents one of the most completely formal and also totally unrealistic compositions of all his work: the Whites are drawn up on a triangular shaped isthmus, with their backs to the river, and are neatly disposed so that their ranks exactly parallel and match the contours of the landscape. The Reds, straggling at first, gradually form into a straight line as they advance; they fire one or two ragged volleys as they march, and a few of the Whites fall; their opponents hold their fire till the Reds are within close range and one volley is enough to mow them all down. The effect here is a distancing one, for we are forced by the sheer unreality of movement, shape, and action to view this culminating scene, not as yet another individual battle, but as a microcosm of the overall struggle and the cold impartiality of death.

In *Confrontation, Red Psalm,* and *Elektreia,* Jancsó sets up a contrast between the rigid formations adopted by the pupils at the seminary, the soldiers, and Aegisthos's subjects; and the freedom of movement enjoyed by the students, the peasants, and Electra respectively. Though the students are highly disciplined and respond obediently to commands and the blasts of a whistle, they are capable of rapid changes of direction and of alternations between circular and straight-line patterns that confuse and bewilder their conventional opponents. In *Red Psalm* the peasants wander in and out of the serried ranks of the assembled soldiers, arguing and debating with them. Much the same happens in *Elektreia,* when Electra walks freely among Aegisthos' people who are drawn up in a pattern of rigidly straight lines that symbolises their pathetic and helpless conformity.

The impassivity and detachment evident in Jancsó's handling of both actors and landscape is present also in the way in which violence and death are treated in the films. Mass deaths and individual deaths are presented with equal objectivity: we are not encouraged to find them heroic, stimulating, or exciting, and there is no lingering on long drawn-out death agonies, facial contortions, or torrents of simulated blood. It is only extremely rarely that death is presented in close-up—one of the few examples is that of the White officer in *The Red and the White* who has hardly had time to begin the killing of wounded prisoners before the tables are turned on his forces. Here the intention seems to be to accentuate the process of reversal, rather than to invite sympathy with the victim. In many cases, the treatment is deliberately totally unrealistic, as with the shooting down of the Reds at the end of *The Red and the White* or the massacre of the peasants by the soldiers and the reciprocal killing of officers, landowners, and priests by only one woman in *Red Psalm*. Individual deaths become even more stylised in the later films, so that the stabbing of the messenger by Electra produces blood neither on his clothing nor on the knife blade—appropriately enough, as he will come to life again later in any case.

From this it might be deduced that death is painless and innocuous in Jancsó's films, whereas, of course, the reverse is true. If the characters show no overt sign of protest or of suffering, it is left to us to provide these responses ourselves. Jancsó forces this involvement on us by the way in which his camera observes and records the killings: instead of urging them on our attention, he presents them from the viewpoint of those perpetrating them, as casual, business-like, routine. Time and again, the camera will show us the preparations for a killing, and perhaps even the beginnings of it, and then it will appear to lose interest and wander off to examine something else instead. This is true of such incidents as the whipping of the girl in *The Round-Up,* where we are informed of her death almost as an afterthought, or the massacre of wounded Red prisoners in *The Red and the White*. This action exactly mirrors the attitude of those who have ordered the killings, and it is left to us, if we refuse to accept that human life should be disposed of in so arbitrary and mechanical a manner, to remind ourselves of its value.

A variation of this technique is to have the death take place just off screen, but in such a way that we are fully conscious of it nonetheless, or to squeeze the killing into a remote corner of the frame while something of greater interest to the participants themselves is happening in the foreground. There is a strange, but wholly successful paradox constantly at work here, for the neatness and "cleanness" of the deaths themselves is set against the disturbing and unsettling context and presentation, making the final impact much uglier in moral terms than more conventional methods that attempt to shock in a purely physical manner. There is one case, however, in which this method is used to obscure rather than sharpen our moral sensibilities and this is the death of the bailiff in *Red Psalm*. The studied ambiguity of the treatment, allowing smoke to billow across the screen at the decisive moment and thus making it unclear whether the peasants *do* in fact throw the man on to the burning pyre (though the implication is unmistakably that this is what takes place), allows Jancsó to continue to present the peasants as essentially pacifistic when they have in fact already committed an extremely violent action.

Many of Jancsó's other characteristic visual motifs display the same basic constancy combined with development and variation in their treatment as his career proceeds. Nudity—both male and female—is a factor in all his major films, but it gradually takes on a positive rather than a negative significance. In *The Round-Up, The Red and the White,* and *Agnus Dei,* nudity is imposed as a humiliation on both men and women, though the circumstances are different in each case. When men are forced to strip, it is generally to render them both harmless and defenceless in a context of war and violence; sometimes they are then set free, sometimes they are killed, and in the latter case their nakedness ensures that their clothing can be utilised by their executioners. With women, the humiliation is more explicitly a sexual one: rape or attempted rape usually ensues, or at best the kind of sly and yet somehow detached pawing performed by the sergeant on the two sisters in *Silence and Cry*. Sometimes, however, as in *The Round-Up* and *Agnus Dei,* nudity is a prelude to death for women as well as men.

Winter Wind, while continuing the element of humiliation and danger associated with female nudity, also introduces a shift of emphasis. At one point one of the terrorists forces the two women, Maria and Ilona, to undress, and then makes Ilona get into a huge wooden bathtub. Maria gets dressed again, and a third woman is brought in; she strips and gets into the tub with Ilona and the two women embrace. They come out of the water, cover themselves with a huge fur coat, and embrace once more. The intruder then leaves and the obviously angry Maria drags Ilona back to the tub and ducks her head in the water. The scene is an extremely erotic one and picks up on the very subdued lesbian implications evident at moments in *Silence and Cry*.

By *Red Psalm,* female nudity has developed into a weapon and a provocation, as well as a symbol of solidarity and—through the medium of touch—communication. No one has to force the women to strip here; they do so of their own free will and taunt or distract the soldiers with their bodies, diverting their attention from other matters and presenting an opportunity for reconciliation rather than conflict. The element of vulnerability remains, especially in shots that show doves and naked women in the same frame, but this also strengthens the suggestions of potential peace and harmony. *Elektreia* continues with the almost casual nudity of many of the female characters (except Electra herself) through much of the film; here, however, it seems to suggest passivity and complicity rather than the positive reconciliation of *Red Psalm,* and there is a return to the use of nudity as punishment in the scene where Aegisthos's closest male and female associates are forced to strip after his overthrow and perform a dance together. This scene is so mysteriously and eerily beautiful, though, that there is little real sense of degradation or humiliation in it.

It is significant that the character played by Andrea Drahota puts on a red shift before eliminating the oppressors at the end of *Red Psalm* and that another avenger, Electra, is never shown naked at all. For women, who play a non-existent or totally subservient role in films like *My Way Home, The Round-Up,* and *The Red and the White,* have become the main agents of resistance, change, and revolution in some of the more recent films. A rather ambiguous transition stage is provided by *Silence and Cry* and *Winter Wind,* where the actions of the female characters generally have a negative effect, though there are suggestions of a bond between the two women in each film that goes far deeper than their relationship with any of the men.

Confrontation presents Jutka as the most idealistic, active, and ideologically coherent of all the student revolutionaries, though her tendencies towards intolerance and authoritarianism are clearly to be seen as defects. In the communal atmosphere of *Red Psalm* the women are treated on a level of absolute equality with the men: they initiate much of the action; they debate, argue, persuade and challenge; they are the main agents of solidarity and resistance; and they emerge as the symbolic representatives of victory through armed struggle at the end. The ambiguity that still persists in this film, between women as representatives of love and harmony and women as agents of defiance and resistance (an ambiguity which enriches rather than weakens the film), is replaced in *Elektreia* by the more single-minded presentation of the heroine as the implacable opponent of tyranny who will allow nothing to distract or deflect her from her chosen course. Though she is clearly as fanatical as Jutka, Jancsó has presented her situation in such a way that we see this as a strength, a stubborn refusal to allow bribes, threats, or contemptuous indifference to deter her from accomplishing what she knows to be right.

The motif of nudity has another ramification in its interaction with the role of uniforms in the films. In *My Way Home* Jancsó had shown a kind of "spiritual nudity" in the relationship between the two boys: forced to confront each other as human beings, they develop an understanding that transcends their nominal allegiance to opposing armies. Ironically, Jóska, at the end of the film, is beaten and rejected by his fellow countrymen when, in a symbolic gesture, he puts on his dead friend's uniform. Uniforms in *The Round-Up* mark a clear distinction between oppressors and victims; the dividing line is blurred at the end when the latter are given uniforms themselves, but this becomes, paradoxically, a means of identifying and isolating them more clearly. Power and authority in *The Red and the White* are constantly represented by the donning and removing of uniforms; ironically, however, once the uniforms have been removed, all men look alike and both Reds and Whites simply become people once more. This, of course, becomes the whole point of the scenes at the field hospital where, without uniforms to guide them, the Whites cannot be sure which of the patients are "friends" and which are "enemies".

Uniformed figures appear, with much the same functions and implications, in all the other films except *Rome Wants Another Caesar* and *Elektreia*. In *Confrontation,* the uniform worn by András Kozák, as the police officer, separates him from his former comrades among the students and puts him in an ambiguous position of alternating suspicion and friendship. At times he mingles with them and joins briefly in their dances; at other moments he represents the authorities who manipulate and confine them. Much the same is true of the cadet in *Red Psalm* whose uniform prevents him from openly associating himself with the cause of the peasants, though he too can join fleetingly in one of their dances.

Another constant symbol of authority and repression in most of the films is the horsemen who circle endlessly round the fringes of the action, always ready to pursue and either cut down or herd back those of the victims who attempt to escape. They are normally associated with the authorities—landlords, the White soldiers, or the pro-Austrian officials in *The Round-Up*. In *Elektreia*, however, the familiar sight of a group of horsemen rounding up a fleeing, pathetic victim is applied to the pursuit of the defeated Aegisthos and is another disturbing indication that Jancsó is now prepared to allow his positive characters to employ methods previously restricted only to the oppressors.

Fire, a relatively new motif that takes on prominence only in the films made in colour, contains an inherent ambiguity that matches the continuing debate on violence and counter-violence that runs throughout these films. Fire can be used as a destructive force by both sides; it can also be a focus for communal rejoicing and festivities by both sides. Jutka and her associates set fire to a pile of dried grasses at the end of *Confrontation* and dance round it. The Whites in *Agnus Dei* heap straw over the bodies of their victims, forming a huge pyre, set fire to it, and dance around it. Both sides in *Red Psalm* use fire as a weapon: the soldiers burn the bags of grain gathered by the peasants, who later retaliate by setting fire to the religious banners carried by the priests, and burning the church. In these, as in all other examples, Jancsó rarely uses his motifs mechanically: their significance and presentation alter according to the circumstances of each individual film and sometimes, as with the role of women, they undergo a radical development over a period of time.

Image/music/sound/colour/movement

Jancsó's films are among the most visually powerful and effective in the contemporary cinema and often, when the exact details of the power struggles and the political conflicts in them have been forgotten, it is particular shots and compositional effects that retain the strongest hold on the imagination. Images exist in a film as much to be experienced as to be interpreted[13] and this is perhaps why *Agnus Dei,* despite its thematic obscurity, remains such an unforgettable film, and why the weakness of *Rome Wants Another Caesar* is to be found less in its structural incoherence than in its inability to provide any really memorable images—with the exception of some shots of the maze-like, mud-walled village in which some of the action takes place.

In the films up to and including *The Red and the White,* although there is a good deal of camera movement and a few quite long tracking shots, Jancsó seems more concerned with formal composition and the interplay of black and white upon the screen, than with the endless camera movements that have since become his trademark. The effect of bleakness and starkness in *The Round-Up* is obtained, not through presenting a dull, grayish image, but through crystal-clear photography (by Tamás Somló) that sharply differentiates between extremes of black and white (an exception to this being

---

[13] This is a variation of a phrase used by Paul Hammond in his *Marvellous Méliès* (St. Martin's Press, New York, 1974), p. 9.

a scene in a rainstorm, where grayness, drabness, and confusion predominate). The dazzling, whitewashed walls of the farmhouse and the stockade are set against the black capes of the officers or, in one particularly striking shot, the black dress and shawl of an old peasant woman. The prisoners themselves are normally dressed in dark gray jerkins and light gray trousers (or rather, these are the "colours" we see on the screen), while the white hoods they are forced to wear at intervals intensify both their sameness and their anonymity. Each shot is carefully composed, either in terms of the patterns of circles, squares and horizontal or diagonal lines already mentioned, or in setting the vertical shapes of the men against the archways and doors of the stockade or the endless monotony of the plain. A striking feature of this film, which Jancsó never again resorts to on anything like the same scale, is the number of extreme high-angle shots that serve to distance us from the action and encourage us to view it as we might a game of chess, noting the overall strategy and the disposition of the pieces.

While *The Round-Up* also employs a good many close-ups, especially of the haunted, tormented face of Gajdor, *The Red and the White* is filmed largely in long-shot, pushing us away from involvement in the action once again and forcing us to watch the interchange of power as some kind of preordained ritual that neither side is able to alter or halt. One of the few significant close-ups in the film is the final shot of András Kozák as he salutes his dead comrades, but generally the effect is deliberately one of anonymity and is heightened by the fact that so many of the characters, stripped of their uniforms, end up wearing white shirts and dark trousers. Composition becomes more abstract, culminating in the final scene on the riverbank, but Jancsó can also obtain some extremely disturbing emotional effects from what are also examinations of shape, planes, and movements within the frame. One example, which is filmed entirely from a static camera set-up, is when a Red prisoner who has attempted escape from the field hospital is recaptured and interrogated. At first he and his captors are seen, together with the nurse who had helped him to escape, at the end of a jetty in the far distance, on top left-hand corner of the screen. The Whites then lead him along the river bank, towards the camera, till they reach a medium-shot position; they force him to sing and he responds defiantly with a Hungarian Socialist song that his Russian captors cannot understand. They take him back to the jetty, make him enter the water, and stab him to death with a boat-hook. The nurse, who had earlier been forced to strip, kneels naked on the pier, covering her face with her hands. The movement between foreground and background here has the effect of making us, as audience, recognize the individuality and humanity of this prisoner before he is sent back to a distant, anonymous death that we are powerless to prevent.

In these two films the predominating effect of bleakness is created largely by the abstract patterning of large numbers of men against the vast backdrop of the *puszta.* In *Silence and Cry* (where János Kende takes over as director of photography)[14] there are only a handful of characters and here it is the impression of isolation that predominates. Stark visual contrasts are achieved by setting the dark uniforms of István or the soldiers, the black, ill-fitting suit of the farmer, and the black dresses and capes of the women, against the vivid whiteness of the farmhouse or the emptiness of the landscape. Strangely enough, the dogs, chickens, horses, and pigs that occasionally wander in and out of the frame serve to accentuate rather than relieve the impression of solitude. And although it is this film that begins the constant camera movement which is to dominate all Jancsó's subsequent work, there is still a strong impression of formal control over the framing of individual shots — more so than in *Confrontation, Red Psalm,* or *Elektreia,* where the impact of the total four or five minute take is more important than any individual stopping-point along the way. One instance of this would be during the conversation between Kémeri and István as the former eats a meal at the farmhouse, where the moving camera brings about, for a few moments, a perfectly balanced composition of the two men and a large dead tree whose lopped-off branches are emblematic of the lack of real communication between them.

[14] Jancsó has said that one of his reasons for choosing to work with Kende (then a very young assistant cameraman) is that, unlike Somló, he prefers to dispense with artificial lighting for outdoors scenes. This gives the director a totally new dimension of freedom in his camera movements and it is thus no accident that the appearance of Kende as director of photography coincides with the drastic reduction in the number of shots used in *Silence and Cry,* in comparison with *The Red and the White.*

In these earlier films the harshness of the visual is reinforced by the bleakness and sobriety of the sound-track. There is virtually no music that does not emanate from a recognisable source within the film: in *The Round-Up* and *The Red and the White* there are military bands, and in the latter film and *Silence and Cry* there are scenes in which one character demonstrates his absolute power over another by forcing him to sing (just as, in *The Red and the White,* the White officers make the nurses perform a dance for them). There are bugle calls in *The Red and the White,* and the Reds sing the *Marseillaise* as they march to the final battle, but, apart from such instances as these, there are only the strains of "Gott erhalte" that open and close *The Round-Up,* and the harsh piano music at the beginning and end of *Silence and Cry.*

There is a good deal of silence in these films, but it is used in a positive manner, to accentuate the threatening, ominous atmosphere and to create a constant mood of tension. When sounds *are* heard, there is nothing haphazard or accidental about their use: the endless wind blowing across the plains, the beat of horses' hooves, the harsh barking of a dog, the crack of whips, gunshots, the quietly monotonous sequence of interrogation and command. A constant motif, which parallels the case of the landscape itself as a setting indifferent to the death and cruelty being perpetrated within it, is that the song of birds is always heard in the moment of quietness that succeeds the committing of a particularly brutal atrocity. This happens in the scene of the killing of the Hungarian prisoner in *The Red and the White,* for example, or after the unexpected execution among the sand dunes that opens *Silence and Cry*.

Confrontation, which in some ways is virtually a musical, integrates songs, music, and dancing into the structure of the film in a manner which is adopted, to a greater or lesser degree, in most of Jancsó's subsequent films. The songs which, like those in *Red Psalm,* come from a variety of sources, all have revolutionary, anti-clerical, or socialist connotations, and they are used both as a means of expressing and establishing solidarity and as an indication of defiance and challenge to opponents. Once again, though, this element is an ambivalent one, for the conspirators of *Winter Wind* have their song of loyalty, and the one seminary pupil who dares to defy the students in *Confrontation* does so by means of a song. In *Agnus Dei* the Whites commit some of their worst brutalities to the accompaniment of a violin, and a group of small children mindlessly chant a hymn of praise and thanksgiving. Electra's defiance of Aegisthos is expressed early in the film by a curse that she sings, condemning him and all those who support him. In all these cases Jancsó has moved a good distance away from the realistic—though stylised—aural texture of *The Round-Up* or *Silence and Cry,* and the soundtrack forms an essential part of the symbolic, non-naturalistic structure of his recent work.

Colour too, which for most directors is simply an excuse for a more "realistic" visual surface or for a display of gaudy pyrotechnics, becomes for Jancsó another symbolic language, refined and pared down to express exactly what he requires it to say. Landscape, in

colour, becomes potentially and almost inevitably beautiful, yet in *Red Psalm, Agnus Dei,* and *Elektreia* the
grass, instead of being green and lush, is usually a
brownish barren stubble, and in *Winter Wind,* the
gaunt trees and greyish snow have a stifling rather than
a liberating effect.

The relatively restricted visual environment of these
later films allows Jancsó to control and limit the range
of colours employed, and generally it is white and red
that predominate. The men almost invariably wear white
shirts, the women white shifts or blouses; when, as often
happens, there are dozens or even hundreds of people
together on the screen, this creates a strong effect of
visual control or harmony. Often the red and white are
combined, when the characters wear red rosettes or carry
red banners; sometimes, as in *Confrontation* or *Red
Psalm,* they wear red shirts or shifts as an indication of
political commitment or involvement. Red is also an
integral element in the blood and fire motifs of these
films.

Although other colours are, of course, employed, they
cover a limited range of the potential spectrum open to
the film-maker, and they are consistently underplayed
rather than emphasised. The uniforms of the soldiers, for
example, are a dull grey or dark green that presents a
contrast to the positive whiteness associated with the
peasant men and women. Yet the peasants too, in *Red
Psalm* or *Agnus Dei,* are often dressed in dull, faded blues
and browns, and the oppositions of bright and dull
colours are usually reserved for moments of crisis and
conflict. It is the intensity of this opposition that makes

Jancsó's films appear more vivid and colourful in the memory than they actually are, and this is in itself a tribute to the manner in which he has manipulated the resources he has chosen to employ. Colours such as yellow, green, and purple are occasionally utilised, but in harmony with the overall pattern: either women wear dresses in faded and subdued versions of these colours that blend into the blues and browns of their companions, or bright banners and streamers appear at moments of exultant rejoicing or challenge. Colour then for Jancsó, as theorists such as Eisenstein have always argued it should be, is a force for further stylisation, for creating a visual code that reinforces the deeper meanings of the film, rather than an aspect of naturalism.

All the developments discussed so far are clearly part of a consistent attempt by Jancsó to make the various formal elements of film—composition, sound, music, and colour—part of an overall symbolic structure. Though there is a considerable amount of verbal debate and polemic in the films that follow *Silence and Cry,* Jancsó's main achievement has been the creation of a visual language in which ideas and emotions are expressed purely by means of images, and it is in this respect that his much-criticised reliance on the extended tracking shot and the long take must be seen as being of fundamental importance.

The Round-Up, like *My Way Home,* contains relatively few sustained takes and probably has something close to the average number of shots overall for a film of its length. And until the last minutes of the film, there are few particularly conspicuous or extended camera movements. Normally the circular movements which are already prominent in the film (men trudging in a circle round the courtyard, or interrogators prowling round prisoners) are performed by the characters themselves, watched by a relatively static camera; the same is true for the scenes of attempted escape and pursuit. This pattern is varied a little towards the close of the film: as the newly recruited soldiers perform their manœuvres or the two prisoners prepare for their duel on horseback with whips, the camera begins to probe and circle in an unsettling, foreboding manner.

In *The Red and the White,* however, Jancsó begins to use the moving camera in an almost dialectical manner, setting up conflicts and oppositions, and then resolving them, within the context of a single shot. The most striking example of this is the shot already mentioned which begins with a White officer ordering the massacre of the wounded Red prisoners; the camera tracks away from this and follows the officer's gaze as he examines some activity on the far bank of the river; as he turns back towards the camera he is suddenly shot from offscreen, he crumples and falls, the victorious Reds are brought into frame and reprisals against the White soldiers begin immediately. Many other shots in the film, however, contain a similar pattern in which the constant uncertainty, the to-and-fro pattern of the film as a whole, is crystallised within one single camera movement. Elsewhere the long, continuous shot can suggest the paradox of illusory freedom and actual entrapment which is also central to the film's meaning: when the captured Red prisoners near the beginning of the film are ordered to run, one by one, across a narrow courtyard and are then shot down by selected White soldiers, the camera films the whole sequence in one take, moving with the victim as he runs, panning back to the soldiers, then moving on to the quiet-spoken, cultured officer who has ordered the whole business, then back once more to the soldiers and the prisoners. Conventional editing in this sequence would allow us some relief or escape; as it is, we feel almost as trapped as the victims themselves are. And even in shorter, less claustrophobic sequences, the moving camera is constantly viewing events from different angles and perspectives, continually readjusting our perception of the characters and their relationships with one another, and so literally creating the atmosphere of tension, unease, and uncertainty that permeates the film.

Silence and Cry takes this process a step further, drastically reducing the number of shots in the film to well under forty and intensifying the closed, restricted environment, the inability of any of the characters to escape from their situation, their fellow victims, or themselves. Now the camera too begins to circle endlessly, accompanying the oppressors as they prowl around their prey, probing for weak spots and assessing their vulnerability. Astonishingly, many shots begin with one group of characters, introduce a second, and end on a third, a process that reminds us of the constant interlinking of the destinies of characters who otherwise have little in common. As in *The Red and the White,* tensions and oppositions are introduced within the context of a single shot, though here the resolution is even more ambiguous and open-ended. One shot, for example, shows the farmer standing with outstretched arms in the yard as he has been ordered to do for some time each day; István approaches warily from hiding and asks him indignantly why he submits to this humiliation; the sergeant reappears, István hides once more, and the sergeant inflicts a further humiliation on the farmer, giving him the choice between "rabbit-jumps" and singing; he goes away again, István re-emerges and runs off across the plain in what is quickly shown to be a futile attempt to escape from this environment of stifling oppression and equally stifling obedience.

In what is perhaps the most extraordinary single shot in the film, one that is completely silent except for the endless wailing of the wind across the plain, Jancsó exposes the ambiguous sexual undercurrents that run throughout the whole film, yet leaves them at the end as mysterious and disturbing as they were before. The shot begins with István and the farmer's wife, seen in close-up but with the static figure of the farmer himself, patiently fulfilling his day's penance in the courtyard, clearly visible in the far distance. The farmer's presence is evident throughout all the action that follows, forcing us constantly to reinterpret the behaviour of the others in the light of what we know about their relationship to him. István and the wife circle each other and briefly touch; he then slips away and the camera moves with him to pick up the wife's sister; they embrace and then the wife herself moves to join them. The camera circles the three of them, constantly altering their spatial relationship to one another in a way that mirrors the ambiguity and uncertainty of their emotional patterns. The three come close together, they embrace, István moves aside leaving the two women holding each other, then he moves further away, out of the frame. The scene conveys more potential tenderness, more reaching out for physical contact and comfort, than any other in the film, but this is qualified by the shifting, impermanent nature of the contact achieved and by the silent presence of the farmer in the distance.

Confrontation and *Winter Wind* continue with this double use of the extended take as an element in the dialectical structure of the film and as a means of crystallising within one series of images the basic tensions of the film itself, making ideas and emotions concrete and visible. *Confrontation* begins, as it will end, with a close-up of Jutka; we move to her fellow students on the river bank as they block the passage of a jeep full of soldiers. The police officer played by András Kozák is with the soldiers; the students circle them and sing, then lie down on the ground, defying the soldiers to move them. The officer, in a gesture symbolising his divided allegiance, lies down briefly beside them, then rises and orders the soldiers to shift the young people out of the way. Unexpectedly the students take the initiative and throw the startled soldiers into the water; they then take off their clothes and jump in too and both sides indulge in some light-hearted horseplay. The camera moves to a close-up of the officer, his hands raised, as he retreats in what appears to be alarm from some unseen threat; Laci, the leader of the students, takes his gun from him, but again the mood is one of jest rather than earnest; the officer retaliates by throwing the students' clothes into the water. All this is contained within one shot, and it brilliantly condenses all the main issues and movements of the film: the oscillation between confrontation and fraternisation on a tactical level; the question of loyalty and divided commitment on a personal level; the sense that, for these young people, politics is a game whose deeper and darker implications they are still incapable of sensing.

Shot 8 of *Winter Wind,* apart from its prodigious technical virtuosity, might serve to illustrate how the very different moods and ideological concepts of this film are presented within the framework of a single take. The shot begins outside the farmhouse, with snow falling; Marko appears on horseback with another man and then enters the house, the camera smoothly following them. A wanted poster with Marko's photograph on it is seen on the wall; his followers argue about strategy and tactics and some insist on repeating their oath of allegiance; the leading objector is led outside and, as the others sing their song of loyalty, one of them breaks the window with his gun and shoots him. Marko tells them all to leave, except one, whom he forces into a closet and then locks the door. A group of women and children appear outside, and then the stranger arrives who claims that he wants to join them. The camera has moved outside again as the newcomer is interrogated and ordered to display his willingness to co-operate by shooting a dog. When he balks at this, he is given an inanimate target instead. By presenting all these events within the framework of one shot, Jancsó intensifies the sense of constant stress and tension under which Marko suffers (no sooner is one problem resolved than another appears) and so makes his almost pathological suspiciousness much more credible, and even inevitable.

A similar technique of concluding, or temporarily abandoning, one line of action to take up and elaborate another within a single shot is evident in other sections of the film. The scene of jealousy between Maria and Ilona that has already been mentioned, for example, is merely the culmination of a series of events that begins with some children taking a bath and playing around with guns as Marko reads to them from Proudhon; he then has some target practice using a photo of the King of Yugoslavia as the mark, and follows this by inciting the children to shoot at the photo too. Here various layers of sexuality and violence are brought into disturbing conjunction within a single framework.

By *Red Psalm,* then, Jancsó had perfected a method of crystallising political and personal tensions and conflicts, and of suggesting complex and ambiguous motives and emotions, within a cluster of images united by the constantly moving camera. *Red Psalm* takes the process a stage further by pushing the images more clearly towards symbolism: Jancsó's method is by now the antithesis of the classical Hollywood style of "invisible" camerawork, editing, and music, with its implication that the audience is somehow watching pure, unmediated reality, a slice of (usually very glamorous) life. Jancsó's stylistic devices cannot be ignored; they call attention to themselves and force the audience to examine and assess the images, instead of passively absorbing them. Moreover, like

Bergman in *Persona* and *Cries and Whispers,* Jancsó has created here a world that exists on its own terms, somewhere on the borderline between what we take to be "real" and what we would normally consider to belong to the realm of fantasy, dream, or symbolism, and, like Bergman again, he has presented this world with such internal consistency that we accept without question events and actions that we would normally reject as flagrantly unbelievable.

Shot 18, for example, has something of the dialectical structure evident since *The Red and the White,* but introduces some purely symbolic elements that crystallise and drive home the political significance of the scene. It follows a debate on the morality of violence in the cause of freedom, and the suicide of an elderly peasant who is unable to come to terms with the direction in which his fellows are moving, and it begins with a shot of the dead man lying in state. The traditional allegiance of the peasants to the Church has not been entirely severed by this stage of the film, and so a religious service is being conducted for him; there is the murmur of hymns, a nun gives a blessing, soldiers, the ultimate guardians of the Church's authority, are visible in the background. The nun speaks in terms of a centuries-long pattern of Christian consolation: those who have suffered and endured misery in this world will find their reward in the next, where Christ will wash away their tears. One of the peasants responds to this by reciting a socialist version of the Lord's Prayer, current at the time in which the film is set, demanding that injustice be redressed in *this* world and tyrants and oppressors punished. This demand is picked up by the other peasants; they too want justice and equality now, not in an afterlife, and, in a symbolic expression of the new, militant mood, the peasant who had been the chief spokesman for passive, peaceful resistance, puts on a shirt with a red rosette. A scene of music and dancing follows, in which children appear for the first time in the film, and the united peasants are seen in confrontation with the soldiers at the end of the shot.

From this point on, the symbolic undercurrents evident throughout the earlier parts of the film come to dominate the remainder of the action. This is clearest in shot 22, at one and the same time the most moving and the most unreal of all the images: the peasants are celebrating their solidarity in a dance that Jancsó films in extreme long-shot, from the top of a hill. As the scene proceeds there is a very slow forward movement of the camera, but we never come really close to the characters and the totality of the action is always clearly visible. The soldiers sorround the peasants in straight lines that form three sides of a square; the military band provides the music for the dancing and gradually the soldiers themselves break ranks and begin to mingle with the peasants and dance with them. The image, of reconciliation and harmony still possible, is one of the most poignant in all Jancsó's work, but by this stage it is wish-fulfilment rather than fact. The harsh call of a bugle breaks into the music; the soldiers obediently hurry back into line; they form an uneven circle round the dancers, close in, raise their rifles, fire. The peasants fall, virtually simultaneously, but the firing continues for a few moments longer, as though to emphasise that brute force is to be seen as the ultimate law.

Two shots later, however, we see what must be interpreted as another variation of the same theme of the defeat of the incipient revolution. The force exerted by the oppressor has proved stronger once again, but this time the peasants remain alive and are being forced to recant. The images and soundtrack are full of the evidence of re-established authority: religious banners, priests and tinkling bells, a military band, men and women waving white rather than red banners. But once again a dialectic movement works itself out between the first and last images of this shot: from indications of submission and defeat, we move to a renewed defiance as the previously uncommitted guitar player is roused to stab the leading apologist for collaboration among the peasants.

The final shot of the film too (27) has something of the same pattern: from symbols of authority, rifles being loaded and bayonets fixed, we move to scenes of the condemned peasants saying farewell to one another. Their death is represented elliptically, the camera simply tracking past some scattered bodies, a bloodstained dove, white shirts with patches of blood on them, the discarded weapons, bayonets and swords, stuck deep into the soil. The victors drink toasts to their success, but one woman, dressed in a red shift, rises from among the bodies; she wrests a gun from an officer on horseback, shoots him and then all the others; she sings of the final victory of the workers' struggle as she raises high the gun wrapped in a red streamer.

As even a brief account of shots such as these should

indicate, Jancsó has made a film that translates abstract ideas into complex, but clearly comprehensible images. Even without words, it would be possible to follow the whole movement of the film, the various conflicts, both internal and external that are expressed and then resolved, the potential solutions that are offered, the unambiguous declaration that is made at the end. Far from being purely mannered or existing simply in a vacuum of its own contrivance, Jancsó's style here is totally integrated into the nature of his material: in a very real sense, the form itself is the narrative.

Much the same is true of *Elektreia,* or of the first eleven of its twelve shots at least (the weakness of the concluding shot having been discussed already). The film is Jancsó's most purely ritualistic work to date and operates totally within the structure of symbolic and visual motifs established in previous films; in so doing it becomes one of the most successful renditions of the *spirit* of Greek tragedy produced in modern times, catching perfectly its sense of strangeness and formality, the paradox of primitive and anarchic emotions and actions being performed within a rigidly hierarchial social framework. Some of the most effective and mysterious moments in the film are those that have little connection at all with the ostensible action, yet hauntingly express its overall mood. In shot 9, for example, while the defeated Aegisthos waits passively under the net Orestes has thrown over him, his leading courtier is ordered to strip and then to give food to the doves: to the sound of a drum, he then begins a dance with his female counterpart in Aegisthos's court (also naked), Electra joins them, the woman places one foot on the kneeling, white-robed drummer and is raised to her full height above him by the courtier; this shot is held for a moment while the head and crest of a peacock fill the lower right-hand corner of the frame. The strange and remote beauty of this sequence is enhanced by the non-naturalistic use of sound: the drumbeat casts its hypnotic spell throughout, while the horsemen circling just beyond the immediate area of the action carry out their manœuvres in utter silence.

Several other shots demonstrate particularly well Jancsó's ability to create a world distanced from us by the elaborate formality with which it is organised and filmed, and yet shockingly close in the immediacy and even barbarity of the emotions represented. From the beginning of the film Electra makes no secret of her intention to kill Aegisthos as soon as a suitable opportunity arises; he replies calmly that, if she does so, she will have no popular support as his subjects prefer a ruler like himself who makes all their decisions for them and will resent a "trouble-maker" who tries to force them to think and choose for themselves. This idea is brilliantly brought to life in shot 6 where Electra, having stabbed the messenger who has brought news of Orestes' death, is brought before Aegisthos for judgement. Flutes play softly in the background, the camera tilts to a balcony above them where one of Aegisthos' mouthpieces pronounces sentence on his behalf, then tilts down to catch the body being carried into the building on a stretcher; horsemen circle as usual in the background as the camera tracks away and the guitar player who appears throughout the film sings a few lines that crystallise the issue at stake here. Electra is brought before the assembled populace, who are drawn up several lines deep in perfect rectangular formation; lying face downwards on the grass, she is told that her life will be spared if she recants and makes public confession of her mistakes. Instead she walks among the people, accusing them of cowardice, lethargy, and treachery; as she reaches each row, the characters rise to their feet in unison and clasp their hands over their ears. Smugly, Aegisthos speaks to them instead of the happiness to be attained by obedience to the established laws. The messenger killed by Electra appears; he is of course Orestes himself and is alive once more because the destined liberator can never be slain. Aegisthos tries to retain control of the situation: his soldiers drive the crowd away from him and then back to him with whips; he says that Electra must die and they should pray for her; the people prostrate themselves before him and horsemen carrying red smoke flares ride around them. Now the camera moves past a line of girls in white shifts carrying lighted torches to centre on Orestes holding a burning knife in his hand; as the guitarist begins a song about freedom, a man throws a net over Aegisthos, forcing him to kneel, and Orestes thrusts the dagger into the ground at his feet.

Within the scope of this one shot Jancsó has condensed and illuminated one of the key issues facing any political activist—the degree of support he can expect to achieve from the people he intends to liberate—and has succinctly visualised the dilemma in a way that a more orthodox and naturalistic film-maker could never have equalled.

The images are bizarre, unreal, and yet true to the inner reality, the essence of the problem, in much the same way as, a little later in the film, Aegisthos's fall from power, his rejection by the people he had formerly oppressed, is given concrete form in the sight of him squatting grotesquely on top of a gigantic ball of animal hide, scrabbling futilely to hold his balance as he is rolled along by a group of naked women, and finally tumbling into the jostling, hostile crowd.

The most thoroughly ritualistic shot in the whole film is probably 3, in which the reasons for Electra's hatred of Aegisthos are given and the tensions between them are vividly established. It begins with a group of small children dancing, some of them holding full-sized swords: then Electra talks to the leading woman courtier of Aegisthos's court, vainly trying to persuade her to rise in rebellion against the tyrant and the usual horsemen circle in the background during this conversation. Next the camera tracks past a group of naked women, a basket of chickens, and the three dwarfs who play a more prominent part in shot 5. More nude women stand in a pool of blood, their bodies ornamented with paint, while to the sound of drumbeats, a man performs an intricate piece of swordplay on the solid ground beside them. Aegisthos's leading male courtier enters the pool and starts to mime the murder of Electra's father, Agamemnon, in his bath, while a woman narrates these same events; at the moment of the stabbing, the courtier falls full-length into the pool while the drumbeats abruptly come to a halt. Aegisthos's soldiers appear, cracking their whips, horsemen ride past, Electra softly sings a curse on Aegisthos and all those who support him; she walks past a line of hooded, kneeling figures towards a group of men holding a white sheet at arm's length between them, the drum starts to play once more and a solemn dance begins. As well as establishing and elaborating some of the major symbolic motifs in the film, the effect of this shot is to create an atmosphere of both bloodsoaked barbarity and moral inertia and to intensify the isolation of Electra herself as she insists on pursuing her quest for justice.

As should be clear from even these examples, there is a logical development and consistency within the overall structure of the film, in which the most bizarre and apparently arbitrary details are finally seen to take their place. The three dwarfs, for example, who might seem an unnecessarily grotesque intrusion into shot 3, are shown to have an important role to play in shot 5, where Electra is forced to undergo a mock marriage with one of them. Similarly the birds and animals that appear in almost every shot both add to the sense of visual strangeness and often perform an important symbolic function. The most obvious example is that of the peacock: shot 2 begins with a close-up of a peacock's feather; the bird itself is seen in shot 5, together with a dog and some other birds, as Aegisthos meditates on the problem of fear; in shot 9 the peacock and a bull are seen close to Aegisthos as he waits under the net in which Orestes has trapped him, and later in that shot the peacock is seen during the dance performed by the courtiers; finally, in the last shot, the peacock is used as the symbol of the new world that (perhaps) may soon be established, in the song that the guitarist sings as Orestes and Electra lead the other characters in their dance of freedom.

Once again, then, form and meaning are identical and Jancsó has created a work which is ruthlessly logical both in its analysis of the nature and effects of tyranny and in its overall visual movement and patterning. The stylisation, the rituals, the symbols, the rejection of conventional narrative structures and psychological analysis, are not empty formal devices, but the necessary tools that enable him to penetrate to the essence of his theme: the nature of despotic control over the minds and bodies of its victims, and the problems faced by any liberator whose first task is to free those that he wishes to rescue from their own worst instincts, their sloth and their cowardice.

One could look, of course, at a film like *The Round-Up* and say that similar or identical themes were present there, but it would be a mistake to assume that *Elektreia* is therefore redundant. Quite apart from the shift in thinking that has led Jancsó to a more overt espousal of revolution, substituting a concern for how to achieve freedom for a meticulous chronicling of the mechanism of repression, the later film is a totally different aesthetic experience and its meaning is irrevocably altered as a result. *Elektreia,* like *The Round-Up,* is memorable primarily as a collection of images, of bizarre and striking juxtapositions, of geometrical precision mixed with the utmost freedom and fluidity of the camera, of sounds and silences, of mysterious and hypnotically alluring (even if often repulsive) actions; yet each of the elements cited is handled in such a totally different manner that the experience of watching them is only remotely or intermittently ever the same.

Chapter Three

The Age of Day-dreaming: István Szabó

Jancsó is a genuine original: whether one likes his films or not, it has to be admitted that there is no director quite like him in the world today. István Szabó, despite a clearly defined personal style and a collection of themes and images almost as obsessive as those of Jancsó, is more obviously in the mainstream of contemporary film-making. His first short film, *Concert* (1961), has something of the surrealist quality of the young Polish cinema of the late 1950's; while another short, *You* (1963), is clearly much influenced by the *Nouvelle Vague* of Truffaut and Godard in particular. His first feature, *The Age of Day-dreaming*[1] (1964), contains several explicit *homages* to Truffaut: the characters play the "Tour-billon" song performed by Jeanne Moreau in *Jules and Jim,* and later we see a poster advertising *The 400 Blows*. In *Love Film* (1970) and *25 Firemen's Sreet* (1973), the intricate flashback structure recalls the work of Alain Resnais, and Szabó admits that, while he still loves Truffaut's work, he now feels that Resnais, together

---

[1] Also known in English as: *The Age of Illusions*

with Bergman, Bunuel, and Fellini, is, in the long run, a more significant film-maker.[2]

None of this need imply, however, that Szabó is a mere imitator or plagiarist: even ten years after its appearance, *The Age of Day-dreaming* still possesses a freshness and charm that owe nothing to the work of anyone but Szabó himself, and his two most rec nt films employ techniques similar to those of Resnais, but with totally different intentions and results that are quite unique. The particularly haunting quality of Szabó's films derives from a combination of total mastery of his medium and an extremely personal thematic pattern that attempts to use the experiences of one figure (always played by András Bálint) as a microcosm of Hungarian history over the past thirty years.

Szabó denies that his films are in essence autobiographical, though he acknowledges that Bálint (whom he describes as his closest creative collaborator) is much the same age as himself and that the films generally cover a time span similar to that of his own lifetime: childhood during the Second World War, adolescence in the early 1950's, young manhood in the late 1950's. The films, he says, are more "the autobiography of a generation" and this is why each of them ends with a scene in which the central character, hitherto rather isolated, is suddenly seen in a context in which dozens of other people are performing the same actions as himself (these scenes will be discussed in more detail later).

[2] Statements attributed to Szabó are based on conversations with the author in July 1973 and July 1975.

The recurring themes in Szabó's work are those of time, memory, self-knowledge, childhood, and the—often painful—acceptance of maturity, with all its compromises and disappointments, as the idealistic and unreal dreams of adolescence fade away. This process is not a defeatist one, however, for confrontation with the realities that lie behind the hazy glow of childhood memories, and rejection of the comforting protective devices that distort the past in order to shield us from ourselves, lead, not to despair or self-disgust, but to a truer understanding of our real potentials and of what we can now go on to achieve. The films thus display an overall serenity in which sadness, humour, courage, cowardice, violence, and tenderness all come together and are assimilated into a wider harmony.

Though Szabó uses many of the editing techniques associated with the work of Alain Resnais—flashbacks that are sparked off by a chance word, movement, or gesture; the repetition of key scenes with subtle variations that suggest the fallibility and uncertainty of memory; the establishment of a visual rhythm that steadily integrates past and present into a process of interaction and reassessment—the overall impact of *Love Film,* for example, is very different from that of Resnais's *Je t'aime. Je t'aime.* To some extent it is a question of viewpoint: the past tends to be less destructive for Szabó than for Resnais, and his characters seem better able to assimilate and come to terms with the discoveries they make about themselves. And it is a matter of temperament, too: Szabó stays close to and is more involved with his characters than the more intellectual and cerebral Resnais.

The unique tone of Szabó's work comes partly from the understatement of his editing: rather than destroy a point through overemphasis, he risks losing it by cutting the moment a perceptive and alert spectator can be assumed to have grasped its significance. Rewarding as this method is, it runs the risk of becoming over-elliptical and obscure, and it is probably true that all of Szabó's recent films gain considerably from being seen for a second time (fortunately the first impression is always positive enough to encourage a second viewing). Linked with this is the subtlety of the soundtrack: Szabó is much less afraid than most other directors of silence with the result that there are no sound effects and no music that do not contribute directly to the emotional impact of the scene. A whisper in Szabó's films can be more emphatic than a blast of trumpets in the work of other film-makers.

Szabó pre-plans his films very carefully: the script contains detailed instructions of exactly where the flashbacks are to occur and how long they are to last, and each shot is carefully worked out in advance with the director of photography. He also likes to keep his collaborators, and especially the actors, completely informed of the overall pattern of the film and the part they play in it. The result of this scrupulous exactness, together with the complexity of the final editing process, is that each film occupies him for a minimum of two years, and his overall rate of production is therefore much less than that of Jancsó, who relies more and more on improvisation while on location and whose editing task is now limited to putting together the best takes of the dozen or so shots that make up the film. Nevertheless, Szabó is capable of adjusting to changed circumstances during shooting, where necessary: he says that he enjoys working with children, partly because they are easier to handle and less temperamental than adults, and partly because if a child, after three or four attempts, cannot play a scene properly, this is a clear sign that there is something wrong with the writing or conception of the scene itself.

*

The Age of Day-dreaming (1964) is the most conventionally structured of Szabó's features and the influence here is more clearly that of Truffaut and Godard than of Resnais. The film begins with a group of newly-graduated engineers, four men and a girl, watching a television programme on which a young woman who has just received her doctorate of law is talking about her plans for the future. The programme is being viewed on half a dozen TV monitors simultaneously, each giving a different perspective on the woman, suggesting perhaps that the clear-cut, straightforward pattern she has marked out for herself is in conflict with the complexities and ambiguities of human personality and experience. At the moment, however, she has no doubts or reservations at all: her generation sees life more clearly and honestly than her elders do, and it is time for all the old prejudices, inhibitions, and hypocrisies to be swept away. The watching engineers agree with her, and they too are confident that they have the potential to put the world to rights and to redress the mistakes of their elders; equally, they are sure that they will never become stuffy and timidly conventional like their old-fashioned bosses.

They begin to put their ideals into practice: they choose a project on which they can work together and celebrate the decision in a scene shot in slow motion, yet full of quick cuts, a method that both prolongs and extends the moment of rejoicing and conveys an outburst of exuberance and delight. But once the hard work of putting the project into effect gets underway, enthusiasm begins to flag: it is really much more fun to go on holiday, to lie on the beach and practice one's Spanish, to ogle the pretty girls that stroll past and attempt to strike up a friendship with them. The cohesion of the group begins to come apart, a process accelerated by the fact that they are now working in different departments and it is an effort to find the time and energy for their work together.

János (András Bálint) at first attempts to keep the original impetus going, but even he finds that personal concerns begin to intervene. After a brief flirtation with the girl in the group, he meets another woman, an ice-skater, and it is in her apartment that they listen to Jeanne Moreau's "Tourbillon" song from *Jules and Jim* while, in another tribute to Truffaut's film, the camera follows the girl round the room in a lengthy panning shot. His friends, meanwhile, have been following much the same course, and one of them is already married.

János, who has kept a vivid recollection of the lawyer

from the opening sequence of the film, unexpectedly meets her at a New Year's Eve party. They leave together, strolling through the crowds of revellers, gradually opening up a succession of common memories and ideals. For a time, everything seems easy: they reminisce about their childhood, they watch newsreels that cover this period of their lives and especially the events of 1956, when Éva's lover decided to leave the country, while she herself stayed. She talks of the difficulties of her job and the sad, helpless people whose problems she attempts to resolve. Wrapped up in this new relationship, János drifts even further away from his former friends, and finds himself having to inquire, on meeting one of them, whether he is married yet. Then, without warning, one of the members of the group dies, and his remorseful friends gather at his funeral, guiltily aware of how far they have neglected the proud hopes and ideals with which they had started. Éva, though not herself one of the group, is particularly disturbed at the vision of loss and futility that this young man's death opens up to her: she flees from the funeral, seen in jerky helicopter shots that mirror her distress and panic.

János too recognises that he has to face up to reality and accepts Éva's decision that it is better for them to separate now, while there is still time for them to do something worthwhile with their careers. A chance encounter in the street brings him into contact with the ice-skater once more, but here too the process of growth and change has pushed them too far apart. The final scene of the film shows János being roused in the morning by the telephone wakening service: we see the girl whose job it is to call him, and then the camera tracks away from her down an endless line of other operators, wakening people all over Budapest, all, in a babble of voices, repeating the same words.

This last shot crystallises the essential mood of Szabó's films as a whole: the situation is mildly incongruous, even ridiculous (at least in its manner of presentation), and we are suddenly reminded that our own situation, whether it involves achievement or failure, pain or joy, is rarely totally unique. Yet this is presented in a spirit of affirmation rather than belittlement: we can gain strength from the realisation that we are not alone, even if this involves accepting that we cannot alter the world on our own and that many of our most powerful impulses have little substance in reality. János has finally to settle for something less than he had originally hoped to achieve, yet he has shown a capacity to learn from experience, to come to terms with his own capacities for self-deception, for neglecting and even hurting other people, and this, in its own way, is surely a victory.

Szabó speaks of Truffaut's films as being *douce* and this word admirably conveys the mood of *The Age of Day-dreaming* itself. There are few outstanding individual images, apart from the closing shot and one extreme long-shot that shows some of the young men floating on a raft in the middle of an empty lake, lustily singing—a shot that has something of the unexpected, bizarre quality of images in later films, *25 Firemen's Street* especially. It is the overall impact of the film that is really memorrable, the truthfulness and honesty of the emotions, the moments of quiet, unstrained comedy, and the warmth and affection with which Szabó brings his characters before us.

Father (1966) has many of these same qualities, but works on a more ambitious level, both in structure and in theme. It covers a period of twenty years, from the early 1940's to the early 1960's, and follows a complex flashback pattern in which fact and imagination mingle on apparently equal terms. András Bálint plays a young man who has grown up idealising his dead father as a heroic patriot and resistance leader. As he has no more than three genuine memories of his father, he fills in the remainder of the story through his imagination, and Szabó presents the boy's wildly exaggerated and unreal concepts with both wit and compassion. As he becomes older he tries more and more to live up to his idealised version of what his father was, but gradually realises that this is beginning to inhibit the development of a true personality of his own. Finally he comes to terms with the fact that, though his father was both honourable and brave, his actual life was a very ordinary one, and he is thereby freed to create an independent existence of his own.

The film falls into two parts: in the first, the son, as a child, uses his invented stories about his father as a means of creating an identity for himself and also of establishing for himself a position of respect and envy among his schoolmates; in the second, the search for identity continues, but in a more subdued and painful manner, as fantasy slowly gives way, as in *The Age of Day-dreaming,* to an acceptance of reality and its unglamorous limitations.

The first section shows Szabó's style of quiet, tongue-in-cheek, sympathetic humour at its best. The child's most bizarre fantasies about his father's activities are presented in a deadpan fashion that might delude an unwary spectator into accepting them as the truth—for a few moments, at least. The boy watches newsreels of war-damaged Budapest and of the execution of war criminals; he tries to place his father in this context and visualises a heroic escape from captivity, against tremendous odds. His stories initially lead him into trouble at school, but as they become more and more elaborate, they begin to fascinate his classmates too and they gradually accept the world he is creating for them as a real one. The boy's naivety leads him into exaggerations and implausibilities that an adult would suspect, but which other children accommodate easily into their own imaginings: as a partisan leader, his father proves capable of executing motor cycle stunts that would do credit to a circus, and it is obviously there, or on the movie screen, both of them more real than reality to a child, that they originate. Carried away by excitement, the other children elect him class leader.

He discovers an old bicycle wheel and learns from his mother that his father used to go for long cycling excursions with friends. In a beautifully lyrical sequence, the boy imagines one of these expeditions, the camera swooping over hills and through valleys with the cyclists. He teaches himself to ride a bicycle, so that he can emulate his father, and makes outings of his own with his friends. At the annual May Day parade, he mentally transforms the posters carried in the procession into portraits of his father, and even imagines his presence in the crowd.

The light-hearted humour of these scenes takes us inside the larger-than-life world of the child, but without
mockery and without condescension. Already, however,
darker undertones have begun to appear: the child
fiercely resists any "betrayal" of his father's memory by
his mother and objects to the attention shown her by
another man. To compensate, he recreates the original
wedding ceremony—in the light of his own knowledge
of this event, and in his own words. At school, too, there
are puzzles just beyond the edge of his comprehension.
One of his friends is from an aristocratic family, and he
cannot understand why this boy should be barred from
joining the Young Pioneers and why his prospects of
further education should be jeopardised. Here, the gener-
osity of spirit that he attributes to his father encourages
him to argue the matter out with his teacher, but with
no success.

The contradictions continue: his father must, of
course, have been a great surgeon as well as a heroic
patriot, and he imagines him conducting a major operation, the camera almost literally waltzing round the
room, the characters moving in grave and beautiful
slow motion. As a patriot and a humanist, therefore, his
father could not have wasted any time on the religious
superstitions that his education has taught the boy to
discredit, yet his mother insisted, despite his protests,
that his father was a profound believer. These tensions
become more pointed as the boy reaches maturity, forcing on him an extensive reassessment of everything he
has taken for granted so far.

Even as a student, however, he continues to move in

the shadow of his father: the more obvious fantasies
have been discarded, but he wears his father's suit and
watch and consciously models his behaviour on the
ideals that have by now become second nature to him.
During the events of 1956, he tries to act in accordance
with his image of his father's bravery: his fellow students,
after a series of debates and arguments, decide that they
need a Hungarian flag to symbolise their solidarity, and
the boy offers to search for one. The camera follows him
through the streets of Budapest in an eerie sequence in
which no overt danger is actually shown, but the constant
sound of gunfire off-screen makes us understand why he
hesitates at corners, summoning up all his courage,
before dashing across an apparently empty street. Finally he finds a flag and makes his way back to the classroom with it; everyone else has gone home and there is
nothing to be seen in the room except a forest of Hungarian flags...

Szabó allows the boy's amazement, and disappointment, to register for a moment, then cuts briskly into
the next scene, but this sequence displays once more the
characteristic feature of his art. The boy's courage is
placed in a wider context, yet it is acknowledged and
credited and in no way belittled; there is a touch of
irony and incongruity about the situation, but this is
presented with warmth and affection, not with mockery.

His father's watch has been broken during this episode and the boy takes it to be mended. When he returns
to collect it a few days later, the watchmaker has shut
up the shop and left the country; once again 1956 provides, as it is to do even more prominently in *Love Film,*

an occasion for meditation and reassessment, on both a personal and social level. Shortly after this, his father's body is exhumed and reburied, and the son is forced to examine once again his relationship to this almost mythic figure.

His awareness that one's role in life is often arbitrary and accidental, that one can adjust with surprising ease to totally divergent circumstances, is strengthened when he finds himself playing a minor role in a film about the Second World War. First of all he is a victim, a Jew, with a yellow star to distinguish him; for him it is all make-believe, but for his girl-friend Anni, who is really a Jew, and whose parents had been deported during the War, even an amateurish production like this is capable of rousing emotions of real grief. Suddenly, his role is reversed: there are too many Jews, and more Fascists are needed instead. The boy finds that he is now an oppressor, wearing an Arrow Cross armband; he runs across a bridge with his fellows, herding the "Jews" together and shouting at them. This experience is perhaps comparable to János's reaction to the death of Laci in *The Age of Day-dreaming:* until this moment of heightened awareness, each has been drifting, content to allow events to take their course and to shape his life for him, instead of taking a realistic assessment of his situation and attempting to act on it.

He decides to investigate more fully the true circumstances of his father's career and to seek out, rather than avoid, those who had known him personally. Was it true that his father was the first man to get the streetcars running in Budapest after the war? He imagines the scene: a solitary figure doggedly pushing a streetcar along the tracks is gradually joined by more and more bystanders; the car fills up, begins to move on its own, and, as the music swells to a joyful climax, others run to stick photographs of missing loved ones on its side, in the hope that someone will recognise or identify them.

The image is still a heroic one, but this is steadily muted as he finds out more and more of the actual details. People's memories vary, but the picture that emerges is very different from the one the boy has carried with him all his life. His father was like most other men, a decent fellow, not very striking physically, certainly not a hero, though not a coward either. For a time, the boy attempts to bolster up his illusions and to maintain the façade about his father that he had presented to others, but the heart has gone out of this and it will serve him no longer. He has a dream in which he vainly searches for his father, attempts to pin him down, and at the end of the dream, reality—and Anni—await him.

He must step at last out of his father's shadow and perform some symbolic action that is unique and personal: he decides to swim across the Danube. The camera watches him in close-up as he carries out this task, then it tilts slowly upwards and widens focus. Two or three other young people can be seen swimming beside him, then half a dozen, then dozens, until the screen is full of them. The image is less naturalistic than its equivalent at the end of *The Age of Day-dreaming,* but it performs the same function of opening up the scope of the film, of reminding us that we have been watching, not so much one individual story as the presentation, through one particular experience, of the universal process of growth and maturity.

Though the essential details of this experience transcend national and social boundaries, *Father* is more clearly a "political" film than *The Age of Day-dreaming*. A work of art does not attain a "universal" appeal by being vague and abstract; on the contrary, the more precise and exact it is in its presentation of circumstance and event, the more likely it is to touch a corresponding nerve in its viewers or readers. Szabó's film gains, therefore, by being so firmly tied to the historical and political events of his hero's lifetime; it is these that have shaped and formed him, and his dilemmas, problems, and decisions are those of his whole generation—both within Hungary and, in their essence, outside it. The major flaw that can be found with the film, and this is true to some extent of *Love Film* as well, is in its length: it is perhaps too relaxed, too meandering in places, and some judicious cutting might have strengthened the overall impact.

Love Film (1970) takes its starting point in the problem touched on in both of the previous films: in 1956 Kata and Jancsi (played, as usual by András Bálint), who had grown up together as children and had since fallen deeply in love, were forced to separate. Kata decided to leave the country and has lived in France since then, while Jancsi remained in Hungary. After a montage of photographs of them as children and a narrator's comment to the effect that "fancy modifies reality", we see Jancsi on his way by train to visit Kata. In *Father* a sense of inner joy and happiness was often expressed

István Szabó

The Age of Day-dreaming: three young men who are going to change the world. András Bálint is on the right

The Age of Day-dreaming: but idealism slowly gives way to the search for a more personal and intimate happiness

Father: the boy attempts to shave with his father's razor

Father: one of the boy's fantasies of his father's career. Miklós Gábor, who plays the father, is to the left of the streetcar

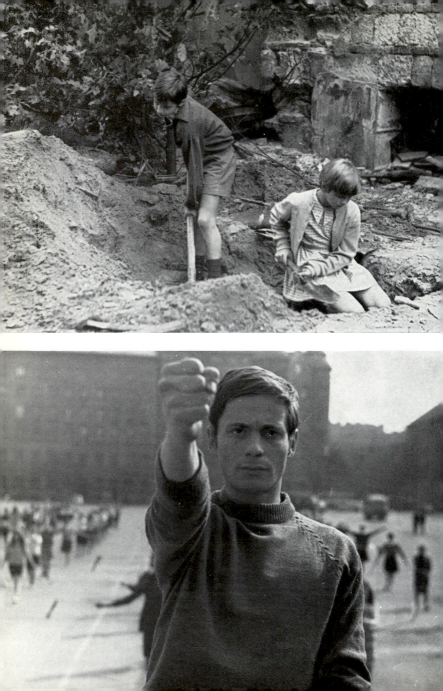

Love Film: the children start to dig their way to Australia

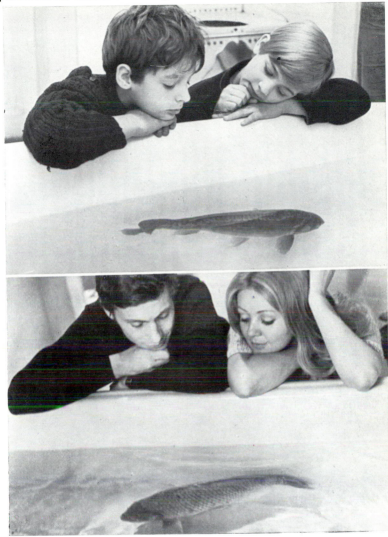

Love Film: a publicity still that juxtaposes past and present within the film

Love Film: Jancsi (András Bálint) in his place for the parade, "solemnly clutching a fistful of empty air"

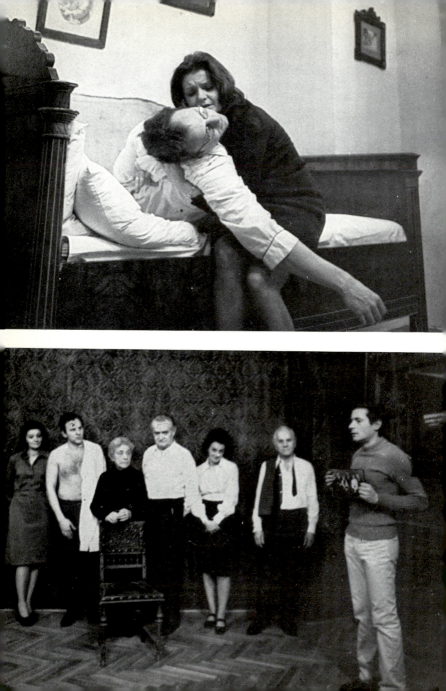

◀ *25 Firemen's Street:* one of the many flashbacks in the film: Maria (Lucyna Winnicka) remembers the death of her husband

◀ *25 Firemen's Street:* one of several scenes in which time past and time present fuse and merge into the same image

25 Firemen's Street: the old clockmaker is left alone with his memories, sitting despondently among a jumble of broken and faceless clocks

István Gaál

Current: a tiny figure dwarfed by the huge trees spaced at regular in- ▶
tervals along the water's edge

Current: Gabi's grandmother, unable to accept that he will never have ▶
a proper burial, draws on her knowledge of traditional folklore to call
him to the surface

◄ *The Green Years:* Márton (Bence Tóth) finds that he no longer fits into his home environment in the village

◄ *The Green Years:* Márton with his friends at university

Baptism: Menyhért (Zoltán Latinovits) and András (János Koltai) begin to acknowledge their mutual antagonism

The Falcons: the boy watches as three horsemen, arranged in a circle, perfect their total control and domination of their falcons

◀ *The Falcons:* an image from the boy's dream of the distorted and all-powerful Lilik

◀ *The Falcons:* the boy (Ivan Andonov) is initiated into the mystique of falconry by Lilik (György Bánffy)

Dead Landscape: the old woman's son arrives unexpectedly for a visit, not knowing his mother has died

Dead Landscape: Anti (István Ferenczi) and Juli (Mari Törőcsik) near the beginning of the film (note the falcon!)

Dead Landscape: Juli walks through the autumnal landscape on her way to market

by bizarre, apparently incongruous images (during the scene with the streetcar, for example, a man is seen doing handstands on the roof of the car); and in *Love Film* Jancsi's excitement and exhilaration are conveyed by an unexpected series of very brief shots, in utter silence, of him in a succession of most unlikely postures, propped somewhere between the luggage rack and the ceiling, and then racing along outside the carriage, turning cartwheels and keeping pace with the train. Then the sounds of normal life return again as the conductor enters the carriage and asks the impassive Jancsi for his ticket. A similar pattern of mental images later in the film shows Kata, dressed in a collection of stunningly exotic costumes, rushing eagerly to meet Jancsi at the station; when he actually arrives, however, the tiny platform is deserted and he is left gazing despondently around as the train pulls away.

Scenes like this make it clear that Szabó is as interested in the tricks and deceptions played by memory and imagination as he is in simply reconstructing the story of Jancsi and Kata's relationship by means of flashbacks. The first half of the film is built up as a dense mosaic of images of past, present and (as in the station scene described above) future, centred on Jancsi's train journey and requiring to be fitted together almost like the pieces of a jigsaw puzzle. Gradually a more or less chronological pattern emerges, taking the children from the age of around six to their early twenties, but even so some of the images come to be naggingly disturbing and even "wrong", especially when, as often happens, key scenes are repeated several times.

Near the beginning of the film, for example, there is a scene that shows Jancsi, riding a bicycle, being stopped in the street in 1956 and searched for concealed arms. When this scene is shown again later in the film, not only is the angle from which it is shot different, but the actions are subtly altered too. A more extreme instance is an image that occurs several times in the film, of Kata as a small child sitting on a swing jeering at Jancsi: not only is this particular memory changed each time it appears, it seems probable that this incident never occurred at all, and that for Jancsi it is simply a way of clarifying to himself one aspect of their relationship.

The most crucial of these "false memories" is that of the execution of the children's swimming instructor during the war: Jancsi himself did not witness this, of course, but he imagines it to himself in various ways and the whole incident has become one of the key events round which he has organised his understanding of his childhood. The teacher herself is represented mostly by a close-up of her face and the strangely hollow sound of her voice as she repeats instructions to the children, and Jancsi has preserved a photograph of her that, towards the end of the film, he shows to a mutual friend that he meets in Kata's apartment in France. "Oh, no", the friend tells him firmly, "that isn't her at all," and she goes on to give her version of the execution, which she claims to remember exactly.

Hints and warnings of this kind about the fallibility of memory accumulate throughout the first part of the film. As the hero of *Father* discovered, we often remember what we *wish* had happened rather than what actually *did* happen; this process is harmless and natural enough on a small scale, but if we proceed to shape our lives and personalities in accordance with these pseudo-memories, the result can be destructive and can stunt or distort our understanding both of ourselves and those close to us. In the second half of the film, once Jancsi has been reunited with Kata, he is forced to come to terms with the fact that the past cannot be picked up again after a gap of ten years as though nothing had happened: each of them has changed, has developed new interests and friendships, and, as they compare their memories and discuss these with friends who had gone through the same experiences, they discover that each has subtly altered the past to suit his own inner needs and there are now barriers between them that make it impossible to recapture or return to the simple and natural relationship that each had imagined existing before — "imagined" because even there tensions existed that memory has smoothed over or neglected.

The structure of the film is thus very similar to that of *Father*: in each case the young hero begins by constructing a version of his past that is a mixture of fact, dream, wish-fulfilment, and subtle distortion of actual incidents; in the second half of the film (which has a more conventional narrative structure in each case and a smaller proportion of flashbacks) he is made to compare this with the recollections of other people, and has to discard the more obvious and comforting fantasies, and come to terms with the realities of the present.

In the early part of the film the various strands of the past are tied together by a flashback technique based on association. Sometimes the link is a verbal one: the phrase "Don't look back" connects the first version of the scene in which Jancsi is searched for arms with an earlier childhood memory in which danger also threatens. Sometimes it is association by image: from Jancsi and Kata gazing at a fish swimming in a bathtub, there is a cut to the face and voice of the swimming instructor. And sometimes a movement or action provides the connection: a gesture begun at the end of one shot appears to be completed, but at a totally different time and place, in the next shot. Once the pattern of the film has been established, however, and the audience can be assumed to recognise that certain types of images will regularly recur, the linkage becomes less obvious and predictable. In one instance, two levels of the past are juxtaposed within one shot (a technique which Szabó elaborates later in *25 Firemen's Street*): towards the end of the film the teenage Jancsi and Kata are seen together, Kata moves away, the image blurs briefly and then, in the same camera movement, we see the two again as children. There is also one fine sequence in which past and present are fused together as at no other time in the film. Jancsi and Kata begin to make love in the latter's apartment in France; there is a series of short cuts of the pair as children playing in the snow and riding on a sledge; these shots become longer as we hear on the soundtrack the muted sighs of the lovers; now the camera is on the sledge rushing downhill in one long continuous motion; gradually it slows down, hesitates, comes to a stop. The metaphor is perfect, both visually and rhythmically, and—unlike most similar metaphors in the cinema—it has the advantage of being an intrinsic part of the characters' experience, and not something totally unrelated to this.

The move from the intricate flashback structure of the first half of the film to the more straightforward chronology of the second may imply that the past is being assimilated and absorbed instead of remaining as a nagging, distracting element in the lives of the characters. On another level, the progress is one from innocence to experience and, as in *Father,* Szabó presents this in both personal and political terms.

Though both children grow up in an environment shaped by the events of the Second World War, they are able nevertheless to pass through most of the normal experiences of childhood. On the one hand, there is the constant threat of air-raids (to the extent that Christmas presents have to be opened one year in a basement shelter); their early schooldays are in an improvised classroom with the black-out paper on the window doing duty as a blackboard; there is the constant struggle for food, the mysterious disappearances of friends and acquaintances. On the other are the incidents that can be paralleled in the experience of almost all of us: Jancsi joining Kata in her attempt to dig a tunnel all the way through to Australia; the couple trying (unsuccessfully) to electrocute a fish in their bathtub.

The social and political problems that follow the end of the war present their own problems—more acute and intractable this time, because the children, as they grow older, are forced to make decisions and choose a moral stance of their own. One of the most disturbing of these incidents comes at a meeting of the Young Pioneer group to which both children belong. The couple are virtually put on trial before their fellows and told that their exclusive attachment to each other is reprehensible and anti-social; they attempt to justify themselves, but their arguments make no impression on the closed minds of their young accusers (themselves hardly more than ten or twelve years old). Szabó shows us close-ups of the sly, smirking faces of the "judges", petty tyrants in the making and proud of it.

Later, Jancsi and Kata are due to participate in a bombastic celebration and parade of the early 1950's, complete with rigorously synchronised marches, banners, and slogans. During the rehearsals, Jancsi puts his banner aside for a moment to go and talk to Kata; when he returns someone has stolen it. The next scene shows him in his place for the parade, solemnly clutching a fistful of empty air. Despite the absurdity of the situation, and the comic treatment of it, this scene is clearly parallel to the earlier one in its comment on the hollowness and rigidity of the political situation of the time.

1956 brings all the strands of the film together: Jancsi and Kata have to make both a political and a personal decision and though each acts in a perfectly honest and straightforward way, the result, paradoxically, is that they have to separate. Kata decides to leave the country and go abroad, while Jancsi chooses to stay, but in the years that follow, their letters and the selective distortions of memory manage to convince them that the breach is not irreparable and their relationship may still be a viable one.

Even in France, however, they find it is impossible to act purely as individuals. Several of their former friends have also emigrated and, as they visit one family for the evening, they watch a television newscast that displays a map of Europe and the parents eagerly point out to their uncomprehending children the tiny dot that is Hungary. Gradually the question at issue between Kata and Jancsi defines itself as their relationship to their country as much as their relationship to each other. Kata is not prepared to leave France and return to Hungary, while Jancsi cannot tear himself away from his emotional roots in Budapest. Once the situation has been presented in these terms, it becomes inevitable that Jancsi must leave.

Once again the final scene of the film expands the implications to take in a wider range of experiences than those of Kata and Jancsi alone. Jancsi has returned to Budapest and is writing a telegram to Kata; slowly the camera tracks away from him to show an apparently endless line of other people, all likewise sending messages to loved ones from whom they too are separated. The sound track fills up with the murmur of voices, greetings and endearments overlapping and blending together, and in the midst of all this we hear the brisk instructions of the children's swimming teacher. The past cannot, and should not, be discarded entirely; rather it must be integrated into the present, but in an honest and realistic manner, not as a system of illusions. The image slowly begins to over-expose and there is a cut to Kata's face, blindingly white, hardly visible at all against the brightness of the screen, as she responds to Jancsi's message.

As she talks, the over-exposure continues, until the image bleaches out completely.

The film is clearly as much about the difficulties of living in a small, fiercely nationalistic country, too often at the mercy of forces it has no means of controlling, as it is about two fictional characters called Kata and Jancsi. Szabó, however, neither preaches or complains, and the richness of the film comes from the fact that both elements can exist together, that we can understand the young couple as individuals and also appreciate the outside pressures that shape and finally thwart their relationship. This was Szabó's first film in colour, and he uses colour to intensify the contrasting moods and emotions on which the film is built; the present, and especially Kata's apartment in France with its blue and green pastel-shaded walls, is bright and cheerful, while the past is softer, darker, less clear-cut, more ambiguous.

This emotive use of colour carries over into Szabó's work, *25 Firemen's Street* (1973) where the images are dark, haunting, and secretive. The film itself is more enigmatic than *Father* or *Love Film,* partly because there is no one central figure with whose experiences all the elements of the complex flashback structure can be associated (though András Bálint appears in the film, it is in a relatively minor role this time). The setting is an old house on the eve of its demolition; during a hot summer night the numerous inhabitants indulge in dreams and recollections of the events of the past thirty years and especially the period of the Second World War. At a first viewing, the film appears almost too dense to be completely assimilated: we are introduced, in quick succession, to at least half a dozen characters and it becomes difficult to sort out which memory belongs to which character and even whether what we are watching is a true recollection or merely a fantasy. Gradually, however, the focus narrows down to the reminiscences of two or three major characters, but even so the film is much more adventurous stylistically even than *Love Film* and achieves some astonishing leaps in time and space— shots that bring together in one continuous camera movement characters from totally different areas of the past, or compress into one unbroken sequence several quite distinct events; scenes, even in which living and dead characters are reunited. Much of this can be justified as reflecting the actual process of memory, which is rarely as neat and logical as film-makers (even Szabó himself) have tended to represent it, but Szabó explains it further by saying that the film should be seen as a dream experienced by the house itself and that, within that context, the fragmentary and often contradictory stream of images has its own logic.

At any rate, whereas one can find a clear thread of narrative continuity in both *Father* and *Love Film, 25 Firemen's Street* works in a more musical structure of theme and variations, with no sharply defined resolution or release at the end.[3] As a result, its beautiful, though often bizarre and puzzling images tend to linger more strongly in the mind than the actual sequence of events

[3] This type of structure perhaps classifies *25 Firemen's Street* as Szabó's most "modern" work and aligns it with such films as Bergman's *Persona,* Fellini's *8 ½,* and Resnais's *Last Year in Marienbad.*

does, and it is significant that the typical "reunion" scene that closes all Szabó's features performs a new function in this film. Whereas in the other films it served to widen out the relatively narrow individual experience by placing it in a context of similar experiences occurring to characters who are introduced for this scene only and are otherwise anonymous, in *25 Firemen's Street* it is more of the nature of a recapitulation, bringing together the various strands that had touched or briefly intertwined throughout the body of the film. Andris (András Bálint) leaves the doomed house and turns to look back at the inhabitants (both living and dead) who are lined up in front of it as though for a group photograph; the camera slowly pans along the line of (mostly familiar) faces, then closes with a shot of the empty house.

The theme too is less that of the persistence of, and escape from, illusions, than simply the concept of survival. The inhabitants of the house have all lived through a shattering and destructive period of history that constantly forced them to make difficult, and sometimes impossible, moral decisions. Without resorting to easy moral judgements, Szabó distinguishes between those who, even in the most desperate circumstances, retained their self-respect and their concern for others, and those who compromised their behaviour to suit the shifting political circumstances.

The film begins with a montage of shots of deserted houses crumbling under the impact of demolition; interspersed between the naturalistic sound effects are scraps of music—a brass band, an orchestra playing popular music of the 1930's. We see the house itself and are quickly introduced to the inhabitants; a young woman speaks directly into the camera, "It's so hot!" Suddenly we see her swimming soundlessly through a series of flooded rooms. (Silence is used as effectively here as in *Love Film:* an eerie, dreamlike quality is obtained from shots that have neither the dialogue nor the sound effects that we would expect, or from scenes in which the camera appears to float effortlessly down staircases and probe into rooms).

Some of the characters are thinking about food: an old woman lovingly describes the recipe for a richly luxurious chocolate cake, while her daughter eats spoonful after spoonful of cream; a man dreams that a former girl-friend talks to him about his favourite soup and we see her settle herself on the bed beside him while his wife sleeps soundly at his side. The dreams and memories thus become as real to us as to the characters, and figures belonging to the imagination take on as much weight and solidity as those of everyday experience.

Others are imagining or remembering romance: Andris opens the door to the bathroom and finds a naked girl standing in the bath; smiling, she shows no embarrassment or fear. Meanwhile his mother Mária, whose story is one of those we follow most thoroughly in the film, is remembering her own youth, the various suitors who courted her, and the suicide of one of her friends. The faces and voices of two of those suitors blend uneasily together; she remembers a dancing class and the endless conversations about marriage; and here we have one of the most complex shots in the film as events that must have taken place over several years are brought together within the framework of one continuous camera movement and the scene ends with Mária talking to the friend who has been dead for so many years.

Other characters are introduced: an old man searches through a series of empty rooms, then opens a door to find himself in a carpenter's workshop, full of small children; he begins to sing to them. Two postmen, their coats covered with snow, stand silently at the bed of a dying colleague. We return to Mária, who remembers her wedding dinner and a story told by her grandmother containing a German phrase that is solemnly translated by one guest to another all the way round the table. Up to this stage, the effect of the film is somewhat disjointed: themes are clearly being exposed, but it is difficult to keep track of them all or to decide which have the most weight or significance. With the introduction of the events of the war, however, the focus sharpens and the memories become essentially those of Mária and Mrs. Gaskóy, the baker's wife.

At first the atmosphere is one of solidarity, most vividly realized in a scene where a man buys a whole truckload of bread and distributes it to the young conscripts who are just about to be taken off to the Front. Soon, however, dissensions become evident; some choose to align themselves with the Nazis or to adopt a posture of passive collaboration that allows them to benefit from the misfortunes of their neighbours, while others attempt to retain some sense of integrity and self-respect. Mária is included among a batch of people due to be deported; she goes from apartment to apartment in the house, leaving some clothes here, some furniture there, asking the neighbours to take care of them until she returns: "Of course we will, and you'll be back soon," they attempt to reassure her. We see her empty rooms: one by one pictures drop from their hooks to the floor. She and the other women are forced to strip and submit to a humiliating body search; the people conducting this are familiar to them, their neighbours too: "Forgive me," one of them whispers. In one of the most powerful scenes in the film the naked women walk in turn through a pool of disinfectant, still clutching their pitiful possessions, some food, a clock, a typewriter; steam shrouds and obscures them, there is complete and ominous silence. Huddled together in a basement shelter, they carefully share out their few scraps of food; there is not even enough for a whole sardine each, and the children have to be provided for first. Mária is lucky: she is told that she can go home and, before leaving, she distributes her winter clothing among those for whom there is no reprieve.

These scenes are fragmentary, interspersed among other recollections, notably those of Mrs. Gaskóy, who shelters fugitives and escapees in her attic and gives them work in the bakery. There are constant searches, interrogations, narrow escapes, fears that the neighbours who know of this might one day betray her. We see a young German soldier walking confidently down the stairs; suddenly a shot rings out, he crumples and falls: the tables have turned at last.

After the liberation, there are those who want to take vengeance on collaborators and traitors, and it is often those who had themselves suffered least who prove the most vindictive. Even Mária, however, despite her contempt for this behaviour, cannot prevent herself from reacting violently when she encounters one of her neighbours, a fat woman who had strutted proudly in her uniform and gleefully supervised the humiliation of those she held in her power. Her bedridden husband, who had survived all the vicissitudes of the war, finally dies. Meanwhile Mrs. Gaskóy has become a heroine: she is besieged with requests for character references and safe-conduct passes: "Please, you have to help me. Remember, I knew what you were doing, and I said nothing about it."

There is a jump in time, a procession takes place outside the house and people who are in reality several thousand miles apart from each other, people who are alive and people who are really dead, reunite and joyfully greet one another. Now we are at the end of the 1940's Mrs. Gaskóy finds that her bakery is being socialised and the woman in charge of this operation is brusque and unsympathetic: Mrs. Gaskóy's heroism belongs to the past and new qualities are needed now. A few years later, the situation is reversed again: it is 1956 and this same woman comes to Mrs. Gaskóy and begs her to protect her.... We see another reversal, sad and ironic this time rather than bitter: the Count in the apartment next to Mária is forced to leave and he asks her to take care of his possessions in virtually the same words as she had used when leaving things with him a few years previously. "Of course I will," she tells him helplessly.

The pattern of the past has worked itself out now and events have fallen into place. History is far from meaning

less for Szabó: it repeats itself with ironic twists and variations and those who adapt themselves too eagerly and
too readily to each change of circumstance find that, even
if they survive physically, they have lost the sense of
dignity and purpose that ultimately makes life bearable.
We return to the present, perhaps even to the future: the
house is being vacated, furniture tumbles in slow-motion
from the windows into the courtyard, the camera travels
slowly through the deserted rooms. In a mysteriously
powerful and haunting image, we see the old clockmaker
whose daughter had killed herself so many years before,
sitting despondently among a jumble of broken and
faceless clocks. There are some flowers in a vase beside
him, he takes a handful, puts them in his mouth, chews
them; then he picks up some broken glass and reflectively
almost tranquilly, munches this too. Many of the other
characters have gathered together in a room where a
cheerful rag-and-bone man is making an offer for their
remaining possessions; carried away by enthusiasm, he
begins to remove even the shoes from their feet and the
coats from their backs: "I'll take this, and this, and this
too." In these scenes in particular, but elsewhere in the
film too, Szabó displays again a fine ability to create
images that function as metaphors, based on a concrete,
factual reality, but working themselves out in a way that
transcends literal representation.

The central figures in this film are rather older than
the heroes of the three earlier works, and this perhaps
accounts for its reflective, almost melancholy, tone.
Whereas in the earlier films the protagonists are still on
the threshold of life at the end of the film and have the

chance to make use of the discoveries they have made about themselves and their potentialities, in *25 Firemen's Street* the major characters have already reached a plateau from which they can assess the significance of a life that is already complete in its essentials. The diffuse structure of the film also contributes towards this sense of resignation: some of the older characters (like the watchmaker) appear to have been defeated by their experiences, while we do not really learn enough about younger figures like Andris to feel any certainty about the direction their future life might take. This is not necessarily, however, a weakness in the film for, despite the fact that it goes over much of the ground covered in the earlier films, it takes in a much wider and more varied area of experience and is thus much less likely to move towards a clear-cut resolution. And if it is less immediately likeable or attractive than *Father* or *Love Film,* it has a teasing, enigmatic quality that makes certain scenes linger and reverberate in the memory.

Like Jancsó, Szabó has shown an ability to develop and expand his stylistic resources while remaining true to a consistent body of themes and recurrent situations. Interestingly enough, despite the obvious differences in their style, the direction taken by both has been away from the realism of *Cantata, My Way Home,* and *The Age of Day-dreaming* towards a more poetic, even at times surrealistic cinema, where the images often function at one remove from reality, in a metaphoric or symbolic manner, and dead characters can either come to life again or mingle with the living in the no-man's land of memory. Jancsó's method of long takes ensures that each individual shot functions in terms of real time and real space, with no possibility for the manipulations for stylistic or functional effect that are normal in the cinema; yet the transitions from shot to shot are often so ambiguous that it is often difficult to tell whether minutes, hours, or even days have elapsed. Szabó's very different, almost antithetical method of fragmentation and flashback strangely enough allows him something of the same double focus: for much of the film we are firmly anchored in a clearly defined space and time and then we are suddenly let loose and left to scramble for our bearings. Each has certainly moved a long way from the straightforward, chronological narrative of his first features, and though Szabó's development is a less spectacular and controversial one, the modest and unpretentious surface of his films should not disguise their profound originality.

Chapter Four

Landscape and Silence:
István Gaál

Photographs tend to make István Gaál look more forbidding than he really is, and his films too are sometimes
taken to be more purely austere and sombre than they
actually are, critics overlooking the vein of sly humour
that runs through all of them, producing moments of
wry comedy at the most unexpected moments. Now in
his early forties, Gaál is one of the Hungarian film-makers
most highly regarded on an international level, and four
of his five features to date have been awarded prizes at
major film festivals: *Current* at Karlovy Vary and Pesaro,
The Green Years at Hyères, *The Falcons* at Cannes, and
Dead Landscape at Karlovy Vary.

Gaál comes from a rural and village environment and
this has proved a decisive factor both in his choice of
subjects and in his handling of them. There is a directness
and straightforwardness in his approach to his characters
that does not preclude sympathy with even the most
vacillating and confused among them, but which maintains a firm distinction between behaviour which displays moral integrity and actions which are morally
corrupt. His second feature, *The Green Years* (1965),
was one of the first to criticise the excesses and the anti-
human tendencies of Hungarian political life in the early

1950s, and he has remained uncompromising in his defence of human dignity against repression and authoritarianism of all kinds. A major theme of all his films is the attempt to preserve basic moral values of justice and humanity in circumstances calculated to suppress or intimidate these, and it is no coincidence that he is a great admirer of both *Somewhere in Europe* and *People on the Alps.*

After he graduated from the Academy of Dramatic and Cinematic Art in 1959, Gaál was awarded a scholarship to study for two years at the Centro Sperimentale in Rome. Like most of his contemporaries he chose to test his mastery of his medium in a series of short films before venturing on a feature, *Current,* in 1963. One of these shorts, *Tisza—Autumn in Sketches,* can be seen as a direct preparation for this, shot in the same settings and making use of some of the people who appear in the later film. These early films, and *Current* itself, were photographed by Sándor Sára, while Gaál changed roles and acted as cameraman on Sára's famous short *Gypsies* in 1962. In the intervals between his features, Gaál has continued to make short films: a documentary on Cuba in 1969, a beautifully edited visual poem—set to music by Béla Bartók—in 1970, and a commemoration of the 500th anniversary of the first Hungarian printed book in 1974.

Despite the intelligence and the moral intensity of his best films, Gaál is primarily a visual poet and the meaning of his films emerges from the nature and juxtaposition of his images, and the relationship between these and the music, natural sounds, or silence that accompany them, rather than from explicit dialogue or debate. In particular he has a very strong feeling for the interaction between character and landscape and an ability to create scenes that emerge as visual metaphors, subtly crystallising the essence of a film far more effectively than words. He prefers, when talking about his work, to discuss style, technique, the sheer difficulty of actually registering the right images on film; questions of intention and meaning depend on these and are shaped by them. As well as writing or collaborating on all his scripts, he is ready to take a hand with the photography (as he did on some scenes of *The Falcons*), and insists on carrying out all the editing himself, physically handling and cutting the film instead of merely supervising this, as most directors do. He controls every detail of the art direction, and has always worked with the same composer, András Szöllősy, one of the leading figures in contemporary Hungarian music. His attitude to film is immediate, sensual, and tactual: he says he loves the smell of raw film stock.

*

Current (1963) gained Gaál immediate critical attention for its sensitive handling of the reactions of a group of teenagers confronted with the sudden death by drowning of one of their friends. The film begins in a light-hearted, almost casual manner, as the six or seven young people drift together on their way to the river, tease one another, joke, and throw a ball around; but there are hints already of tensions and jealousies behind the façade of comradeship. The characters, however, are not very clearly differentiated and it soon becomes difficult to hold them separately in one's mind as individuals; though this appears a fault to begin with, its purpose becomes evident as the film proceeds. Once at the river, a few of them begin to swim while the others lounge on the beach; gradually all are drawn into an increasingly competitive and risky diving contest. As the afternoon progresses, they tire of this, return to the shore and light a fire; some of the boys daub mud on their faces to look like "savages" and they begin a mock tribal dance round the fire, a soundtrack of throbbing drums adding the first non-naturalistic element so far to the film and signalling a change of mood, a sense of menace. One of them decides to take a photograph of the group and it is only then that they (and we) realise that someone, almost as anonymous to themselves as he is to us, is missing.

The hitherto sunlit and carefree setting now takes on an atmosphere of uneasiness as twilight falls and, in a grove of trees that surround them at weird and ominous angles, they begin a search for their friend. The camera follows them from the far bank of the river as, reduced to small and isolated dots, they try more and more frantically to find him. Some of them dive repeatedly into the water in search of his body, the camera bobbing under the surface with them, their shouts and splashing uncannily replaced by utter silence. Splash and silence, splash and silence, interminably repeated. Finally they gather once more round a dead tree silhouetted starkly against the skyline and put on their clothes, hardly exchanging a word. They return apprehensively to the darkness and silence of the sleeping village.

The engine of a police motor boat cuts into the quietness as the search for the boy's body is resumed the following morning. His friends are stunned by what has happened; they listen uncomprehendingly as a police officer lectures them on their foolishness and irresponsibility in taking such chances in an area of the river known to be dangerous. He later comments to one of his helpers on how similar all the young people's faces had looked to him: Gaál wishes to stress the utterly random nature of what has happened and that it could be any of these carefree, unthinking teenagers who is now lying at the bottom of the river. As the search continues, the others slowly attempt to come to terms with their experience: one of them, a shop assistant, suddenly finds himself the centre of attention for the first time in his life. Everyone wants to hear his story and, as he tells it, he begins to embroider it, altering the facts, exaggerating his own role in it.

Laci, a doctor's son, rather more intellectual and thoughtful than his friends, tries to discuss with his parents the meaning of what has happened, but his parents are too busy and, in any case, are not particularly interested in the death of someone whose family belongs to a much lower social stratum of the village. He then turns to Luja, the drowned boy's best friend, but neither of them can make very much of it on their own. Gaál now signals another turning point in the emotional structure of the film by once again combining music and images in a very formal, almost abstract manner: in a piece of virtuoso editing reminiscent of the beautiful scene in the blacksmith's shop in *Gypsies* (which Gaál edited as well as photographing), he shows us the objects in the dead boy's bedroom, cutting the images together to the rhythms of a Vivaldi concerto.

The formerly cohesive group of friends begins to break up, the tensions that were signalled earlier in the film now coming to the surface under the stresses they have gone through. The two girls quarrel with each other, and one of them breaks with her boy-friend—who had innocently set in motion the chain of events that led to the accident by daring a potential rival for the girl to the diving contest. He is unable to understand her actions and even when she leaves the village to start a new life in the city he follows her to the station, still eager to marry her, and numbly watches the train leave.

The mood of the film becomes darker and more elegiac: Gabi's grandmother, unable to accept that he will never have a proper burial, draws on her knowledge of traditional folklore to call him to the surface. In the strangest and most haunting sequence of the film she sets out at darkness along the bank of the river, a tiny figure dwarfed by the huge trees spaced at regular intervals along the water's edge; a rowing boat takes her out to the centre of the stream and she places a loaf of bread with a lighted candle on it to drift with the current: the bread will stop over the boy's corpse and draw it to the top. Two of his former friends, a boy and a girl, watch from a cliff overlooking the river, and the poignant, dignified Baroque music completes the atmosphere of a formal and age-old ritual.

The next day the boy's friends go to identify his body in a small hut high above the river where it has been taken; they realise, to their horror, that they too are already beginning to forget what he looked like and that the unity of their group and their feelings for one another were based on much shallower and more arbitrary foundations than they had suspected. Their growing self-awareness is counterpointed by the casual attitude of the policeman on duty, to whom all this is merely part of the day's routine. It is the grandmother's loss that is felt most deeply and, in another of the set pieces in which Gaál manages to combine aesthetic formality with deep and genuine emotion, a montage of the house in which they had lived together, the dark trees surrounding it, and the objects that will always remind her of her bereavement, is placed against the sound of her keening lament for her grandson.

For the others, life continues: policemen put up notices forbidding any more bathing at the spot where the drowning occurred; Laci, uneasily aware that something within him has been tested and found wanting, leaves the village for the university; we see the photograph of the carefree group taken just before Gabi's absence was noticed; finally the camera focuses on the placid, treacherous waters of the river and zooms slowly away from them.

Current can be faulted in several respects: it follows a rather *too* schematic structure perhaps, that leaves the set pieces, for all their effectiveness, somewhat apart from the style and tone of the rest of the film; and there is some unevenness in the acting (most of the performers were still students at the Film School). Yet it demonstrates most of Gaál's characteristic strengths and especially his ability to convey emotions and psychological development *visually,* by means of setting, structural rhythm, the counterpointing of image and sound, and the creation of scenes that work through what he has called "realistic abstraction"—maintaining a firm basis in physical reality but taking on, through the images or the editing, a dimension beyond this.

The process of self-discovery, of painfully coming to terms with the fact that one's capacity for deep and loyal friendship or for moral courage is much slighter than one had imagined it was, is followed up in Gaál's next two films, *The Green Years* (1965) and *Baptism* (1968); and, more explicitly than *Current,* both are also concerned with the tensions that arise between young intellectuals and the rural background that they are forced to abandon in order to continue their careers.

Gaál denies that *The Green Years* is in any way explicitly autobiographical, though the general situation in which the hero finds himself must have been very familiar to anyone who was a student at a time when arbitrary and dogmatic political decisions could alter or destroy a person's career overnight. The film begins with Márton leaving his native village on his way to university: he takes farewell of his family, all of them crowded together in the same small room, and walks through the still sleeping village to the station; the atmosphere of desolation and starkness remains to condition our response to what follows in the film. On the train he meets another student, intending, like himself, to study medicine; on their arrival in Budapest they gaze in wonder at the ubiquitous loudspeakers ready to spew forth propaganda and now weirdly issuing the applause from a political rally, and stare at the monuments and statues on the public buildings. Then they encounter their first shock: the medical faculty is full and each is arbitrarily shifted to another, less crowded area of study, so that Márton finds to his amazement that he is now destined to study French for the next four years.

Gradually Márton comes to terms with the strangeness of his new environment: in the student hostel he is able to use running water for the first time in his life and he moves cautiously, and then delightedly down the washroom, turning on all the taps in the basins and in the showers, and finally, in a way that is both comic and touching, standing back to admire his handiwork. He attends lectures at which, packed in with several hundred other students, he is expected to note down religiously every word that falls from the professor's lips. Slowly a pattern of crushing authoritarianism begins to emerge: even in such minor matters as their compulsory physical exercise the students are hectored by a constant stream of instructions; one, who cannot swim, is brusquely ordered to jump into the pool nevertheless and almost drowns. This particular student turns out to be one of the many peasants who have been sent to university, despite a stunning lack of aptitude or scholastic talent, simply because the government insists dogmatically that peasants fill a certain proportion of university places. Fully aware of his own incompetence, he struggles on desperately nevertheless, terrified of the shame and dis-appointment his failure would bring to his parents.

Márton does what he can to help him; he is vaguely aware that injustices are being committed but, as none of them affect him personally, he feels that all he has to do is to stand aside. When Laci, a friend of his, is unanimously "elected" secretary of the Faculty's Youth Organization, Márton, puzzled by the blatantly undemo-cratic nature of the proceedings, tries to salve his conscience by not joining in the general applause, but pushes the matter no further than this. He becomes disturbed, however, by Laci's excessive zeal in discover-ing and routing out "enemies of the Party" and the first challenge to his moral neutrality is forced on him when his own girl friend is publicly accused by Laci of "im-morality" (having an affair with one of her instructors) and is expelled from the Youth Organisation. Once again he compromises: he defends the girl's reputation against those of her former friends who turn against her, but, believing the accusations and resenting her betrayal, he refuses to have anything more to do with her.

Returning home for Christmas he finds that the ele-mentary sophistication he has acquired in his few months away has altered his relationships with his family and set up barriers between them. He begins to question aspects of their way of life he had taken for granted before and becomes particularly sensitive to the resent-ment and frustration of his sister, who sees herself trapped, without choice or consultation, in the dead-end of marriage, child-rearing and domestic drudgery.

Back at the university Márton tries to talk things over

with Laci, who is disturbed at the further persecution of the girl (she has now been expelled from the university), and agrees that it is unfair to punish her so savagely while allowing her lover (who has meanwhile abandoned her too) to go scot-free. Laci forces a confrontation with the instructor, an influential Party figure, and is summarily arrested for his pains; a web of half-truths and rumours is woven around him to explain and justify his disgrace. These scenes are movingly counterpointed with another that shows Márton being summoned from a classroom to give information about Laci while the professor is reading a passage from Shaw's Preface to *Saint Joan* and talking about the need to maintain human dignity and self-control; the resigned, despairing look on the teacher's face as Márton leaves sums up the tensions and complexities of the situation better than any dialogue could.

Once more Márton compromises: he refuses to give evidence against Laci or to join in his persecution, but he cannot bring himself to defend him publicly. He visits Laci's wife and offers her financial assistance, deliberately suppressing his awareness that his moral support would be much more valuable to her. Walking away from this encounter through the deserted streets, he suddenly becomes aware of his shadow, monstrous and distorted, thrown on the walls around him. He stands outside the classroom as his fellow students unanimously vote to expel Laci from the Youth Organisation; without waiting for them to disperse, he runs away down the long corridor, towards the camera. The moral tensions suggested by these, essentially visual, scenes, come to a head when he is offered Laci's job as secretary and turns it down.[1]

The relief that results from his having finally made some kind of moral stand is reflected in the upward movement of the film from this point on. Listening to the radio in his room, Márton is told that his mother has come to visit him; his happiness is mirrored in the sudden blast of joyous music that mysteriously emerges from the radio. In a scene full of charm and sly social satire Márton makes modest use of his newly acquired ability to stand conspicuously aside from the crowd instead of merging quietly into it: he takes her (still in her peasant dress and scarf and clutching her basket of supplies in her hand) to one of the most fashionable restaurants in Budapest, enjoying the discomfiture of the waiters and at last making use of his French to order the most expensive meal on the menu.

The closing scenes of the film employ Gaál's method of "realistic abstraction" to suggest that Márton's conflicts are a reflection of the wider problems of his society as a whole. His family debate as to whether to join the new farm co-operative being set up and Márton leaves the discussion to walk through the fields that were once so familiar and have now become so alien. He meets Laci's wife, who explicitly accuses him of moral cowardice in his behaviour at the university. He watches as the

---

[1] This is the only aspect of the plot that appears contrived or unreal: it seems very unlikely that someone like Márton, who has taken no active part whatever in the political life of the university, should be offered this post. But, within the thematic structure of the film, it does allow him to make an unambiguous moral decision at last.

villagers carry out a traditional folk procession that was arbitrarily banned as "superstitious"[2] the previous year and has now been equally inexplicably permitted. The procession is being filmed and the film crew constantly give instructions to the villagers as to how to carry out the ritual "properly" and make it more picturesque. From the burning effigies thrown into the water, Gaál cuts to Márton once more on the train back to Budapest: rain streams down the window and he opens it, thrusting his face into the downpour in a gesture of cleansing and purification; the throbbing noise of the engine becomes louder and merges with drumbeats and the scream of the train whistle.

Perhaps the most remarkable aspect of *The Green Years* is Gaál's refusal to pass explicit moral judgements or condemnations on any of his characters. It is easy enough to be smug about other people's dishonesties and compromises from a safe distance of ten years; it is totally different to have to live through the situation oneself, and Gaál meticulously adds detail to detail to produce an authentic and convincing record of the moral atmosphere of a whole era. Though his style is much more sober than in *Current* and there are few of the earlier film's virtuose effects, much of the impact comes from scenes that must be seen both as realistic and metaphorical simultaneously: Márton's confrontation with his shadow, which comes immediately after the

---

[2] Religious imagery is fairly strong in this film, especially in the opening scenes and in the Christmas service in the village church. Gaál displays in other films an equal awareness of the importance of religion in village life and of its shaping of the outlook of the characters.

most serious and most disturbing of his betrayals, or the scene of the folk procession that provides a microcosm of the film's main themes: the conflict between past and present, the pressures of change, the pervasive authoritarianism that assumes that ordinary people are incompetent to make any decisions at all for themselves.

The Green Years employs a traditional linear narrative pattern to tell an essentially straightforward story; in *Baptism* Gaál wishes to present a direct confrontation and interaction between past and present, and the result is a fragmented time-scheme and an extremely complex flashback structure. Basically the film moves on two different time levels: in the "present" action, set in the mid-1960s, two old friends are reunited in their native village as they participate in a christening celebration; in the course of the day they talk together and with relatives and friends, recalling old times, and gradually finding earlier antagonisms between them rising to the surface. Cut into the chronological pattern of this section of the film are a series of flashbacks, from both Menyus's and András's point of view, to scenes from their childhood, their experiences during the War, and their diverging lives in the late 1950s, when Menyus went to live in Budapest and András continued to live in the village.

The flashbacks follow an associative rather than a chronological pattern: a familiar sight within the village or a chance remark will spark off a memory within one or other of them, Menyus, for example, glancing at the statue in the village square as they pass and remembering a childhood incident that took place there. The two

boys, standing barefoot in the crowd at a political meeting, were brought forward to have their feet measured
by the speaker, who then pledged that each child in the
village would have new shoes once he was elected (the
father of one of them shrewdly interrupting to point out
that they will have grown by then and will need a larger
size). But Gaál does not adhere strictly to this pattern
throughout and, especially near the beginning, the flashbacks seem to be thrown at us without much warning
and it is some time before the narrative method becomes
fully clear. It may be that Gaál intends to combine the
characters' memories with a purely objective or impersonal selection of key incidents; there are some scenes
in which neither of the men participate (one, for example,
in which a group of old women reminisce about an
incident which is then shown to us in flashback) and
where the images cannot be connected directly with
their present actions. The result, in any case, is that,
while the overall pattern is perfectly clear and the method
justifies itself by the results it obtains, several of the
specific temporal juxtapositions are unnecessarily confusing.

The first series of flashbacks shows us the two men as
small boys, sometimes friends, sometimes belonging to
rival gangs. In parallel incidents each boy is captured by
the opposing gang and tied to a tree; mud is thrown at
András but, when his turn for revenge comes, he refuses
to retaliate physically and is content to denounce Menyus
as a "traitor". Short flashes from these scenes are set
against the leisurely opening to the contemporary story,
where the atmosphere is one of friendship and welcoming

hospitality. But even here tensions of a kind are visible: Menyus arrives in a conspicuously new foreign car, accompanied by a glamorous girl friend; it is so long since he has visited the village that he has to ask the way of a peasant by the roadside and he continues on his way shaking his head sadly at the stupidity of country dwellers. Yet he himself comes from a peasant family and it is his brother's child who is to be baptised in the village.

As the convivial christening meal gets under way, another series of flashbacks shows us the two men forced to join the Fascist armies during the War; from their train on the way to the front they watch an endless line of closed cattle trucks roll past, carrying Jews, some of them from their own village, to the concentration camps. Then we go back to a childhood memory: Menyus, persecuted in school by a sadistic teacher for being a "stupid peasant", is forced to run round and round the schoolyard, the other boys looking eagerly on, the only sound his ever more painful breathing and the slap of his feet on the ground, until he collapses. From his falling body there is a cut to Menyus, András and a friend throwing themselves exhausted on the grass after they have deserted from the Fascist army. Then comes another attempt at escape as, in 1956, Menyus tries to persuade András and his wife to join him in crossing the border; they refuse, he leaves on his own and, a few hours later, ignominiously returns, having been spotted and turned back by a guard.

The interaction of the tranquil, peaceful present with these fragments of violence, prejudice and hostility from the past, creates an undercurrent of anxiety that remains submerged in the overt responses of the characters as, having finished the meal, they begin to wander round the village, pointing out significant landmarks from their past. Menyus shows his girl-friend the now abandoned house in which he grew up; she cannot believe that a whole family could live together in such cramped surroundings, sharing one room between them, but, all the same, she finds it rather "quaint". And they look at the attic in which the men hid after their desertion and from the roof of which the boys had dared each other on in a jumping contest until one of them was injured.

The flashbacks, while continuing to resonate against the increasingly false harmony presented in the contemporary action (though not a word spoken by the characters betrays this tension and it is conveyed entirely through the juxtaposition of the images) now begin a complex interaction amongst themselves. András, imprisoned during the early 1950s for imaginary political offences, is seen, on his release, tentatively following a woman in the street. She looks round at him apprehensively, hurries on, looks back again, recognises him, and rushes into his arms. A cut shows him timidly following the same woman, both of them younger, as he begins his courtship of her in the village. Another cut shows her, now his wife, walking just ahead of Menyus and himself on the day of the christening. Slightly later on, a similar series of parallels demonstrates Menyus's crumbling relationship with his wife, as, now a successful sculptor in Budapest, he becomes increasingly arrogant and self-centred; and sets this against an earlier, more contented phase, when he still took others as much into consideration as himself.

Menyus's failure in personal relations is linked with his essential failure as an artist; despite his fame and the critical acclaim it has achieved, his work is hollow and empty. András and his wife watch him on T.V. as, a typically dreadful specimen of his art beside him, he pontificates on the need for art to remain in close contact with reality and states that only his personal experience as a railway worker made it possible for him to create that particular statue. Knowing that the closest Menyus ever came to railway workers was to visit András when he worked as a labourer after the war, the couple dissolve into tolerant, almost admiring laughter at his fraudulence.

But Menyus's betrayals have been more serious than this. Another scene shows him, newly established as an officially approved artist, wriggling embarrassedly away from an encounter with András in Budapest. Later he explains why: it would damage his career if he were to be seen associating with a former political prisoner: surely András must understand? András does, for he has come up against the same kind of evasiveness when trying to publish the diary of his prison experiences. The publisher admires it intensely: it is as good as Solzhenitsyn, he tells him. But... there are some passages... under the circumstances, you know... couldn't he just delete them?... later on, of course, when things became easier... surely he can understand? András refuses and returns to the village, where he has earned his living since as the local schoolmaster,

Most of these memories arise as the two men visit their former headmaster, drink some wine with him and talk about highlights of their earlier friendship: the night they got drunk together after passing their university entrance exams, or their graduation. Menyus suggests an expedition to the local vineyard to sample some more wine; they gather together all the other guests, who are to follow on foot, and Menyus and András set off in the car. (Before they leave, Menyus's brother comments admiringly on the car and talks about how much money he too could earn away from this dead-end village).

The move away from the village to the open setting of the vineyard perched on top of a nearby hill acts, in combination with Menyus's increasing drunkenness, as a catalyst to release the antagonisms and resentments that have been recalled and intensified by the day's events. Menyus, unable to escape this confrontation with his own moral cowardice and his emptiness both as man and artist, retaliates by taunting András. The latter walks away from him and Menyus watches him till, a tiny figure in the distance, he has almost disappeared; then he takes off in the car after him. András tries to avoid him by leaving the road, but Menyus hunts him down until, in desperation, he is forced to take refuge in the crook of a tree, squatting there, in full view of the road, ridiculous and pathetic, blinking stupidly at his pursuer. Goaded beyond endurance by the vulnerability and passivity of the man who has emerged as so much his moral superior, Menyus utters a shout of triumph and begins to hurl mud and rocks at him, reverting to the immediate and easy solution of their childhood battles and openly acknowledging the conflict that has existed all their lives. András endures this for a few moments, then closes with him, and the two wrestle ineptly in the mud until the other guests catch up with them. "We were only playing," they explain sheepishly, separating and brushing down their clothes. In the gathering darkness they return to the village, side by side.

Baptism seems to be considered something of a failure by most Hungarian and foreign critics. While acknowledging that Gaál could have made the overall narrative pattern more consistent by either linking *all* the flashback to the memories of the two men, or by adopting more clearly the attitude of omniscient narrator, I find the film one of the most interesting and subtle that he has made. He conveys an extremely complex series of relationships and conflicts, both personal and social, in a manner that is almost entirely visual and hardly ever resorts to explicit verbalisation: this is particularly important when the whole structure of the film depends on an *unspoken* tension that neither of the characters is willing to acknowledge openly. Once again, he passes no explicit judgements: both men are ultimately failures, in terms of what they might and should have achieved, but each had to contend with social pressures over which they had no control as well as with personal weaknesses. But András at least made some attempt to accommodate himself to his past while Menyus, in trying to deny or evade it, succeeded only in destroying himself. And yet the scenes that show the "stupid peasant" Menyus being bullied as a child make it understandable that he should be constantly seeking to escape—from the village, from

Hungary, from himself—and that, when all these fail, he should settle for the kind of empty façade that society is only too eager to reward him for assuming.

The Falcons (1970) was Gaál's first feature in colour and, with typical thoroughness, he ensured that colour became, like landscape, an expressive element within the film, and not a mere decoration. The setting of the film —bare, flat plains, broken only by clumps of trees—has inevitably been compared to that of Jancsó's work: certainly Gaál, like Jancsó, makes use of landscape as a metaphor for the bleakness and coldness of the moral behaviour of his characters; but Gaál constantly maintains an interaction between the human beings and their setting, the tone of the landscape (as in *Current*) changing as they change, whereas Jancsó, having established one kind of relationship, proceeds to exploit the formal possibilities of this, playing off vertical and diagonal movements of his people against the vast and unchanging horizon.

It is a film that demands to be interpreted on more than one level throughout, with the surface action constantly pointing to another, metaphorical dimension beyond it. Though it is usually spoken of as an allegory, this is somewhat misleading, for it suggests that, as in most allegories, the basic story is contrived, vague, or unreal and has significance only as a stepping-stone to the "higher" or "truer" meaning beyond it. In fact Gaál takes great care to give the central action of the film an almost documentary authenticity of detail, so that it takes on a legitimate fascination of its own; his method, once again, is that of "realistic abstraction", and there is not as much difference between the technique of *Current* or *Baptism* and that of *The Falcons* as may appear at first sight.

A young student arrives at a camp at which falcons are being trained to keep the local bird population under control. The head of the station, Lilik, views his task in mystical, almost religious terms, and has imposed a rigidly authoritarian system to ensure that it is carried out with maximum efficiency: he divides his birds into "superior" and "inferior" categories and imposes a vast gulf between them and the creatures they are trained to hunt; he constantly extols the virtues of obedience, order, control, the maintainance of a strictly established hierarchy in which everyone knows his place and his duties. The boy is fascinated at first by the skill of both trainers and falcons, the cold, hard beauty that results from the discipline imposed on them; he is shocked, however, then disgusted and repelled by the methodical cruelty and suffering that is taken for granted as part of the total pattern, and these drive him finally to leave the station.

It is obvious that even a summary of the film that attempts to be as neutral as possible must suggest that it is as much about the mentality of totalitarianism as it is about the training of falcons. What gives it its unique and ambiguous quality, however, is that there is no point at which one element drives out or blatantly outweighs the other: the study of authoritarianism is carried out *by means of* an analysis of the technique of training falcons, and the film remains immediate, physical and concrete from its first frame to its last. The boy's growth to moral awareness parallels that of the heroes of Gaál's three previous films and, as in them, it is presented through an accumulation of specific incidents, through what *happens* to him, rather than by means of discussion or explicit analysis.

The movement of the film is steady and controlled throughout and even the climactic scenes are examined with gravity and restraint, are understated rather than emphasised. The characters are constantly, and unobtrusively, defined by the settings they are placed in or that they themselves create: Lilik, for example, has constructed the training station so that the buildings take on the arrangement of an encampment or a fortress, with his own quarters set apart in a position from which he can supervise the others. The dominant colour scheme of the film is one of cold and muted yellows and blues, with the faded green of the landscape as a daytime alternative to the darkness and flickering firelight of the camp at night. Throughout the film the characters are dressed in yellow, blue or white; the only exceptions are outsiders—a group of farmers in red denims—and Teréz, Lilik's woman, whom he generously shares with his fellows on the nights when he has no need of her. She is an archetypal Gaál character, aware that she is co-operating with something evil, yet believing it is really none of her business and that she can remain detached from it all; though she stays on in the camp after the boy leaves, she has been affected by his example and, when we last see her, she is wearing a faded pink blouse instead of her familiar white.

Music is used to heighten our awareness of the moral

dimension that lies behind the physical action: a soft haunting theme accompanies most appearances of Teréz; while the first scene of the training of the falcons, the opening of the scene in which they are set to work to rout a few magpies from their hiding place in a haystack, and the bizarre scene in which Lilik arranges a nocturnal military funeral when his favourite falcon dies, are all given a warlike, marching rhythm, based on drumbeats. The theme associated with the boy mixes woodwind and drums, suggesting the tension within him between the potential humanity contained within the woman and the inhumanity of Lilik. Most of the film, however, dispenses with music to create a haunting aural atmosphere of the tinkling bells of the falcons, the harsh cries of command, the whirring of wings, the throb of hoofbeats, the wailing of the wind, the bleating of sheep, the mysterious purr of telephone wires that opens and closes the film. Silence too is used for powerful emotional effect, especially in the scene in which Teréz first comes to the boy's room to offer herself to him: the quietness of their lovemaking stresses its strangeness and the remoteness between them.

As usual Gaál obtains some of his most striking effects through editing, but he also moves the camera much more freely than usual, and a distinctive pattern of sweeping circular movements emerges as the film proceeds. The camera prowls within the circle of the trainers as they prepare for the first demonstration of their skill; it explores the contents of Lilik's room with the boy; it circles the haystacks within which the frightened magpies have hidden themselves; it swoops round the boy and Lilik as the former holds a crippled heron on which a falcon is to be perfected in the art of killing; it follows the boy as he walks round the fire at which the trainers gather in the evening; a 360 degree pan searches the barren field in which Lilik and the boy have hidden in an attempt to entice back an escaped falcon; as Lilik rushes frantically to save his precious birds during a thunderstorm, the camera circles the yard with him; and, it follows him as, like an ancient Germanic warrior, he urges his horse round and round the dead falcon as it lies in state.

In addition to this, Gaál makes a point of cutting emphatically on movement as often as possible through the film, creating a forward rhythm that is both fluid and remorseless. Long lenses are frequently used, both to distance us from the characters and to assimilate them into their background: Lilik and the boy galloping soundlessly over the plain to save a falcon that is being beaten to death by indignant farmers (it had entered their territory and was torturing its prey); and throughout the final scene in which the boy leaves the camp. Only one scene, however, employs an obvious visual distortion: the boy's nightmare, filmed in black and white and slow-motion, where an extreme wide-angle lens monstrously exaggerates the shape and movement of Lilik as he advances on him, birds perched on his arms and shoulders.

A brief analysis of a few of the key scenes in the film should serve to illustrate how Gaál combines camera movement, cutting, music and colour to create an effect that is simultaneously concrete and metaphorical. Soon after his arrival the boy watches as three horsemen, arranged in a circle, perfect their total control and domination of their falcons. The birds are hurled from one man's wrist to that of his fellow and are given no chance to pause or rest before being thrown to the next man: they are being taught the virtue of submission and that they have no will apart from that of their master; the parallel to the methods by which authoritarian regimes break down the resistance of their opponents is there for those who wish to perceive it, but no one in the film draws it and it remains implicit in the physical construction and movement of the sequence. It is built up from dozens of short cuts: the birds in flight, the moment of throwing, the moment of receiving, repeated over and over again. At first the shots are quite long and follow a segment of the action in its entirety; gradually they become shorter and shorter till the effect is that of a continuous whipping motion in which the birds are allowed no respite at all; a relentless and endless physical persecution. (Gaál says that he envisioned this scene in the form of a spiral, with wide circular movements to begin with, narrowing as it reached its apex.) The only sounds are the trampling of the horses, the shouts of the trainers, the jingling bells and beating wings of the birds. Occasional cuts to the admiring face of the boy show that, as yet, he perceives only the aesthetic dimension of what is happening and that its moral implications escape him.

The boy's moral education is taken a stage further in the magpie hunt where the falcons' training is first put to use. Once again the effect comes mostly from the cutting as a couple of terrified magpies are relentlessly harried from their hiding-place within a haystack; they take refuge among a flock of sheep and hop in bewilderment among the animals' feet; finally, after a disproportionate expenditure of energy, one of them is killed. Then the boy is given the task of holding a hooded heron to the ground as Lilik sets a falcon to attack it again and again; the dissonant music mirrors his moral confusion, the bells of the falcon, the flutter of the victim's wings keep up a constant pressure on him; finally he tells Lilik that the bird has suffered enough and can take no more. "It must," Lilik replies grimly, and the camera tracks slowly in on the boy's anxious face.

The scene that makes the boy fully aware of his complicity with something both brutal and futile is that in which he and Lilik set out to recapture Diana, an escaped falcon that has taken on a mythic significance in Lilik's mind and has become a symbol for him of something fierce and independent that must be admired and yet tamed. Each man conceals himself in a shallow pit, clutching in his hand a pigeon whose beating wings should draw Diana within close enough range to be seized. The boy waits and waits, the bird stirs feebly in his hands, he searches the intense blue sky for a sign of life, the camera zooms gently in on him across the barren field, and at last Diana appears: the camera zooms down on the fluttering, terrified pigeon in a series of violent shock cuts and the boy releases the bird. He staggers from his hiding-place, tearing the protective bandages from his hands, clutches his stomach as though he is about to vomit, then runs across the field, the only sound that of his heavy breathing. The camera zooms back and away from him, stressing his isolation in the vast landscape, and the noise of a train cuts harshly into the silence.

His departure from the camp is delayed for some time longer, though this incident makes him aware that he can preserve his moral sanity, his self-respect, only by leaving (none of this is ever stated in words and once again it is the visual progression of the film that tells us what is happening to him). It is early morning when he goes, a dark silhouette in the mist, birds rustling and chirping in the trees. The camera zooms steadily away from him as he makes his way through a wood, creating an almost black and white effect as it outlines him against the trees. There is a cut to the camp where Teréz, in her pink blouse, begins the task of feeding the falcons, opening another day in the cold routine of the camp: "meat and two pigeons". The camera returns to the mist, the boy withdraws from him as he begins to run; there is the hum of telephone wires, the song of birds; a further zoom back and he leaves the frame; then a zoom in, slowly, on the telephone wires till they fill the screen; their humming becomes louder, there is the steady beat of drums. It is an ending that is mysterious and ambiguous and, as so often in Gaál's films, the landscape survives the characters. It is better, I think, for not being explicit, for maintaining the subtlety of the remainder of the film and, if it is argued that escape is too passive a solution, at least it is better than conscious or unconscious collaboration, and more useful than a brave but futile resistance against overwhelming odds. Gaál's films and characters constantly work towards self-knowledge and an understanding of the groundwork for action, rather than indulging in romantic gestures of defiance.

Not all of the film proceeds solely through the visual and aural suggestiveness that makes these particular scenes so memorable. Lilik is quite articulate about his philosophy of life, sometimes rather too much so, as when, several of the falcons having strangled themselves in their leashes trying to escape from the flooding of their cages in the storm, he warns that this is what comes of too much freedom of movement and that henceforth he will have to keep them on a tighter leash. But generally the film moves by means of implication rather than direct statement, creating the obsessive need for order, domination, ritual unanimity and rigid planning (Lilik needs to fulfil a certain quota of birds killed to justify his work, and keeps the legs of his victims to provide accurate statistics) that characterise the authoritarian mentality in all its manifestations. It is a mentality based on fear, and Lilik betrays this in his insistence that the people of the surrounding countryside are conspiring against them; external danger, of course, justifies even stricter control within the camp. People are treated as no more than objects: Teréz satisfies Lilik's need for power and enables him to make benevolent gestures towards his subordinates; sex is a means of control, not communication. Cruelty and torture are inevitable and even welcomed as essential means towards the achievement of the great design. This, and much more, emerges without strain or over-emphasis from a film that is also, to all intents and purposes, a documentary on the rearing of falcons, and a lyrical and poetic meditation on figures within a landscape.

Gaál's following film, *Dead Landscape* (1971), continues his investigation of the ways in which people adapt to, or resist, the pressures of an environment that is alien or inhuman: here, as the title indicates, the landscape is predominantly a physical one, though the crises provoked by it demand a moral resolution. And once again he ensures that the film's metaphorical implications rise out of an exactly defined and credible setting: the film was shot in a small, depopulated village, whose inhabitants, like those of so many other rural areas of Hungary, had gradually drifted away to live in the larger towns. On one level, then, the film is an account of a social phenomenon of acute importance within contemporary Hungary, while, on others, it becomes a study of the need for community, to know that there is somewhere where one belongs and has roots, and of the psychic disorientation that results when that community crumbles or is withdrawn.

The film deals essentially with three characters: a young couple who have chosen to live on in the village and to send their young son away to school during the week, and Erzsi, an old woman who refuses to leave the place in which—with the exception of a visit to Canada to see her son and his family—she has spent all her life. From this journey she retains a few treasured souvenirs in a battered Air Canada flight bag, and awe-inspiring memories of Niagara Falls that fascinate the little boy. Juli cultivates vegetables in a greenhouse and sells them at the market in the nearest town; Anti works for a forestry company nearby. Of the two, Juli is most anxious to leave the decaying village, and tensions between her husband and herself mount as the film proceeds. Erzsi's death leaves her totally alone during the day and her loneliness and frustration precipitate a crisis that leads to her death—possibly by accident, possibly through suicide.

More than in any of his other films, Gaál here makes the landscape into an active participant in the fate of his characters: there is no escape, either by day or by night, from the silence, the decay, the crumbling walls, the flaking plaster, the boarded-up windows of the dead village. Juli in particular is constantly under the influence of her surroundings, and each stage of her desperate attempt to define herself and the reasons for the kind of existence she is leading is set against a further deterioration of her physical environment, creating a sense that it is slipping further and further away from any control she can hope to impose on it.

At first the loneliness and emptiness of the village are a challenge: they offer freedom, a chance to control one's own destiny without interference from outsiders, and the opening scenes are light-hearted as Anti and Juli play hide-and-seek in the empty streets and joke with the officials who come to board up and seal the public buildings like the school and the police station. Even away from the village, Juli is constantly integrated into a landscape of another kind, and the shots of her carrying her goods to the local market invariably place her against a golden setting of autumn woods that comes to take on a more and more elegiac connotation as the film continues. Her contacts with the outside world, while providing a relief, also make the monotony and isolation of the rest of her life more unbearable. The scenes at the market centre round her relationship with the old man who has the stall next to her and who offers to sell her a volume on the coming Apocalypse put out by the Jehovah's Witnesses. She declines but, when he leaves her in charge of his stall one day, she manages to sell the book at an exorbitant price to one of her customers. The old man is taken aback at first: "What will I read now?" he asks plaintively; but the sight of the money cheers him up and he philosophically accepts his loss.

Quarrels between Juli and Anti become more frequent and even at night the silence of the village becomes oppressive and frightening, occasionally bringing Juli to the verge of hysteria as she insists that Anti get up and track down the sounds that she thinks she hears outside. After Erzsi's death, she wanders round the old woman's empty house, her own isolation once again made stronger by the contrast of the companionship she has lost, then waits for Anti to return in the gathering darkness. Another quarrel between them is provoked by yet more signs of the inexorable decay continuing around them, as even their own furniture begins to break and collapse and cupboard doors come apart as they try to open them. A visit by Erzsi's son and his family, who arrive after the old woman's death, merely exaggerates her awareness that she has no one left with whom she can communicate; this scene is followed by a montage of crumbling walls and boarded-up windows, and then

Juli walks away from the village, seen in extreme long-shot, pauses, and returns.

She walks through the misty autumn woods to the town once more, but this time enters the church and, in an atmosphere set by the semi-darkness of the confessional and the muttered voices of the worshippers, tries to explain her fears, her loneliness, her terror that she is incapable of love to a young priest who, for all his attempts at understanding, can advise her to do no more than attempt to recapture the "moment of grace" she recalls experiencing in her childhood. She goes back through the wood and past an abandoned quarry, to attempt a reconciliation that night with Anti; they drink and smoke together in celebration, he sings a favourite song, they dance and, still happy, she goes outside into the dark, abandoned village, and there she can only weep. A cut takes us to the next morning and Juli, walking along the street, starts back in horror as a section of a house crumbles into dust before her eyes. Desperately she runs into the woods to meet Anti, but resists when he tries to embrace and reassure her; they stand together in the rain as a group of ragged gypsies makes its way past them.

Juli's waning control over the pattern of her life disintegrates completely when an initially trivial incident gets out of hand: she allows the pigs to escape from their sty and finds herself unable to round them up. She chases them in ever more futile and frantic desperation, sobbing and shouting and slashing at them with a stick, in a scene of psychological crisis that is made even more horrifying by the banal nature of the event that provokes it. Back in the house she studies herself in the mirror, noting the ravages that strain and loneliness are beginning to etch on her features. The next morning she has vanished; Anti leaves the village in the early morning mist to search for her, the camera stressing the beauty of the decaying year as he runs among the ripe, golden foliage of the trees; he finds her near the edge of the quarry, there is another dispute, she turns to leave him, her foot slips, she falls over the cliff. The last, long-held shot, is of the crumbling face of the quarry, the stones sliding and settling in a cloud of dust that recalls the disintegrating façades of the houses.

As in *The Falcons,* some of the motivation of the characters is provided through dialogue, especially that of Anti, who wishes to remain in the village because they can live cheaply there while he works nearby, and thus save money for a new house in the town. More effective, though, are those scenes that show Juli's disintegration visually, paralleling it with the erosion and decay of the setting from which she can find no escape. In addition a contrast is established between her restlessness and dissatisfaction and the calm acceptance of Erzsi, who realises that her life is behind her and that she can now only wait for death among the surroundings she has known all her life. The first intimations of death come to her as she is working in her yard; finding her strength slipping away from her, she sits down and, calmly and contentedly, takes a full and unhurried look at the world she is going to leave.

In the most moving sequence of the whole film, Juli and Anti take her to a doctor in town by cart. The music is soft yet almost impersonal; the only other sound is the creak of the cart and the noise of hoofbeats. A subjective shot from Erzsi's viewpoint shows her house as she passes it for the last time; we see her face, then the leaves and the trees under which she passes; these shots alternate in a rhythm that conveys the beauty of the landscape and her full enjoyment of it even now. The sound of this sequence overlaps to the scene of her burial and here too there is loveliness, the sunlight pouring through the trees as Anti and Juli leave the graveyard.

The scene in which Erzsi's son and his family come to visit her brings to the surface the theme of community, and the contrast between the past (now gone for ever) where Erzsi could spend seventy years virtually in one place, and the forces that inexorably disrupt this stable pattern, bringing economic benefits but also the kind of psychic and spiritual emptiness that torments Juli. The son had not warned his mother that he was coming and, having been out of touch with her for some time, is not even aware of her death. He is stunned by the news and at first can feel nothing but shame and guilt, responding vaguely to the attempts at consolation offered by Juli and Anti. It is his Canadian wife, shrill voiced and already impatient with the time they are wasting in this desolate, primitive setting, who takes control: her husband's memories mean nothing to her and she is concerned only with keeping her children quiet and getting away as soon as is decently possible. She and her husband go off to visit the grave with Anti, while Juli hurriedly prepares a meal. The children, with not a word of Hungarian between them, make tentative contact with Juli's little boy; they gape in wonder as he rides a real live horse round the yard and, used to eating food that comes already carved and enclosed in plastic bags, they ask in disgust if they are really supposed to eat that bird that Juli is plucking. The oldest boy and Juli's boy settle down to playing happily at astronauts on the roof of the barn, but the apprehensive shrieks of the returning mother bring them down. Juli sets the chicken on the table and they sit down, but the visitors can't eat and can't stay; they leave the food untasted and scramble back in embarrassment to their huge American car and drive off. The scene works in two ways, intensifying Juli's sense of isolation on the one hand, and yet displaying the kind of existence that might be in store for her once she moves away from a setting that she understands. Erzsi's son is the most pathetic character in the whole film (and perhaps in all of Gaál's work): a human being with no sense of direction left at all, allowing himself to be carried along by forces he no longer even pretends to control.

He is, however, an exception for, time and again, Gaál quietly returns in all his films to an insistence that human beings must take responsibility for their actions, that even the most restrictive or depressing circumstances offer no excuse for moral inertia. *Dead Landscape,* though not perhaps his best film, is the one in which he tries to present his characters and their dilemmas most subtly and obliquely, relying on the melancholy of the dying village and the autumnal landscape to take the place of dialogue and verbal analysis. He says that he sees this film as a turning point in his career, the logical conclusion to his themes and stylistic development to date. More than Jancsó or Szabó, perhaps, he has the ability to move beyond a relatively narrow (though richly and intelligently exploited) range of images and subject-matter, and the next stage of his career may well be crucial in demonstrating this.

Chapter Five

Horizon: The Sixties and Early Seventies

Although Jancsó, Szabó, and Gaál remain the best-known of contemporary Hungarian film-makers, individual films by other directors have been well received abroad over the past decade, confirming the depth and solidity of the country's film industry. These works have come from both "older" and "younger" artists, and would include such titles as *Love,* by Makk, *Twenty Hours,* by Fábri, *Cold Days,* by Kovács, *Ten Thousand Suns,* by Kósa, and *Horizon,* by Gábor. One of the most striking aspects of the cinema of the 1960's, in fact, has been the process of interaction between the established film-makers and the newcomers: Fábri and Makk, in various ways, helped to break the ground for the examination of Hungarian history and society carried out so enthusiastically by the younger directors; while their own style, and that of Kovács too, has often been clearly influenced by Jancsó and Szabó.

The best of these films continue to explore the Hungarian reality of both past and present; one could even say that, in a sense, they are all "historical" works for, in many cases, the action takes place in a setting that is contemporary in terms of numerical dates only, its mentality, behaviour, and social structure being hopelessly obsolete. A good many films deal with conflicts of this kind: the stresses and tensions faced by those who move to the city, abandoning the traditional patterns of life of the countryside; the attempts to bring new technologies and ideas into a rural environment; the mental gulf between those whose habits of thought have grown rigid and ossified and those who wish to introduce new ideas, to take risks and experiment. Once again, film is viewed, not as an escape from the problems of everyday life, but as a means of understanding them better.

One of the key films in this respect is Zoltán Fábri's *Twenty Hours* (1964), a complex panorama of the twenty years of Hungarian history since 1945. As a journalist interviews the inhabitants of a small village, their memories spark off flashbacks of the jealousies, tensions, hostilities, and conflicts involved in the immense social and political upheavals of the period. The film centres round the inter-relationships of four friends who had been responsible for carrying out the agrarian reforms of the late 1940's and in establishing a village co-operative, but whose friendship had been disrupted by the growing dogmatism and authoritarianism of one of them, Varga, who was also the local party secretary. The tensions which have been established come to a head during two successive evenings in 1956 and result in the killing by Varga of Kocsis, who is, ironically, the only one of the four who had not quarrelled with any of the others and had constantly tried to mediate between them.

Individual scenes in the film are very powerfully presented, especially the climactic encounter between Varga and Kocsis in the main street of the village and the subsequent confrontation between Varga and the silent, intimidated villagers. And overall the film is of the greatest importance historically as being the first to expose the struggles for power, the dishonesties, the time-serving, the arrogance, the personal vindictiveness disguised as social justice that too often characterised the attempts to bring about a new social order in this period. One might question, however, whether the ultimate effect of the film matches its admirable intentions and ambitions: Fábri opts for a complicated flashback structure that is clearly modelled on the technique of Alain Resnais and, when this is combined with an intricate and complex series of events and a large cast of characters, the result is that the film is often impenetrably confusing and obscure. (This, it is true, might also be said of Szabó's *25 Firemen's Street,* a film which I have already praised, but there is the difference that Szabó's work is structured as a series of variations on a few central themes; once this is realised, the film becomes much clearer on a second viewing. The same—for me at least—cannot be said of *Twenty Hours*).[1]

Nevertheless, this remains Fábri's strongest film since the late 1950's; he has been one of the most prolific of Hungarian directors and his films are almost always worthy of serious attention. It would be difficult to deny, though, that—as is true even of *Merry-Go-Round* and *Professor Hannibal*—they always tend to be more effec-

[1] For a more sympathetic treatment of Fábri's work since 1960, and of this film in particular, see: Claude B. Levenson, *Jeune Cinéma Hongrois* (Premier Plan, Lyon, 1966).

tive in isolated scenes than they are as a complete artistic unity; in recent years this defect has been compounded by an increasing heavy-handedness in driving home the main "message" of the film and by an over-electric adoption of the techniques of other directors such as Bergman, Fellini, and Resnais, that seems to have inhibited the growth of a style that can be said to belong to Fábri alone.

Over-emphasis, for example, destroys much of the impact of *Two Half-Times in Hell* (1961) and *One Day More or Less* (1972). In the former, a group of Hungarians deported to a German labour camp in the Ukraine are ordered to stage (and of course lose) a football match with their guards in honour of the Führer's birthday. At first, those who have been chosen for the team appear fortunate and privileged: they are given extra rations and excused certain work duties. This leads to charges of collaboration by their fellow prisoners and, to refute these, they organise an abortive attempt at escape. They play the match, therefore, in the knowledge that they will almost certainly be executed at the conclusion; they are dispirited and apathetic until the team captain, a former professional footballer, inspires them to a performance that is both a show of defiance and an assertion of their own human dignity. They take the lead in the match, arousing frantic enthusiasm among the watching prisoners, and are immediately shot down on the orders of the enraged and frightened visiting General. Once again, although the intentions behind the film are impeccable, the ponderous pacing, the lack of subtlety in distinguishing between "good" and "evil" characters (the chief

German guard, for example, is grotesquely and bestially obese) and, especially, the closing moments of the film where the camera lingers endlessly on each of the dead bodies littering the playing field, tend to turn the film into a lecture rather than an artistic experience.

One Day More or Less displays the same characteristics: its structure depends on the audience being kept just as much in the dark as to the central character's motives and intentions as the other figures in the film are, but the waiting is dragged out to such lengths that one is finally bored rather than intrigued. The "hero" is a former collaborator with the Germans who has just been released from a twenty-five year prison sentence; he returns to a village where he had participated in a war-time atrocity and attempts to pick up some of the threads of his past life. Frustration, resentment, and drunkenness combine to lead him to another murder, a small-scale repetition of the original crime.

The Tót Family (1969) is rather more successful and benefits from an excellent leading performance by Zoltán Latinovits. The situation is one of Kafkaesque proportions: during the Second World War an autocratic Major spends his leave with the family of one of his soldiers and, in their desire to dispose him favourably towards their son, they allow him to acquire despotic control over every aspect of their daily behaviour and force them to carry out totally meaningless and absurd tasks. What they do not know, however, is that the boy is already dead. At its best, the film is a blackly comic version of some of Jancsó's basic themes: the Major issues a constant stream of interrogations and commands:

he is dependent on the unquestioning co-operation of his victims and is destroyed the moment this is withdrawn; his endless aggressiveness allows him to create a series of "double-bind" situations in which the answer "yes" and the answer "no" are both equally wrong; and he is always twisting perfectly innocent statements into confessions of guilt and subversive intentions. Fábri unleashes a barrage of technical effects—freeze-frames, fast motion, jump cuts, tricks with space and time that produce miraculous transformations of clothes or setting or allow a character to appear in two places within the same shot—that are sometimes effective, but too often are overdone and eventually become tedious. The film is virtually a compendium of the best and the worst that Fábri has to offer and ultimately one simply has to accept it on these terms.

Fábri's most ambitious recent work (there are others over the past decade that I have not seen) is *The Unfinished Sentence* (1974), based on a massive novel by Tibor Déry. The film is a panoramic survey of several decades in the life of a member of a wealthy bourgeois family who gradually becomes aware of the injustice and inequality on which his own comfortable way of life is based, but who is too thoroughly conditioned by his upbringing to make more than a few futile gestures towards atoning for and remedying this. Visually the film is probably the most beautiful that Fábri has yet achieved, with its sumptuously furnished interiors, elegant costumes, and radiant, sun-drenched exteriors; it is also the one that draws most heavily on other film-makers to achieve its effects. There is a Fellini-like mixture of fantasy and reality (often within the framework of the same shot) and, in particular, a strong dependence on Resnais's technique of repeating key events from the past, or within the protagonist's memory, with significant variations each time: this is especially evident in the numerous scenes that return to the central incident of the film, in which a young worker is murdered by Fascist thugs. The film moves back and forwards in time, warning us of the future deaths of the characters or combining several different time levels within one continuous camera movement. Despite this virtuosity, however, one never feels that Fábri is totally at ease with these modish devices; it would be instructive to compare this film with Andrzej Wajda's thematically similar *Land of Promise* to see what happens when a director is totally in command of a style which, however flamboyant, is unmistakably and uniquely his own.

Károly Makk is another "veteran" who is still producing interesting and significant work, though his career has fluctuated much more wildly than that of Fábri. The early success of *Liliomfi, The House Under the Rocks,* and *The Fanatics* was not followed up; instead Makk produced throughout the 1960's a series of commercially oriented works that led even his warmest admirers to conclude that his career as a significant film-maker was over. Then, quite unexpectedly, *Love* appeared in 1970. Based on two short stories by Tibor Déry, it is set in 1953 and deals with the relationship between a bedridden old woman and her daughter-in-law. The old woman believes that her son is a successful film director in America, whereas in reality he is a political prisoner in Budapest; to shield her from this knowledge, the daughter-in-law (played by Mari Törőcsik) concocts a series of letters that describe, in increasingly fantastic detail, the son's supposed activities abroad. Towards the end of the film, the man is released from prison but, by the time he reaches his mother, she is dead.

The film creates and sustains a mood of its own that perfectly conveys the mixture of respect, affection, and exasperation with which the younger woman handles the often autocratic behaviour of her mother-in-law, while at the same time she has to cope with the atmosphere of suspicion, hostility, and petty persecution that her status as the wife of a political prisoner has brought upon her. The film is quiet and restrained throughout; there are no towering confrontations, no scenes of denunciation or accusation, and yet—or perhaps because of this—its indictment of the arbitrary exercise of power in the early 1950s is all the more effective.

Makk begins the film with a series of quick cuts of the old woman (beautifully played by Lili Darvas) and the objects and photographs with which she has surrounded herself in her bedroom. This is accompanied by the tinkling of a musical box and, throughout the film, fragmentary scraps of music, and moments of silence are used in brilliant counterpoint to the old woman's memories and fantasies. As we follow through the daily routine of her existence, we are given glimpses of her memories of her youth and of her son as a small child: there is a sense of softness and fragility to these images and they are subtly and almost imperceptibly distorted by wide-angle photography. When she imagines her son's career in America, she does so in the only way that will make his hardly conceivable alien world recognisable to her, and transfers the clothes, furnishings, and settings to her own youth and her own memories of luxury and happiness. The result is, of course, wildly anachronistic, but though it is comic, there is no sense of condescension in the film-maker's attitude towards her. The sense of unreality is further heightened by photographic distortions, most notably in a scene where she imagines her son riding on horseback with a group of admiring companions.

In counterpoint to this, we see the grim realities of the daughter-in-law's struggle to make ends meet: she is dismissed from her job at school because her husband is a prisoner, she has to sell some of her most treasured possessions simply in order to keep alive, and she has to cope with police spies claiming to be "telephone engineers" rummaging around in her apartment. Despite this she maintains her sense of responsibility to the old woman, though there is no trace of the martyr or the saint in her behaviour towards her: tenderness and concern co-exist with moments of completely human and natural impatience and even hostility.

In the final sequence of the film, Makk creates another, totally appropriate stylistic framework to match the experience of the son in the first few hours after he has been released from prison. He is given his freedom in a sequence that is deliberately confusing and disorienting; no explanations are offered for his release, just as, presumably, none were given in the past for his arrest.

As he makes his way by streetcar and taxi to his wife's apartment, he begins, with bewilderment and almost disbelief, to reacquaint himself with the sights, sounds, and textures of ordinary life. In his final reunion with his wife—only to learn that his mother has just died— there is a very effective use of a method of time-dislocation that Makk uses at other points in the film: the wife opens the door and sees him; we see them embracing; and then we see her still standing, disbelieving, in the doorway. The ending of the film is in tune with the sobriety and restraint that has characterised it throughout; its understatement, however, co-exists with extraordinary technical skill and maturity.

Makk's next film, *Catsplay* (1974), was eagerly awaited, but it proved something of a disappointment to most critics. It is almost as though he were trying too hard to repeat the success of *Love,* for once again the film centres round the memories, illusions, and fantasies of an old woman. Erzsi lives in Budapest, her sister Giza in Germany; they exchange letters and childhood reminiscences, while Erzsi tries to handle her relationship with her fickle, aging beau Viktor, a once famous singer. The film (in colour this time) is certainly extremely beautiful, and Makk once again presents hazy, soft-focus images of an idyllic past that contrasts with a much less satisfactory present; the cutting is subtle and intricate and builds up an almost dance-like rhythm of its own; yet, with the exception of one or two scenes like that in which Erzsi finds Viktor dining with a hated rival and proceeds methodically, and with ominous calmness, to demolish the meal, the crockery, and the glassware, the

András Kovács

Cold Days: the soldiers discuss how best to carry out the killings, while their victims wait and listen

Károly Makk on the set of *Catsplay*

Love: the doctor offers advice to the old woman (Lili Darvas), while her daughter-in-law (Mari Törőcsik) looks on

Catsplay: tender memories as Mrs Orbán (Margit Dayka) listens to Viktor (Samu Balázs)

Ferenc Kósa

Snowfall: a lyric winter landscape
Snowfall: the son finds his father and almost immediately loses him again

Sándor Sára

The Upthrown Stone: Balázs (Lajos Balázsovits), on the left, surveys the body of his dead friend, the Greek

Identification: József Madaras, as the Commissar, attempts to cope with the problem presented by the returning soldier with no official identity (György Cserhalmi)

Imre Gyöngyössy directs

Palm Sunday: an image with characteristically religious associations from ▶
one of the last sequences of the film: black robed women come to identify the bodies of their menfolk, hanged from the branches of trees

Legend About the Death and Resurrection of Two Young Men: a shot from ▶
one of the "potential" conclusions to the film: the Gyspsy painter (Sándor
Oszter) is drowned

At the End of the Road: the embarrassed, shame-faced girl leaves the ▶
train and is seen in extreme long-shot as she walks across a barren, misty
landscape dominated by a distant, solitary poplar tree

No Man's Daughter (László Ranódy). The little orphan girl (Zsuzsa ▶
Czinkóczy) furtively snatches a bite to eat

Sindbad: the hero (Zoltán Latinovits) in his prime, in an appropriately
sensual environment

Football of the Good Old Days: an explicit acknowledgement of the influence of Chaplin on this film

Romanticism: Kálmán (István Szegő) near the end of the film, ironically ▶ a "noble savage" at last

Holiday in Britain: the old and the new: the anxious parents are separated ▶ by a portrait of Che Guevara

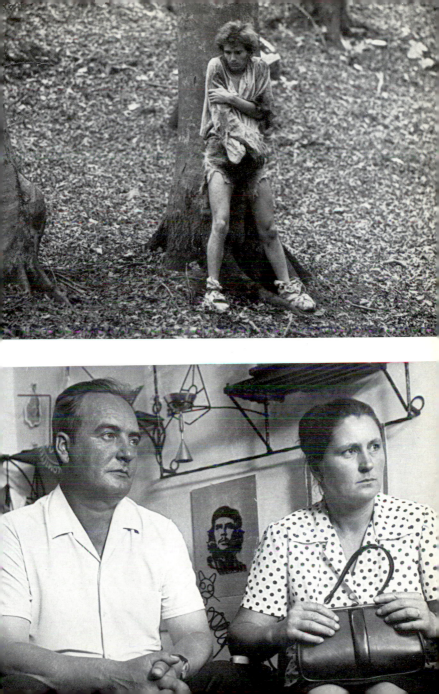

Márta Mészáros, with Jan Nowicki and Lili Monori

Adoption: The central character in her workshop

The Two of Them: Julia tries to come to terms with the emtiness of her existence

The Two of Them: Lili Monori as Mary and Marina Vlady as Julia share a moment of understanding

film never really comes to life—or perhaps it is just that we feel we have seen it all before.

Although András Kovács did not begin making films till 1960, he was born in the same year (1925) as Makk and thus belongs to the same generation as Makk and Fábri. His first important film was *Difficult People* (1964), a series of *cinéma-vérité* interviews with inventors whose ideas, often original, valuable, and eminently practicable, had been suppressed or ignored by officials who ought to have been aware of their importance. The film makes use of a clip from Makk's *The Fanatics* at one stage, and aligns itself with that work in its attack on bureaucratic indifference, cowardice, and arrogance.

Two years later came *Cold Days* (1966), a fiction film based on a historical event, the massacre, by Hungarian soldiers, of several thousand Jewish and Serbian inhabitants of Novi Sad in 1942—an extremely courageous subject to tackle, in view of the embarrassed silence that, till then, had shrouded Hungary's role in the Second World War. The film is structured round the memories and self-justifications of four men involved in the massacre as they await trial in 1946. Each, of course, denies his complicity or responsibility for the events—either he was just obeying orders and thus had no choice in the matter, or, in one case, he simply helped dispose of the corpses rather than actually taking part in the killing. (Any validity the first argument might have is negated by a scene that shows one officer refusing point-blank to be involved in the killing of civilians).

Though the story is rather too neatly patterned, with each of the four characters turning out to have played a crucial role in the actions of at least one of the others, many of the images of the film remain unforgettable, and the stark black-and-white contrasts provide an atmosphere of coldness, remoteness, and detachment that is worthy of Jancsó. Like *The Red and the White* (released, incidentally, a year later) it chronicles the way in which ordinary people can find themselves responsible for the lives of total strangers: a railway clerk is ordered to pick out all those she recognises from a group of arriving prisoners; uneasily she obeys but then, realising that those she identifies are to be spared, she frantically begins to select them all, attempting to save them. There is also a Jancsó-like fatality and passivity in the manner in which the victims accept their fate; patiently they wait shivering on the river bank as their executioners hack a hole in the ice to dispose of their bodies. Shots ring out constantly in the background and the soldiers scramble out on to the ice, half swallowed up in the mist that hangs over the river. The film is particularly effective in displaying inhumanity as something casual and almost routine: disappointed to hear that the authorities have belatedly ordered an end to the killings, a corporal suggests that, nevertheless, they could "finish off" the remainder "before lunch" if they hurried.

Blindfold (1974) is perhaps closest to this in quality among Kovács's subsequent films. Once again the style is sober and unobtrusive, the black-and-white images stark and clear. Based on an actual incident towards the end of the Second World War, it studies the spiritual torment of a young priest who believes that his prayers to a minor saint have brought about a miracle that saved the life of a confused, simple-minded soldier condemned to be shot for desertion (the man's defence is merely that he wanted to go home and see his wife again). Just as the execution is about to take place, a bombing raid occurs and, when the rubble is cleared, there is no trace of the potential victim to be found. Later events force the priest to modify his belief that a miraculous intervention occurred, but by then it is too late to halt the rumours that have swept through the army; he finds himself caught in a conflict between expediency and truthfulness, between dogmatic belief and a faith that admits the possibility of honest doubt. Brought before a tribunal that refuses to allow him to speak honestly and demands a simple "yes" or "no" to all questions, he is driven inexorably towards madness.

Péter Bacsó, another member of this generation, who enjoyed a prolific career as a scriptwriter before turning to direction in 1963, seems more interested in studying present-day society in his films; to a large extent, in fact, they seem intended almost as documentaries of life and work in today's Hungary. Following in the line of *The Fanatics,* Bacsó typically takes a subject that deals with inefficiency or dissatisfaction within the social framework and explores the results of this. The best of his films that I have seen is *Outbreak* (1970), whose hero is a disenchanted young worker who begins to protest, with increasing vigour, at the perennial housing shortage which makes it impossible for him to take a girl home for the night, and at the boring and stultifying nature of his work. Meeting with little success here, he becomes still more outspoken, and, finding himself interviewed on TV as a "typical worker", seizes the chance to attack the stupidity and ultra-conservatism of the management in his factory and to demand more real power for the workers themselves. His behaviour antagonises many of the older workers in his factory, as well as the bosses, but he is sheltered for a time by the patronage of a liberally-inclined manager (with whose daughter he has meanwhile fallen in love). Under pressure, however, the manager deserts him, and he loses his job; the girl leaves her parents and goes to live with him for a time but, as his fortunes decline more and more, she too finally abandons him. At the end of the film, in an overtly symbolic incident, the young man, eating in a restaurant, tells the waiter that there are too many fish in the vivarium and they are choking; the waiter shrugs his shoulders and tells him not to look at them if it worries him. He responds by buying all the fish and, with the help of the one fellow-worker who had stood by him in his troubles, throws them back into the Danube while his friend advises him that he has to "learn to navigate".

Present Indicative (1971), which is in many ways an updating of the twenty years old *Anna Szabó,* deals with a conscientious factory manager who attempts to instil a sense of responsibility and pride into the generally shiftless group in his charge. His efforts are met with hostility and resistance at first, but, once he has proved himself to them by showing that he can carry out hard physical labour just as well as they can, he wins their admiration and respect. In *The Last Chance* (1973) an inefficient factory manager decides, most unusually, to take full responsibility for his mistakes and insists on demoting himself to the rank of an ordinary workman. Everyone treats him as some kind of madman, and the film explores his attempts to convince others that responsibility must be earned, not merely once, but throughout one's whole career.

Bacsó's method is one of almost pure documentary: he prefers to work with non-actors, the settings are those of real factories and offices, great attention is paid to the details and routine of working life. This imposes considerable limitations on his films and means that, though they may be fascinating sociological analyses, they rarely overstep these boundaries to take on the permanence and universality of art. The problem lies not so much in his "realism" (which he justifiably compares to that of Lumière)[2] as in the fact that it is not quite rigidly enough maintained and elements of banal love interest or spurious melodrama too often intrude to destroy the atmosphere of authenticity he has created.

A final representative of this "older generation" is Tamás Rényi, whose best-known film is probably *The Valley* (1967). This is a strange, semi-allegorical work about a group of Hungarian deserters from the Nazi armies who take refuge in a mountain village inhabited only by women and children, the men having been deported to serve in the German army (though no explanation seems to be given as to why there are not even any *old* men left). Reluctantly the women agree to shelter them, friendships and love affairs develop, but the secret is discovered and the village wiped out in reprisals.

*

[2] In a conversation with the author in June 1973.

Fábri, Makk, Kovács, Bacsó, Rényi, and Révész (whose *Land of the Angels* was mentioned in a previous chapter) had all begun their work in film in the 1950's (or, in Makk's case, even earlier), as scriptwriters, assistant directors, or directors of short or feature-length films. Other important figures from the 1950's such as László Ranódy, Felix Máriássy, Frigyes Bán, and Imre Fehér, continued to make films throughout the following decade³, but without ever matching the quality of the best of their earlier works. The "younger generation" of directors can be said to date from the graduation around 1960 of a whole host of talented young men and women from the Academy of Cinematographic Art and the subsequent connection of most of them with the Béla Balázs studio. Though some of them waited until almost the end of the decade before making their first feature films, there is enough continuity of mood and outlook to justify examining their work as the expression of a new and different sensibility.

István Gaál and István Szabó have already been discussed in some detail elsewhere; to my mind, the directors among their contemporaries who come closest to matching their achievement are Sándor Sára, Ferenc Kósa, and Imre Gyöngyössy. Sára is known primarily as a cameraman and, in that capacity, is already one of the most outstanding figures in world cinema: his credits include *Current* (by Gaál), *Father* and *25 Firemen's Street* (by Szabó), *Sindbad* (by Zoltán Huszárik), and the first four of Ferenc Kósa's features. In 1962 he directed

---

³ Bán died in 1969, Máriássy and Fehér in 1975.

the famous short film *Gypsies,* which Gaál photographed. This is a powerful and moving presentation of the plight of the gypsy population in Hungary, allowing them to present their own case in their own words, and showing the imminent destruction of a still viable traditional culture in the name of an often brutal and thoughtless attempt at "assimilation". Something of this is carried over into his first feature film, *The Upthrown Stone* (1968), which is set in the Rákosi era of the early 1950's and deals powerfully and honestly with the injustices of that period, though, like Gaál's *The Green Years,* it handles them from a viewpoint that is not limited to one particular place or time.

Balázs, the young hero, is the son of a stationmaster in a small village who commits the "crime" of arranging an unscheduled stop of an official train so that a veteran of the First World War can meet an old comrade who is now a General. For this he is imprisoned and his son finds that, as a result, he too is politically suspect and he is denied admission to study at the State Film School. He takes a job as a surveyor instead, though he has to lie about his father in order to establish himself as politically reliable, and is sent to help in the farm collectivization movement of the period. The film brilliantly creates both the physical setting and the mental atmosphere of the period, with "traitors" confessing to their crimes over the radio and newsreels showing children performing grotesque dances and singing praises of Rákosi.

Balázs makes friends with a Greek Communist exile who is helping to establish the co-operative and together they try to allay the fears and suspicions of the peasants at this new development. Other officials are either less patient or less scrupulous; they prefer to bully the peasants into compliance rather than even to attempt to explain what is going on. Resentment builds up and results in an outbreak of violence in which the Greek is—quite wrongly—blamed for a particularly callous piece of behaviour and is killed in retaliation. Sára makes of his film a meditation on the nature of idealism and the conflict between achievement and intention, and its most powerful sequence is emblematic of its meaning as a whole: a band of gypsies suffer, on an even more brutal and arbitrary level, the indignities meted out to the peasants as, without warning or explanation, a group of public health officials descend on them and, protected by armed police, proceed to delouse them, clipping and shaving their heads as though they were animals, in a brusque and impersonal manner. The gypsies, knowing they are powerless, submit silently and the whole scene has no dialogue, merely the unrelenting snip of the clippers and then the brisk powdering of the shaven heads, with the rapid, objective editing emphasising the inhumanity of the whole process. Only Balázs protests and attempts to photograph and record what is happening; he is driven away but, by the end of the film, has managed to make the movie we have just seen and thus to use the photographic image as a means of stating the truth, and also to escape from the kinds of films "dripping with optimism" that he had earlier denounced. He has discovered that "history must answer to man" and that a society which humiliates and degrades its members in the name of historical necessity has got its priorities fundamentally wrong.

Sára has directed only one subsequent film, *Pheasant Tomorrow* (1974) and, though on the surface this is a much more light-hearted film, it too presents, in allegorical fashion, a critique of the authoritarian mentality. Here we are in a contemporary setting, where a group of young people on a carefree holiday—casual, disorderly, untidy, but also happy—allow a middle-aged man and a group of his friends to begin to organise and control their activities. At first it is all comparatively harmless: he organises dances at which the older and younger people can get together; he persuades them to tidy up the camping ground a little and begin to work out a routine for the day's activities. Before they quite realise what has happened, the young people find themselves in a rigidly ordered environment, with their tents arranged (by colours!) in neat rows and their days divided up into a series of formal activities to which they are summoned by brusque blasts of a whistle. And always there are rationalisations: if the streets of the tent village aren't given names, children will get lost; if you swim beyond the limits laid out for you by the authorities, you are liable to be drowned. It is all for your own good and if we have to employ a little force to save you from your own worst impulses (like hauling a vagrant swimmer into a rowing boat by means of his long hair), then it will teach you to behave more circumspectly in the future.

As the film proceeds, the satire sharpens and becomes more ferocious. The "Leader" and his cronies consolidate their position and the sexual and material privileges that accompany it; their every move religiously recorded for posterity by a team of photographers. The campers are instructed to dig a swimming pool a mere ten yards from the river in which they had swum so freely a few days previously. The new elite set out on a hunting expedition that is filmed in a way that subtly mixes farce and a sense of genuine horror at the cruel, savage expressions on the hunters' faces: they succeed only in shooting a cow (which is duly photographed) but turn this into a victory with a triumphant procession back to camp with their trophy. A banquet follows at which the Leader and his friends exchange garlands of flowers and mutual congratulations, while the audience wildly applauds their every remark. Retribution is at hand, however: flushed with confidence, the Leader attempts to take a second mistress, rousing the jealousy of the young woman who had opportunistically attached herself to him the moment that his climb to power began. He is publicly humiliated and forced to flee ignominiously down the river in a boat. Even before this, however, signs of discontent had manifested themselves, and one disillusioned young couple had already made preparations to leave; with the Leader's departure, his whole artificial power structure crumbles and we are left at the end with the empty, disorderly camp site, rubbish blowing idly in the wind and harsh, discordant music on the sound track. Amusing as it is, the film leaves a rather bitter aftertaste, and one wonders what alternative Sára is proposing to the extremes of tyranny and chaos with which he has presented us. Perhaps he is simply suggesting that if the natural and harmless behaviour of the young people had not been interfered with at the start, a situation need never have emerged in which only extreme positions could be adopted.

Ferenc Kósa's *The Ten Thousand Suns* attempts, like *The Upthrown Stone,* to come to terms with the injustices committed in the early 1950's in the name of Communism. The film was completed in 1965 and released in 1967 and takes its title from the ten thousand days of the thirty-year time span that it covers (though the young peasant in the film talks also about his vision that he would one day see "ten thousand suns" bursting into flame above the sea). The film begins and ends with this young man, meditating on the value of the sacrifices that have been made to realise the vision of Communism, and questioning how fully this has been achieved and whether even the purest intentions have the right to demand so much suffering to fulfil them. In the body of the film, the life of the boy's father is outlined, beginning with his own youth in the mid-1930's. Though István Széles and his wife suffer humiliations at the hands of their landlord, his dream is the eternal peasant dream of obtaining land for himself rather than the vision of equality and co-operation presented by his Communist friend Fülöp Bánó. With the coming of a Communist government, therefore, and the establishment of co-operative farms, Széles, like many other peasants, resists fiercely and eventually finds himself implicated in a murder. After some years of penal servitude he returns to his village, still unrepentant in his political views; his friendship for Bánó, however (who had attended to his son's education while he was in prison), leads him to help save the other's life when most of the local party officials are murdered during the 1956 uprising. The unresolved tensions of his life, his awareness that he and others have benefited by the changes that he still views as morally wrong, lead him finally to attempt suicide.

The film is one of the most open-minded and honest produced in Hungary in the past decade, centering on the eternal moral debate of whether the ends (which Kósa, like most of his contemporaries, accepts as beneficial) can ever justify the often brutal and authoritarian methods used to achieve them. But it is very much more than a tract, however intelligent; Kósa, like Gaál, is a visual poet who transforms his moral conflicts into a series of astonishing images that often recall the work of Dovzhenko in the Russia of the 1920s. He calls upon the whitewashed farmhouses, bare fields and wrinkled, resigned peasant faces made so familiar by the work of László Ranódy and others in Hungarian films of the 1950's, and incorporates them into a rich visual mosaic where the stark black and white imagery takes on an almost sensual quality.

The film is a succession of images as striking and forceful as any the contemporary cinema has offered us and Kósa (and Sándor Sára) employ the starkness of black and white and the width of the Cinemascope screen to maximum effect. Long lines of men reap wheat in immense and endless fields; women bury their children up to their necks in the ground so that they will be safe while they work; a line of horses trot along a street, then crosses a bridge against the skyline; a woman clings to the beams of the ceiling above the bed as she tramples on her prostrate husband's back, to massage him; a man carries out his sentence of forced labour in a barren, rock-strewn landscape; the local policemen and Party officials stand immersed to their waist in the river while those who have briefly seized power in 1956 debate whether to kill them; the camera tracks along a beach as the peasants enjoy themselves swimming in the water—with their hats on.

Kósa has also been compared to Eisenstein in his compositional effects and his handling of mass movement on the screen; an image which justifies this comparison occurs quite early in the film: Bánó is attempting to arrange a fair distribution of grain after the harvest, while Széles and the other peasants insist on taking what they judge to be their rightful share. The situation gets out of hand; the peasants seize as many bags of grain as they can carry and start to run with them across the open fields, Bánó vainly trying to stop them by firing his pistol over their heads, and shouting that the grain belongs to them in any case. The camera tracks with him as he runs after them, then cuts to an extreme long-shot that shows a long zigzag line of peasants stretching into the far distance, lying where they have collapsed under the weight of their burdens.

I have not seen Kósa's second film, *Judgement,* which deals with the peasant uprising led by György Dózsa in 1514. Hungarian critics seem to consider the film an almost total failure, though Kósa himself says that he thinks its last thirty minutes include some of the best work he has yet done.[4] *Beyond Time* (1972) proved to be

---

[4] In a conversation with the author in July 1975.

one of the most controversial films made in Hungary in recent years: the setting is a prison in 1929 in which a well-intentioned but weak prisoner governor tries to put into effect some mildly liberal reforms, but finds that his muddled political thinking leads him to handle symptoms rather than causes and leaves him at the mercy of the crude, but effective Fascism of his chief warder, Babella. Also, the highly motivated Communist political prisoners who form a tiny minority among the ordinary convicts, are not willing to be fobbed off with Christmas parties at which nuns sing "Silent Night" to men still cooped up in cages, or excursions into the countryside during which trusted prisoners are allowed to paint landscapes to decorate the governor's office: they go on a hunger strike and contemptuously reject the governor's pleas for compromise and reconciliation.

Gradually the situation escalates: the governor comes under increasing pressure from the Minister of Justice to put an end to the hunger strike; while he vacillates, Babella starts to take matters into his own hands and, one by one, the Communist prisoners are beaten up or murdered. Events are seen largely through the eyes of Kallós, a non-political prisoner who shares a cell with the Communists and is gradually driven into sympathy with their cause; he has his own methods of protest however, and one scene shows him in hospital recovering from an operation in which he has swallowed a dangerous object in what appears to be a routine attempt at suicide. The doctor shows him a display case in which he keeps an astonishing collection of similar objects removed from the stomachs of other prisoners over the years.

Meanwhile disorder spreads through the prison and even, as the news of the hunger strike circulates, into other prisons. The governor is ordered again to put an end to it by the Minister, but still attempts to do so in a reasonable, conciliatory manner; the prison is by now in a state of almost complete chaos, with Babella mistreating the political prisoners with impunity, and the climax comes during an official inspection when an ordinary prisoner who has managed to escape from the isolation cell makes his way to the top of a water tower and from there urinates on the assembled dignitaries. After this the governor is forced to retire and is replaced by Babella. In a scene that mirrors the Christmas Eve sequence that opens the film, Babella addresses the caged prisoners: he tells them that things are going to be different now, but that they will be encouraged nevertheless to think and act for themselves. "Now you can clap," he concludes sardonically, in an illustration of the kind of freedom they can truly expect. The style of this admirable film is sober and restrained; the only obtrusive element, the use of black-and-white[5] for scenes within the prison walls and colour for those outside, is not perhaps totally necessary but is effectively handled nonetheless.

Snowfall (1974) begins magnificently with an urgently-edited sequence of a group of soldiers running what appears to be an obstacle race across a barren, reddish-

---

[5] Strictly speaking, the film has a bluish tinge rather than normal black-and-white.

brown landscape. The camera catches the sense of physical effort and strain they are undergoing as they scramble and slide over the loose and treacherous gravel. Suddenly a fight breaks out between the two men in the lead; one knocks the other down (we learn later that he has killed him) and goes on to win the race. The prize at stake is a pass for a few days' leave, and the young man then sets out with his peasant grandmother to search for his parents, who have disappeared in the confusion of the closing stages of the Second World War (the period in which the film is set). The various stages of their quest are superbly photographed, with Sándor Sára's camera creating a constant impression of tiny figures picked out by a means of a telephoto lens and isolated among the bleak and awesome scenery of Transylvania.

The couple finally arrive in an area of the mountains that has been sealed off by the military and are promptly arrested. Here the style of the film abruptly changes and a long Jancsó-like sequence follows in which Csorba is constantly interrogated by an officer with whom he builds up a relationship of mutual respect combined with suspicion. He is finally allowed to leave and, with the grandmother, continues his search. In an extremely obscure final sequence, he finds his father, who is almost immediately killed when the soldiers attempt to arrest them again; Csorba retaliates by attacking the barracks single-handed, only to find them empty, and the film ends with a slow zoom-in on the grandmother as she waits patiently for him in the snow-covered mountains.

Kósa, whose wife is Japanese, says that the structure of the film is based on Japanese traditions in which old people used to be sent off into the mountains to die; even if this is so, it does not throw much light on how we are to interpret several crucial sequences and the film finally leaves the viewer frustrated and tantalised. Nevertheless, Kósa's skill as a film-maker is never in doubt and, of the younger directors, he seems to me the one most likely to make a truly great film one day.

Imre Gyöngyössy's first feature, *Palm Sunday* (1969), is clearly influenced by Jancsó in both subject-matter and style, and deals with the repression, in the aftermath of the Councils' Republic, of an essentially peaceful popular movement. The focus of the film is on the inner torment of a young priest who identifies with the suffering of his flock and is willing to break with his ecclesiastical superiors to express this, but who cannot bring himself to condone or advocate violence. On the one hand, he can suggest to a shocked and horrified bishop that Church lands should be divided up and given to the peasants, yet he cannot agree with his brother that, when the Church refuses to do this, the only alternative is to seize the land by force.

The Jancsó-like element in the film comes most obviously to the surface in the closing sequences, which chart the massacres and reprisals carried out by the authorities once the revolution has been suppressed: the starkly black-and-white images are composed with extreme formality, expecially in a scene where black-robed women come to identify the bodies of their menfolk, hanged from the branches of trees. Earlier, a group of prisoners have sadistically been made responsible for the life and death of their comrades by being forced to suspend a huge rock over their heads that will fall and crush them the moment they relax or weaken.

Legend About the Death and Resurrection of Two Young Men (1971), however, displays a totally original film style that, if anything, is closer to Eisenstein and to Szabó than to Jancsó. Here the images are systematically fragmented and dislocated, then reassembled in a pattern that moves with the utmost freedom in time and space and proceeds more in the associative manner of a lyric poem than as a conventional narrative. The film is both virtually a documentary of gypsy life and a conscious attempt to present this in the form of a myth;[6] it has been criticised for not being wholly the one or the other but, like Jancsó in *Red Psalm,* Gyöngyössy has evolved a style of "lyric realism" that allows him to create an imagined world that works on multiple levels simultaneously, partly through the editing, and partly through a stylised use of songs and dances.

A young gypsy painter returns to his native settlement with a friend, anxious to help his compatriots out of their traditional squalor and ignorance. He is resented, however, as an outsider and his attempts at assistance meet with open hostility. When he intervenes to put an end to what he sees as the community's self-abasement in cheapening and prostituting its traditions for the sake of a group of prying tourists, he is judged to be a traitor and suffers the penalty of having his tongue cut out,

---

[6] In a curious way, the two central characters appear literally to live out the roles of two legendary figures described to them in the course of the film.

while his companion, who has been working on a building site, is drowned by his gypsy co-workers in a trough of concrete.

This, at least, is what *appears* to happen and, on this level, the film is a fascinating and authentic record of the tensions still existing in an often oppressed and still unassimilated minority within Hungary; but it is also far more than this. Through the barbaric splendour of his imagery, with its concentration on the natural forces of water, forests, sun, flowers, birds and animals, and an ambiguous and provocative editing structure, Gyöngyössy gives his film the dimensions of a myth, of a pre-destined and yet liberating ritual. The opening scene of the arrival of the two men is filmed and cut so that it can be interpreted as being either naturalistic or meta-phoric; constant cutting forward within the body of the film to the climactic scene of the blood-letting creates a sense of tension and also inevitability. When the climax arrives, we are given several options, each of them equally valid, as to what actually happened: either the sentence was carried out, or the man was saved by the intervention of the woman with whom he had been living, or he chose to drown himself instead, or he was brought back to life by his mother and his lover. The film thus expands from the chronicling of a particular injustice to a reflection on violence, dignity, exploitation, sacrifice, and the liberation from self-distrust and self-contempt. At the end of the film one of the gypsies approaches Gera as he sits naked on the river bank and admits: "We need you."

Like Jancsó in *Red Psalm,* Gyöngyössy is able to allow the metaphorical and the literal to co-exist on the same

level of visual reality within the film, although his means
of achieving this are utterly different and, instead of the
cold, hard images that he creates for Jancsó, János
Kende here produces effects that are sensual, dreamlike,
even delirious: a black horse rolling over and over in the
sunshot waters of a river; a young girl standing in a
field of sunflowers; a water-melon ripped open by a razor
as the punishment inflicted on the young martyr's be-
trayer is re-enacted; birds and flowers scattered by the
explosion as the workers blast stone at a quarry; the
young gypsy's friend drowned by his fellow-workers in
a trough of slaked lime, then rising, a white, ghost-like
figure to walk through green, sun-dappled woods and
cleanse himself in the river.

Sons of Fire (1974) is loosely structured round the
"Stag Boy" legend that is the subject of a major poem
by Ferenc Juhász, and deals with the attempted escape
from prison of a group of Communist captives towards the
end of the Second World War. Once again, individual images in the film are magnificent and the associative pattern
of the editing produces some dazzling effects, but, even
more than with *Legend,* the film is so complex that a
first viewing produces an impression of obscurity and
confusion overall. This is particularly true of the second
half of the film, much of which must be interpreted
metaphorically rather than literally: at one point, for
example, two lovers among the escaped prisoners spend
the night in a hut which is burned down over their heads.
In the morning, however, they are discovered unharmed
among the smouldering ruins and the apples, bread, and
corn they have brought in with them are also untouched.

The central sequence of the film, nevertheless, in which the escaped prisoners are hunted down like animals by the local landowners, while images of dying birds and deer, together with scenes of the fruitfulness and calm placidity of nature, alternately supplement and contrast with the violence of their deaths, remains an astonishing *tour-de-force*.

*

The most highly praised film of the past few years within Hungary is probably *Sindbad* (1971), directed by Zoltán Huszárik (it remains his only feature film to date).[7] It was photographed by Sándor Sára and has claims to being one of the most visually beautiful films ever made; like Gyöngyössy's work, it makes striking use of extreme close-ups of natural objects—flowers, dew-drops, water, flames—that are cut together in a series of very brief shots, both at the opening of the film and at later intervals throughout it. The intention of these images is very different here, though, and Huszárik is concerned above all to create a sense of physical texture, to capture both the immediate beauty and the fragility, the evanescence of nature itself.

This is fully appropriate to the subject of the film, which deals with the last few days in the life of an aging hedonist, a man who has lived only for the sensual pleasures of women, food, and drink, and who now tries

[7] Huszárik entered the Film School as early as 1949, but after three years was unexpectedly advised to leave. With the help of Károly Makk he was able to return to his studies in 1959 and graduated in 1961. He then made several short films, notably *Elegy* (1965).

to recapture in memory some of these vanished delights. Often an encounter with a former lover will start off a series of recollections of their time together in the past, though, as the film proceeds, the logic of the flashbacks becomes rather haphazard and appears to follow no particular pattern. Several of these images are astonishingly beautiful: two girls dancing in a sunlit glade, the camera swirling in graceful arabesques around them; a sleigh ride that achieves, in colour, the stark contrasts of black and white; finest of all, perhaps, a girl in a red scarf skating in waltz-time on a frozen river before gradually moving away and vanishing into the mist. The images capture both the beauty and the transience of the experience and this is accentuated by the predominance of winter and autumnal landscapes in the setting, and the fact that most of his memories deal with scenes of parting and farewell.

Gradually an emotional pattern emerges from these images, a portrait of an essentially shallow personality, incapable either of offering or responding to a truly loving relationship. The crucial episode here is that of the suicide of a young flower girl with whom he had briefly amused himself before discarding her, but most of the other affairs contain this basic element. Towards the end, the moralising becomes over-explicit, though one fine image does much to capture the sense of the futility and pathos of the pursuit of sensuality into old age: as Sindbad sits in the salon of a brothel, musing on his past life, the camera watches an old man pawing at a girl sitting on his lap, in a gesture that mirrors exactly the position of two young lovers in a painting behind him. A much longer sequence, that has something of the same effect of conveying pleasures that have lost their original savour, shows Sindbad eating a huge meal in a restaurant, the camera focussing obsessively on every detail of the greasy, over-rich food—the surface of a bowl of soup, the sloppy interior of a marrow-bone, froth on a glass of beer, a stuffed pheasant, potatoes, globules of beef in a thick tomato sauce.

On a first viewing, I found the film almost like that meal, too rich to absorb at one sitting, perhaps too concerned with its own formal beauty and the surface recreation of a luxurios setting and environment. On seeing it again, however, I found it much more satisfying; the ambiguity inherent in the nature of the images themselves is much more subtle than I had thought it and the lushness of the imagery is crucial to the meaning of the film and not merely a superficial aestheticism.

Another extraordinarily beautiful film, this time photographed by János Kende, is *Romanticism* (1972), directed by Zsolt Kézdi-Kovács. Set in the period of the Enlightenment, it deals with a young man who returns to his father's estates imbued with the new philosophical principles of the brotherhood of man, the noble savage, and the natural goodness of humanity. Offended by the coarseness of rural life and humiliated as a weakling by his hard-drinking, hard-riding father, he becomes fascinated by the glamorous figure of a local bandit, whom he identifies as natural man, uncorrupted by civilisation, and runs off to join his gang. When the bandit dies after an accident, the rest of the outlaws turn on the newcomer, beat and strip him, and leave him for dead. The film ends with the naked, half-crazed young man wandering through the forest, ironically at one with nature at last, and finally caught up in the panic of a stag hunt led by his father. Like *Sindbad,* the film comes dangerously close to sheer aestheticism at some stages, though its visual beauty can generally be seen as functional and as a commentary on the young man's delusions, and the final image of the naked boy peering through the leaves at the magnificent yet utterly alien stags reminds us that those who distort, ignore, or idealise facts will ultimately be destroyed by them. Much of the film is shot with a telescopic lens that allows Kézdi-Kovács to follow a sequence of action without interruption by cuts—a legacy, perhaps of his earlier career as assistant to Jancsó.

Temperate Zone (1970), an earlier film, displays this stylistic element even more clearly and is full of long, sustained takes where the camera observes a complicated series of movements. The setting is contemporary, though it deals with characters who are haunted by their actions during the 1950's. The central figure is a doctor who held an influential post during the Rákosi period and still keeps a bust of Stalin on his desk, and who attempts to apply the mentality of that period in a totally different set of circumstances, with tragic (and somewhat melodramatic) results. The film has some powerful sequences, but is rather too schematic in its structure, with the plot manoeuvres that make possible the fatal shooting at the end much too clumsily signalled and contrived.

Pál Sándor's *Sarah, My Dear* (1971) also presents the differing outlooks of the older and younger generations as a frivolous and totally apolitical young man is forced by circumstances to spend time with his aunt, a Party worker who had devoted her whole life to the service of the cause. The old lady becomes ever more lovable as the film proceeds and though at the end Sándor makes some attempt (in a series of *cinéma-vérité* interviews with genuine party veterans) to pose the basic question of just how people of integrity could allow the cause they believed in to be responsible for such flagrant injustices and even crimes, he seems satisfied with the standard reply that "it was a difficult situation" and, as Communists, they had a duty to support the Party leadership.

Sándor's first film, *Clowns on the Wall* (1967), is both less tendentious and more interesting. A teenage boy who has taken shelter from a rainstorm in an empty house finds himself trapped inside when the owners unexpectedly return. While he waits for friends to rescue him, he remembers, or fantasises (the dividing line is never fully clear) incidents from his earlier life and his relationships with his parents, girl-friend, and classmates. The film creates a genuine sense of freshness and exuberance (almost all the actors were non-professionals), while conveying some of the tensions, disappointments, and regrets that are inseparable from adolescence. Stylistically too, the film is quite inventive, with trick photography and mock *cinéma-vérité* effectively used in some of the more high-spirited incidents.

Football of the Good Old Days (1973) combines the interest in visual experimentation with a more overtly political theme to produce the most interesting of those of Sándor's films that I have seen. It is set in 1924 and concerns the attempt of a small-time football manager to put together a team that can defeat the traditional local rivals. His main problems centre round satisfying the demands of his two star players, the goalkeeper and the outside right; he is forced to sell the latter to a local entrepreneur (in a scene that shows him literally crawling under a long table to reach and talk to the man), and he finally ends up keeping goal himself in the vital match (he was previously himself a player of international standard). The tone of the film alternates rapidly between slapstick and seriousness, with several reminders of the political tensions of the period—the sabotage of a ferry-boat full of workers returning from a day's outing, or the closing scene in the Budapest railway station where a disgruntled crowd greets the return of the humiliated Hungarian Olympic soccer team with shouts of, "We need new leaders!" The main interest of the film, however, is in its impeccable period reconstruction and its affectionate pastiche of the style of the silent cinema of the time: Dezső Garas in the leading role is a Chaplinesque figure who often, in fact, recreates situations and poses from such films as *The Cure* and *The Kid;* there is much use of tinkling piano music, fast motion, comic chases and an inevitable—and unfortunately overdone—fight with cream cakes. An interesting sub-theme of the film compares the problems faced by a football manager with those of a film director, notably in the areas of choosing, disciplining and inspiring their collaborators and in the need to produce tangible (preferably financial) results.

Sándor was one of the group of highly talented young

directors who graduated from the Film School in 1961. Another was Pál Gábor, whose films to date display a strong influence of trends in film-making in Britain and America. *Horizon* (1970) tackles the theme of disaffected youth that was familiar in such British films of the late Fifties and early Sixties as *Saturday Night and Sunday Morning*. The hero is a teenage boy who refuses to settle for the boring routine of a factory and the life of "quiet desperation" that he sees his mother leading. He resents official reproaches and admonitions, and his response to war veterans who tell him how lucky he is to have a job and to remember the sacrifices that were made for him, is that he didn't ask anyone to die on his behalf. He lives with his mother in a grimy industrial suburb and enjoys with her a relationship based almost equally on affection and hostility. Inspired by sitting through *"If... "* twice, he makes a break for a freer life of his own but has no real idea how to set about doing this effectively; society re-establishes its stranglehold over him, sending him for psychiatric tests and returning him to his work in the factory, no more reconciled to his fate than he was before. *Journey With Jacob* (1972) is a more relaxed work and here the influence is that of such American "road" films as *Easy Rider*. Two young men appear to have found the kind of more open existence the hero of *Horizon* was searching for: they travel together all over Hungary, carrying out their ludicrously easy task of inspecting fire equipment in small towns and villages. Yet, inside, each secretly longs for respectability, to settle down, get married, and find a steady job.

Márta Mészáros's best film to date may still be her

first, *The Girl* (1968), though all of them deal in an interesting way with women who find that social conflicts and prejudices prevent them from realising their full potential as individuals. In this particular film, Mészáros shows how the overt repression of women in the older pattern of village life has been replaced by the more subtle sexual and economic exploitation inherent in the apparently much freer existence of young girls in a contemporary city. The rather vague and unsettled heroine works in a factory and lives in an orphanage; during the film she visits her mother who has remained in her native village and whose still youthful features are smothered and negated by the black peasant costume tradition forces her to wear. On her train journeys to and from the village she is constantly being accosted by young men; she takes up with one of them, but in a curiously dispassionate manner, quietly telling him, "I like you, but I don't love you." There is a rather unsettling coldness and detachment about the whole film, in fact, as though Mészáros is wanting us to *understand* her character, rather than merely sympathise with her. The episodic structure of the film is held together by the girl's attempts to find her father; she is finally approached by a shabbily-dressed old man who cadges a meal from her and then claims, totally implausibly, to be the person she is looking for. In her rather haphazard way, she tolerates his lies and decides to accept his story: at least it is better than no father at all.

Binding Sentiments (1968) and *Riddance* (1973) are less successful, largely because of weaknesses, or even downright implausibilities in plot construction. The former concerns a middle-aged woman (beautifully played, as always, by Mari Törőcsik) obsessed by memories of her recently-dead husband, and her relationship with her son and his girl-friend, who try to bring her back to an interest in the present and the future. She resents the freedom and potential for future happines that the girl, in particular, represents, though, ironically, she had never been particularly satisfied with her marriage and had admired rather than loved her husband. After an inconclusive and rather rambling series of incidents, the young people manage to establish some kind of contact with her, though she remains essentially isolated throughout. In *Riddance*,[8] a young factory worker pretends to be a student in order to impress the boy with whom she is in love, and his snobbish family. The film is of interest in exposing class and social tensions that still exist within Hungary, but the mechanics of the plot and the motivations of the characters remain unconvincing and arbitrary.

János Rózsa and Ferenc Kardos made their first feature, *Grimace* (1965), in collaboration, and each has since produced two or three films on his own. Rózsa's *Dreaming Youth* (1974), which is based on an autobiographical novel by the poet and film theorist Béla Balázs, has been harshly criticised within Hungary[9] for failing to give any indication that the young boy at its centre possesses exceptional qualities that destine him

---

[8] Also known in English as *Good Riddance*.

[9] See the review by József Tornai in *New Hungarian Quarterly*, No. 57 (Spring 1975).

for a great literary career; though this is true, it does not seem to me sufficient reason for condemning the film out of hand. Rózsa's main concern appears to be with the child's growing awareness and comprehension of injustice, bigotry, treachery and cruelty, within the framework of the slow decline of the secure, comfortable, bourgeois world of his parents. All the major episodes, whether ostensibly public or private, contribute towards this understanding and the deliberately dreamlike atmosphere of endless sunshine, green leaves, white dresses and parasols, darkening only towards the end, is crucial to an understanding of the theme of illusion and awakening. One episode, in which the child joins his fellow townsmen at a primitive film showing, to watch a series of short newsreels projected inside a tent, contributes in particular to his realisation that there is a larger, bleaker world outside: riots, demonstrations and barricades in far-away cities replace the opening images of the townspeople themselves relaxing at the fairground; gradually the remainder of the audience melt away, but Herbert remains, fascinated, to the very end.

By contrast, Kardos's most recent film, *Unruly Heyducks* (1974), remains almost inaccessible to a foreigner. The story concerns a cattle-drive by Hungarian patriots in the early Seventeenth Century, in an attempt to raise funds for their anti-Hapsburg rebellion. A group of mercenaries (Heyducks) assist them, in return for promises of grants of land once the drive is over. Kardos, however, provides so little information about the complicated political struggles of the period, and shows so little interest in the motives and personalities of his characters,[10] that the film is left with little to offer except magnificent photography by János Kende and an intriguing musical score. The final scenes, which show the massacre of the patriots and mercenaries by the Hapsburg army are also unavoidably—and uncomfortably— reminiscent of Jancsó.

Judit Elek also belongs to the group of 1961 graduates; her best-known film to date is *A Lady from Constantinople* (1969), a delightful and moving portrait of an old woman who has to move out of her over-large apartment and advertises that she wishes to exchange it for a smaller one. Eager applicants invade her rooms and, in the most memorable scene of the film, gradually an impromptu party begins, with singing, dancing, and drinking and an atmosphere of genuine warmth and gaiety. This cannot last, however, and the old woman is left alone once more; she moves into a pleasant new apartment, with all her possessions around her, but her fundamental loneliness is inescapable. The film also contains some good-natured satire on the housing situation in Budapest—perhaps a legacy from Elek's earlier work as a maker of documentaries.

Pál Zolnay, who is a few years older than these directors, began as a maker of fiction films like *The Sack* (1966), but has now come to see these as outdated and is search-

[10] I realise that, once again, I appear to be condemning one director for elements of style or method that I have praised in another, namely Jancsó. The difference is that Jancsó offers a distinctive viewpoint and tone to replace his neglect of conventional narrative and psychological interests; Kardos (here at least) does not.

ing for a style of film that is neither fiction nor conventional documentary.[11] He is currently working on a film which is to be almost completely improvised according to the circumstances that he encounters in following up the basic situation that provides its starting-point (two young men travelling across Hungary and observing the various "social rites" that give society its cohesion and its traditions). An earlier work, *Photography* (1972), can be seen as a first step in this new direction: the two leading figures are actors, but the remainder of the cast are not, and the film was shot without a regular script. Two photographers travel around taking pictures of ordinary people, listening to their life stories, and, increasingly, attempting to cope with the problem of whether they should present their subjects as they really are, or retouch the prints to conform to the customer's own vision of himself. Gradually they become involved in trying to find out the truth behind an old scandal in which a woman was accused of killing her two daughters; the conflicting accounts given by the participants in this confirm the evidence of their photographic work: that each person sees himself and his actions in the most favourable possible light and values this more than objective or abstract truth.

The films discussed in this section so far display a healthy variety of subjects, settings, and styles and include individual works of considerable quality. Almost all of them work within the Hungarian tradition of using

[11] According to an interview in *Hungarofilm Bulletin* 75/1, pp. 11-14.

film as a weapon of social criticism—either obliquely, in a period setting, or directly, in a contemporary environment, and even if the comment is not to be found on the surface of the film, it will be discovered tucked away in a corner for those who care to search for it. Two recent films, both of them first features by new directors, could hardly be more different in tone and atmosphere, yet each is, in its own way, making a valid comment on present-day life in Hungary.

At the End of the Road (1973) is directed by Gyula Maár and stars his wife, Mari Törőcsik. This is a bleak, harsh, disquieting work and is clearly much influenced in its pacing and the organisation of its black-and-white imagery by the early films of Antonioni and Bergman. Essentially it is a study in failure: on the first day of his retirement, a former factory manager tries to come to terms with the decline of his career after its peak several years before, and with his inability to understand or communicate with his son, despite the genuine affection that exists between them. The film is at its best when it creates its theme obliquely, by inference rather than direct statement: the son constantly conveys important messages to his father by means of a tape recorder instead of personal confrontation; the father goes to an appointment in a café with a colleague, but the camera focuses on an old man patiently chewing his food rather than on the ostensible subject of attention; and, in the finest and most powerful scene of the film, the central character stands helplessly in a train corridor while, in the carriage he has just vacated, a brash and self-confident younger man quickly and confidently seduces a young woman. At the end of this sequence, the embarrassed, shame-faced girl leaves the train and is seen in extreme long-shot as she walks across a barren, misty landscape dominated by a distant, solitary poplar tree—an image that crystallises perfectly the mood of this, admittedly uneven, film.

In contrast, István Dárday's *Holiday in Britain* (1974) provides a refreshingly comic treatment of the perennial subjects of leadership, change, and individual initiative. Here a young boy or girl must be chosen to complete a contingent of young people on a trip to Britain: the successful candidate must possess a pleasant personality, be a member of the Young Pioneers, and be mildly, though not exceptionally, talented as a musical performer. The film shows the process by which a youth, Tibi, is selected and then the resulting confusion when his mother changes her mind and withdraws her permission for him to travel. It is difficult for an outsider to pick up all the subtleties involved in the arguments that follow, but Dárday is clearly very much concerned with the totally different mentalities of the peasant environment to which the mother belongs and the more politically sophisticated world of the officials organising the trip, as well as with the further split between the world of Tibi and his young friends, and that of his parents. Much of the apparently casual, merely scene-setting imagery that opens the film announces this conflict: modern posters and photos of contemporary personalities and events are contrasted with religious images and ornaments; later in the clean bright offices of the bureaucrats, with their Che Guevara posters, are set in opposition to the clutter of traditional souvenirs, photos and ornaments with which Tibi's mother surrounds herself. She fears that her son will be "changed", made different by the experience offered to him, but in particular she resents the insensitivity of the officials who dragged her away from her work in the fields and made her give public approval to a project she hardly understood, while still in her bare feet. She has her way in the end, stubbornly forcing her husband to fall into line with her, and oblivious to the despair of the officials who openly criticise her for stupidity and privately lament their impossible task of bringing enlightenment to such people.

Dárday has fun with the attitudes of both sides and with the closed mentality that each exhibits; Tibi, caught in the middle, is little more than a cipher and he is finally replaced, in the one unnecessarily cruel touch in the film, by a plump, blonde young accordionist who is even less talented musically than he and who accompanies the other successful candidates on to the plane to the strains of inspiring music. Much of the film was apparently improvised, with many of the characters playing the roles they perform in real life; despite its surface casualness, however, it is very carefully organised and contains some finely comic moments.

*

An English critic has noted that the characteristic strength of Hungarian films is that they give "a sense of the heights to which ordinary men and women can rise in response to demanding circumstances."[12] Even if there are individual exceptions to this (such as *Holiday in Britain*) it seems generally true that the best of these films, from *People on the Alps* through *The Upthrown Stone* and *The Falcons* to *Love,* celebrate those characters who hold doggedly to their vision of what is just and humane behaviour, despite all the pressures brought on them to compromise or at least maintain an acquiescent silence. Even in the midst of Jancsó's blackest visions, there is usually at least one person who balks at the brutalities in which he is expected to participate, or who defends his human dignity by a stubborn and honourable resistance to humiliation and oppression. And these are indeed "ordinary" people, men and women who find themselves caught up in sweeping historical changes but who insist on demanding, against all the odds, that history must, first of all, concern itself with mankind.

[12] Suzanne Budgen, "The Festival of the Hungarian Feature Film—Pécs, 1969", *Screen,* Vol. 11 (1970), p. 58.

Chapter Six

Consolidation:
The Mid-seventies

Since mid-1975, when the viewings that form the basis
for this book were completed, Hungarian cinema has
neither given the world many surprises, nor revealed
much unexpected new talent, though the overall level
of production has remained high and some films, recently Fábri's *The Fifth Seal* and Sándor's *Improperly Dressed,* have received major prizes at important festivals
(Fábri at Moscow and Sándor at Berlin, both in 1977).
The impression is of a production that is marking time,
and the next leap forward will probably come either
from Jancsó or Gaál, both of whom have new features
in progress, or from some of the restless young graduates
of the Béla Balázs Studio, eager to work within the new
genre of mingled documentary and fiction, pioneered
so successfully by István Dárday in *Holiday in Britain.*

Jancsó, meanwhile, has continued to alternate between
Hungary and Italy, where *Private Vices and Public
Virtues,* an Italian–Yugoslav co-production made in 1976,
has proved to be far the most successful, both aesthetically and financially, of his "foreign" films. To be sure,
part of the financial success has come from its being

billed as soft-core pornography throughout most of the Western world, but, despite its explicit and powerful eroticism, it develops and elaborates some of Jancsó's most deeply-felt themes in a novel and exciting way.

Conscious no doubt of the charges of "mannerism" brought against him, in particular with respect to *Elektreia,* Jancsó has moved abruptly away from the film based on a couple of dozen sequence shots to something that is much closer to the editing pattern of the normal feature. Yet most of the familiar themes, revolt, power, authoritarianism, humiliation, eroticism as both a political and a moral challenge, remain, and the film as a whole, in its visual beauty, its formal compositions, its interaction between characters and setting, and its iconographic motifs (uniforms, masks, dances, and so on) could have been made only by Jancsó.

It is loosely based on the notorious Mayerling affair of the last days of the Austro-Hungarian Empire, and deals with the young prince's increasingly desperate attempts to defy and scandalise his father, the Emperor, and so expresses both his personal detestation and his opposition to the whole political system which he wishes to reject, yet within which he is trapped by his heritage. It opens with the incongruous spectacle of the naked prince running around the garden of his palace while a military band dutifully conducts a concert in the background; he expresses his hatred of both his father and his wife by defiling objects associated with them, and proceeds to flout sexual taboos by an open relationship both with his former nanny and his half-sister. These scenes are backed up with a use of revolutionary music, notably the "Carmagnole", familiar from *Red Psalm* and *Confrontation,* but the prince's revolt—like that of the young students in *Confrontation*—is essentially little more than privileged game-playing: he is, as yet, taking no real risks and, when some of his friends are arrested, his status renders him immune.

He therefore attempts something more far reaching, and plans a party at which drugs and alcohol will break down the inhibitions of the young aristocratic guests, while he and his accomplices photograph their actions. In the scenes that follow, Jancsó employs some of his most dazzling sequence shots, as the camera follows the gorgeously costumed guests as they wander around the gardens, mingling with the music and dancing of a troupe of folk-artists. The plan works, and the party degenerates into a debauch, while the prince incites, not only sexual license, but overt mockery of the Emperor. A messenger from his father, meanwhile, is first of all kept waiting and made to witness the spectacle, then is systematically humiliated, is made to take off his uniform and jump the length of the banquet table, and is then forced into sexual congress with a hermaphrodite specially provided for the occasion.

Yet all this, too, is futile, if it is to be seen as an attempt to change the social structure rather than, from a position of relative security, to defy some of its most obvious taboos. The film now takes on an almost dreamlike quality, marked by the use of slow motion in several sequences and fragile, soft-focus images—in one scene soap-bubbles are used to accentuate the sense of something fleeting and evanescent. The prince's actions become more desperate and include a pretence of madness, while the forces of authority implacably consolidate their position and typical images of young people singing and dancing within a circle of uniformed soldiers begin to appear. Much of the last part of the film is taken up with a long love-scene between the prince and the hermaphrodite backed by deliberately lush and romantic music and creating an unexpected sense of despairing, yet genuine, tenderness and affection. The prince's open accusations of crimes committed by his father, however, have made him at last too dangerous to the security of the state: in a characteristically ritualistic scene, he and his closest companions are shot down by the soldier (all falling together, each with a neat bullet hole in his forehad), after which the Emperor announces that the prince committed suicide and a military band helps to restore an atmosphere of discipline and order. The final slow-motion images of the funeral cortège, however, suggest that the prince's revolt, though futile and misdirected, was not without its own beauty and dignity. The most powerful impact left by the film, in fact, is that of the trap in which the prince (like so many other Jancsó figures) finds himself: his attempts to resist oppression are conditioned by the limited circumstances within which he can operate, with the result that he can achieve no more than a purely personal defiance and a personal and temporary (though genuine) freedom. Jancsó seems here to have moved away from the relative optimism of *Red Psalm* and *Elektreia,* back to something closer to the bleakness of *The Round-Up* and *Silence and Cry*.

When compared to an earlier Italian-made film like *Technique and Rite* (1972), *Private Vices and Public Virtues* displays a welcome richness and complexity that suggests that Jancsó is far from played-out as a major film-maker. Despite moments of great visual beauty, especially in its combinations of colour and its use of a barren, seashore setting, *Technique and Rite* offers little more than a repeat of the major themes of *Winter Wind* endless suspicions and loyalty tests, elaborate oaths and ceremonies that are almost immediately undermined by arrests and executions, a maniacal insistence on unquestioning obedience and fidelity on the part of Attila that leaves him at the end with some half-dozen followers with whom he, rather optimistically, intends to conquer the world. *Technique and Rite* suggests sterility, whereas *Private Vices and Public Virtues,* despite moments of excess, indicates that Jancsó is still open to innovation and experiment.

István Szabó's new film, *Budapest Tales* (1976), has been much less successful and, indeed, has been greeted rather harshly, both by Hungarian critics and by audiences at international festivals such as Cannes. The main complaints brought against the film are that it is too much of a reworking of Szabó's favourite themes (without the kind of innovations found in *Private Vices and Public Virtues* that makes us look at Jancsó's themes in a new way), and that it is both too overtly, and too obscurely, allegorical. Certainly one is constantly forced to consider the events of the film as pointing to something beyond their surface meaning: a mixed group of civilians and soldiers, in the last days of the Second World War, come across an abandoned streetcar by the side of a river; they start it working again and set off for Budapest.[1] They pick up passengers and stores on the way; there are quarrels and dissensions within the group and conflicts with some of those who want to join them; sabotage is suspected, carried out, and punished; after successfully fighting their way through natural and man-made obstacles, the group almost give up when confronted by an impassable stretch of river, but finally decide to take the tram apart, ship the pieces across on rafts, and reassemble it on the other side; at last they come within sight of the city and, in an almost inevitable closing image, are joined by dozens of other trams, all heading towards the same destination.

The film is thus clearly an allegory of Hungarian history since the War, with its brave ideals, its setbacks and frustrations, its need for solidarity and cohesion if the goal is to be attained. Some of the episodes are obviously linked to specific events in that history, such as the political tensions of the late 1940s and early 1950s, and the conflicts of 1956: the river scene appears to refer to the latter, and the episode in which a doctor takes over leadership of the group, only to be brutally beaten and murdered by a band of soldiers who have previously

[1] The mystery of why a tramline should extend so far out into the countryside, several days' journey form the capital, is explained (for the purposes of the film, at least) when one knows that, in Hungary, the gauges of tramlines and railway lines are identical and Szabó was thus able to run his streetcar on railway tracks.

failed in an attempt to commandeer the train for themselves, seems to stem from the former. In this case, as with a
subsequent scene in which a man sacrifices his own life
to allow the tram to continue, the group calmly, and
somewhat callously, go on their way without any thought
of helping their stricken comrades: indeed they are soon
completely forgotten, as when one of the characters
later remarks in puzzlement, "Wasn't there someone
with us once who knew about colours?"[2]

Each of the main figures (as in *25 Firemen's Street,*
there is no one character at the central focus of interest)
is allowed a monologue in which to chronicle his or her
particular concerns or obsessions, and there is the obli-
gatory birth scene, representing new life, that in this
case produces twins who are nine or ten years old by the
end of the film. The speeding-up of the time-scheme as
the film proceeds is one of the clearest indications that
it is not to be interpreted naturalistically: the early
scenes might, just possibly, be acceptable on a literal as
well as an allegorical level, but once the river is reached
and the tram has been disassembled and flawlessly put
together again with not a bolt missing, Szabó abandons
any pretence at a realistic sequence of events. This seems
to be one of the features that has most irritated critics,
together with the fact that the film often seems to work

[2] The exception to this is the character played by Maya Komorowska,
who single-handedly digs a grave for the doctor and then tries to commit
suicide; throughout the film she displays a higher sense of moral responsibility than any of the other characters and, no doubt significantly,
is presented as being excessively short-sighted and, without her glasses,
virtually blind.

as a puzzle, challenging interpretation and analysis, more than as a narrative.[3]

Nevertheless, the film contains many beautiful sequences that display Szabó's characteristic subtlety in handling image and sound, both in combination and in counterpoint, and, whether one follows all the significant details or not, the overall pattern of the film is perfectly clear. The moral and political issues raised have a general and not simply a local validity: How far can a society seeking solidarity tolerate individual viewpoints and actions? How, and to what extent, can potentially disruptive elements be assimilated within the total framework? When, and to what degree, is violence acceptable as a means of safeguarding society? Is a kind of moral callousness, a refusal to linger on the sufferings and sacrifices of the past, a necessary precondition if a tolerable future is to be attained? Implicitly at least, most of these questions are answered within the very progress of the film itself, as the characters find themselves faced with these problems and come up with a pragmatic solution to them; yet their solutions are not necessarily those favoured by Szabó himself and there is no reason why we, as audience, should not be prepared to continue the discussion ourselves.

The Hungarian director whose reputation has grown most rapidly in the past two years is probably Márta

---

[3] In contrast, for example, to Gaál's *The Falcons,* where realism and allegory work hand-in-hand throughout.

Mészáros, whose films are now in great demand at festivals all over the world. Part of this interest is no doubt attributable to the current interest in women film-makers in general, and in the debates about the role of women within society that are going on throughout the industrialised world. Yet, though Mészáros is most definitely in favour of greater female independence and self-sufficiency, she is also far from taking the extreme feminist position that rejects women's traditional role as mother, though there is a good deal of ambiguity as to whether motherhood should necessarily involve marriage. The heroines of her three most recent films are all the victims of unsatisfactory sexual or marital relationships; all wish to be free to pursue their own careers and find their own kind of happiness; yet all wish also to have children, and it is from the incompatibility of these three elements that the tensions of the films arise.

In *Adoption* (1975), which is aesthetically and psychologically the most satifying of the three, the central figure is a middle-aged widow who is in the midst of an affair with a married man. She wishes to bear his child and is quite prepared to look after it herself without insisting that he abandon or divorce his wife, but he refuses to agree to this. She strikes up a friendship with a young girl from a nearby community home, and thinks for a time of adopting her as her daughter. The girl, however, has a reputation as a trouble-maker, and the authorities attempt to discourage the friendship. The older woman persists, and the girl starts to spend nights away from home, sleeping in her house, often in the company of her boy friend, whom she wishes to marry. She requires her parents' permission, however, and this is finally, and grudgingly, granted only after the older woman visits them and pleads on the young couple's behalf. In the finest scene of the film, the wedding takes place, with dissension already evident between bride and groom and its ultimate failure already perfectly evident. The older woman has meanwhile applied for permission to adopt a child of her own and, in the closing scenes of the film, is seen carrying the baby along the street, a lonely figure in a bleak and deserted urban landscape. As in all Mészáros' recent films, the woman who has fought to achieve her independence and to attain her goals finds herself faced with a series of totally new problems to cope with, and there is certainly no pretence of an easy or satisfying resolution.

Nine Months (1976) and *The Two of Them* (1977)[4] are more open to the charges of implausibility and weak plot construction that marred some of Mészáros' earlier work. The heroine of *Nine Months,* a young factory worker, starts a new job and is immediately hounded by the foreman, a rather older man, who follows her after work and persistently asks her to come for a drink. Despite her refusals, he forces himself upon her and, on their first time out together, he asks her to marry him and produces two rings. Not unnaturally, she refuses. He is undeterred by this, however, and finally they become lovers. János is suspicious, possessive and demanding and, when she refuses to move in with him, he follows her one weekend and discovers that she has a child,

---

4 Also known as *Women.*

who lives in the countryside with her parents. The discovery leads to quarrels and explanations, with János persisting, nevertheless, in his determination to marry her. Juli becomes pregnant once more, but is still hesitant about committing herself to marriage. She takes and passes some exams at the local university, at which her son's father teaches. The knowledge that she is still on good terms with this man rouses János's jealousy and leads to more quarrels. At last, while they are together with his family in the house he is building himself, János brings the existence of Juli's child into the open; his family, predictably and over-melodramatically, reject her and, though he tells them to leave, he then rounds on Juli, beats her, and throws her out. He warns her not to have the child and says that he will not support it; when he later regrets this decision, he cannot find her: she has gone to another town where, in a final sequence that intercuts the birth with scenes of János grimly and despairingly back at work, she has the second child. (The actress involved, Lili Monori, was pregnant when shooting started, and it is the birth of her own child that is shown on the screen.)

The Two of Them deals with a relationship very similar to that of *Adoption:* Mary, the middle-aged supervisor of a home for girls in an industrial town, befriends the younger Julia, a rebellious and defiant woman who insists, against the rules, on having her child live with her. Mary allows her to share her own room during the week and takes her home with her at weekends. Julia's husband is a well-intentioned, but weak-willed man, who drinks heavily and is constantly fighting with her; Mary's marriage has been virtually dead for years, though she and her husband maintain a pretence of affection for each other. Julia's presence, and the disruptions caused by her husband's attempts to reclaim her, force Mary into a realisation of the emptiness and lovelessness of her own existence (most effectively presented in a love-making scene in which she remains totally limp and impassive throughout); meanwhile János, after an attempt to give up drinking, succumbs once more and has to be taken to the hospital for treatment. The film ends bleakly with Mary and Julia together in the snow outside the hospital, faced with the questions posed by Julia's child about her father's behaviour and failing in their attempts to lie to her and convince her that everything is really all right.

Both films show considerable psychological insight throughout, and *The Two of Them* in particular demonstrates how all the characters are very good at analysing other people's problems and proposing plausible solutions to them, while being totally incapable of understanding or coming to terms with their own difficulties. Mészáros has a fine understanding of the unspoken tensions between men and women, and also of the moments of insight and tenderness that bring a genuine, though temporary, understanding. She is also, of course, very good at presenting friendship between women, a friendship that occasionally—as in the shower scene in *The Two of Them*—has sexual undertones. Though her films are rarely exciting visually, they are functionally effective in presenting personal relationships and in using background and setting as an indication of the characters' states of mind. Nevertheless, some very real problems remain. The main one is the strange disparity between Mészáros' concern for realism of detail, for presenting ordinary, unexceptional people in their every-day working and living environment, and the wildly im-plausible progression of her plots. János's obsession with Juli in *Nine Months* is a handy device with which to get the film started, but it has little similarity to the way in which relationships develop in ordinary experience; the concept of the "secret" child and the reactions of János's parents to this are likewise products of melodrama rather than reality. In *The Two of Them,* the drunken husband motif is also disproportionately emphasised and, even if alcoholism is a genuine social problem (and many contemporary Polish films also dwell on it at considerable length), it is handled here in a way more appropriate to the nineteenth century stage. Finally, one might remark that, welcome as Mészáros's presentation of strong-minded, independent women might be, it is too often achieved at the expense of making the men, especially János in *Nine Months,* into mere caricatures who are observed with little attempt at sympathy or understanding. It could be objected, of course, that the opposite situation has been true of male-dominated cinema for the past seventy years, but simple reversal of an aesthetic defect does not automatically turn it into a virtue.

Judit Elek's two-part film, *A Hungarian Village* and *A Commonplace Story,* covers something of the same ground as Mészáros's film, but in a style that avoids many of these pitfalls. Elek presents the social, economic, and personal conflicts and difficulties encountered by young people in contemporary Hungarian society, but in a semi-documentary fashion that observes the problems, instead of inventing them. Elek's method is not that of *cinéma-vérité* or of contemporary American documentarists such as Frederick Wiseman: although she deals with real people and the problems that arise out of their everyday relationships, the technique of the films seems to leave little to improvisation or chance. Much is presented through an interview pattern in which the questions have generally been edited out and only the answers remain, while the editing itself is usually very smooth and the multiplicity of angles suggests either that some scenes were shot several times or two or more cameras were used for much of the shooting.

The two films cover several years in the lives of two families in a fairly large village, and concentrate mostly on the conflicts between parents and children and between tradition and modernity. The daughter of one family, Ilonka, wishes to marry her boy-friend Laci, a miner; her parents feel that she is too young and that the boy is too poor; his parents also oppose the marriage. The couple stubbornly continue to meet, in the village café or at dances, and Ilonka talks to the film-maker about her frustrations at being so inhibited by the traditional moral and social patterns, and of her lack of freedom within a system that gives the parents the last, and only, word (a system, incidentally, that is justified by her married sister, who agrees that women don't need any particular attention or education as they will work for only a few years before getting married and raising a family). The personal conflict is reflected within the film as a whole, as Elek contrasts scenes of the villagers setting out to work in the fields or relaxing in the café afterwards, with the music and clothing of a younger generation unwilling to follow blindly in their parents' footsteps. Ilonka finally becomes pregnant and attempts to commit suicide, after which her parents agree to the marriage and to her having the baby.

Towards the end of *A Hungarian Village,* this story begins to alternate with another, which becomes the central focus of *A Commonplace Story.* Marika, another young girl, is more interested in a career than in marriage: she studies in a technical school and works in a factory, while living with her widowed mother (who, in one powerful sequence, talks about the time her husband hanged himself, while the camera explores the setting where the death took place). One night, two youths attempt to rape her, and she faces the ordeal of giving evidence against them in court. Under the stress of this, and other experiences, she gives up her training and works for some time as a scullery maid; she also begins to quarrel violently with her mother, who had forced her to bring the youths to trial. Gradually, however, she decides to attempt a career again and is accepted for training at a nurses' college in a nearby town. Her mother, too, decides to leave the village, and this involves asking her sister to take care of the family's bedridden grandmother, who is thus also taken away from her familiar environment. Elek seems to view the process of change as inevitable, sometimes, as with Ilonka and Laci, sympathizing with the young in their struggle for independence; in other cases, she is aware of the strength and security of a traditional pattern of existence as opposed to the rootlessness and anonymity of the new industrial towns. The rather colourless young couple seem to have little to look forward to apart from each other, and yet their village environment can offer them nothing that is suited to their particular needs: they are the product—and the victims—of the vacuum that results when a social group is unwilling, or unable, to make the changes that are necessary to ensure its own survival.

Ferenc Kósa, too, has, moved into the newly-popular documentary field with *The Portrait of a Champion* (1977).[5] This takes the form of a series of interviews with a famous Hungarian athlete, an Olympic medal winner in the pentathlon. He talks to Kósa at great length about his own experiences as an athlete and his views on society, emphasizing the fact that he believes rewards and privileges should be granted solely according to the criterion of merit, and criticizing Hungarian society for its failure to operate on this principle. He also speaks of his belief that his refusal to cash in on his fame as an athlete, and to accept the sinecures open to him, has led to his being penalized and forbidden to follow the career best suited to him. The film is probably best appreciated by a Hungarian audience, to whom the

[5] Having recently had the opportunity to see *Judgement,* which it would be out of place to deal with at this point, I should offer my opinion that it is a largely under-rated film, despite weaknesses in casting and in an unnecessary obscure chronological structure, that contains some scenes as fine as any Kósa has ever produced.

subjects being discussed are of vital and immediate concern, and it has certainly proved to be a great popular success.

Imre Gyöngyössy's *Is This The Earth?*, a television film made for a West German company, is also a documentary, in this case the story of an old peasant woman determined to visit her son in England before she dies, that emphasises Gyöngyössy's belief in the necessity of preserving the values associated with traditional rural life. His feature-length drama, *Expectation* (1975), is rather less successful: set in a large family mansion towards the end of the Second World War, it concerns two women, one of them the mother of sons who have died during the War. She refuses to believe, however, that they are dead and is constantly seeking them among the refugees that pour past the house each day and to whom her sister offers what food and comfort she can. She ends up taking three young men under her wing, all of whom humour her belief that they are her children, until more deaths, including that of her sister, force her to accept reality.

Pál Sándor's *Improperly Dressed* (1976) has brought him to the front rank of contemporary Hungarian directors, and is certainly his finest film. It is set in the aftermath of the Republic of Councils in 1919–20, and deals with a young Communist fugitive who is forced to take shelter in a fashionable sanatorium, disguised in female clothing, while waiting for an opportunity to cross the border into safety. He takes a job as a nurse and is subjected to a series of disorienting experiences that force him to adopt more and more thoroughly his female *persona*. He has an affair with one of the women patients, but is also accosted by one of the soldiers searching for fugitives like himself and is forced to kill him to preserve his secret. Another man is accused of the crime and executed for it. Finally, the youth and another activist attempt the border crossing, but the film ends with shots of their dead bodies.

Sándor handles this extremely tricky subject with delicacy and taste—as well as a good deal of wry humour—and, although he does not explore the young man's identity crisis quite as fully as Kon Ichikawa, handling a somewhat similar theme in *An Actor's Revenge,* he creates a fine awareness of the moral and personal confusions under which the youth suffers. One wonders, however, just how necessary the political framework is to the story: an equally powerful film could have been made without recourse to this, and there is a case for claiming that, in this and some other recent films, the historical setting is essentially a relic of a strategy that is beginning to outlive its usefulness to contemporary film-makers.

This is quite clearly the case with *Requiem for a Revolutionary* (1975), a first feature by Ferenc Grunwalsky, a former assistant to Jancsó. Dealing with the trial and execution in 1932 of a prominent figure in the 1919 revolution, this is an almost intolerably lugubrious and high-minded piece of work that presents a naively heroic and one-dimensional portrait of its central figure. Much better is another first feature, *Identification* (1975), directed by László Lugossy, in which a group of prisoners-of-war returning to Hungary in 1947 are being integrated into the new socialist society. One of them, András Ambrus, had been given the name and number of another prisoner while in the camp, and now refuses to accept the documents and papers that are given to him in his "new" name. As nothing, of course, has been prepared for "András Ambrus", his refusal causes administrative problems, and when he doggedly insists on reclaiming his own identity, he rouses the antagonism of the official in charge of the transit station, as well as the hostility of his fellow soldiers, who resent the delay and questioning that they have to undergo as a result of his intransigence. He is finally allowed to leave and returns to the farm where his adoptive parents live; he is greeted with apparent warmth, but soon discovers that, in his absence, his foster-father has appropriated his allocation of land to himself. When he protests at this, the farmer incites a group of young labourers to beat him up. In desperation, Ambrus goes at night to the home of the official and threatens to kill him; he is disarmed, but the official, who has been brooding over the affair, at last agrees to take responsibility for him and do what he can to help. The film is disconcerting at first in that Ambrus's stubborn refusal to "co-operate" may seem as irrational and unnecessary to us as it does to the characters in the film, and we may share something of their frustration and anger at him; his doggedness, however, wins our respect in the end, even if the final resolution is rather facile.

Zoltán Fábri's *The Fifth Seal* (1976), set in the closing days of the Second World War, deals with a group of friends who meet each evening in the local café to talk and exchange ideas; one night an incautious political remark is betrayed to the local Arrow Cross soldiers, and they are all arrested. Their abstract philosophical discussions about human freedom and dignity are put to the test when, after a period of physical torture, the Arrow Cross commandant attempts to destroy their self-respect by offering them freedom if they will slap the face of a dying Communist partisan. Three of them, even those who had earlier maintained that physical survival was the highest moral good, balk at this and are taken off for execution. One, however, consents, but only because he is sheltering in his house a group of Jewish children who, without him, will certainly perish. He is released, but will have to live forever with the knowledge of what—for whatever good motives—he has done. The moral issues that the film raises would, however, have been more effectively handled in a more low-key presentation. After an interesting beginning that conveys the atmosphere of the café and its customers in a relaxed and casual manner, Fábri pulls out all the stops as the film proceeds and the final sequence is too over-played and melodramatic to be totally successful.

A final "historical" film is *No Man's Daughter,* by the veteran László Ranódy (1976), based on a story by Zsigmond Móricz. An orphan girl of seven or eight (superbly played by a little girl of around the same age) is subjected to a series of hideous mistreatments by the various farmers who obtain her services from the orphans' home, including both physical violence and insults about her lack of parents. She develops a fantasy about her lost mother, who she believes is coming one day to reclaim her, and manages to make friends with an old man who is eventually poisoned by the girl's employer, who has tricked him out of his property and fears that this will be discovered. After a final bout of mistreatment, the child, partly by accident, sets fire to the farm, destroying both it and, presumably, its inhabitants. Melodramatic as the plot may sound, it is given credibility and intensity, partly by the child's performance and partly by Ranódy's concentration on the physical and external aspects of her experience, which give the film a concrete and vivid reality.

Of the group of recent films with a contemporary setting, the most interesting is *The Sword* (1976), directed by János Dömölky, who has worked to date mostly in television. A Hungarian couple on holiday in Vienna spot an ancient sword up for auction that the husband recognizes as having national importance in Hungarian history. He phones the National Museum and suggests that they purchase it; when they refuse, he decides to sell his own car and buy it himself, hoping that the museum will make an offer for it later. On their return to Hungary, far from being thanked for his altruism, the man is charged with currency violations and the sword is impounded. In the sequence of serio-comic events that follow, Bojti is hounded by his boss and colleagues at work, threatened with imprisonment (*"You're* going to be a national treasure for the next few years," a police official assures him grimly), and even his wife is dismissed from her job for "irresponsibility". Bojti finally sets up his own museum to display the sword and then, sick of the whole business, throws it into a nearby river—at exactly the time when a journalist friend has managed to rouse public interest in the affair and the National Museum has belatedly decided it wants the sword after all. A huge crowd assembles on the river bank to watch as dredgers search for the relic; it is finally recovered, and Bojti is interviewed on television about his experiences. "Would you do all this again?" he is asked. "Yes, of course," he replies with obvious lack of conviction, and adds, when the interviewer comments on this, that he is "not a very good actor". The film is made with a refreshing wit and irreverence that mark Dömölky as a director to watch in the future, and contains an excellent performance by Péter Haumann in the leading role.

Another fine piece of acting is that of Ferenc Kállai in *On the Side-Line* (1976), directed by Péter Szász. He plays a middle-aged baker's delivery man who enjoys a "secret life" as a football referee on Saturdays, revelling there in the sense of importance and authority that is denied him in his everyday existence. One weekend, everything goes wrong: he is assigned a new, and insubordinate linesman; his normal hotel arrangements are disrupted and he is thrown into the company of some unknown women; and his decision to allow a disputed last-minute goal against the home side to stand almost causes a riot at the end of the match. He meets one of the women afterwards and develops a tentative friendship, but his natural timidity and lack of self-confidence prevents him from following this up. A quarrel with the linesman in the train on the way home leads to reconciliation and possible friendship, though the final image of the film leaves the exhausted Ivicz slumped under a tree in the middle of a wood, staring bleakly at the camera. The most effective scene in the film is a virtuoso set-piece in which Ivicz delivers a monologue about his experiences in Auschwitz during the War, when he attempted to save the lives of two Jewish children.

When Joseph Returns (1977) by Zsolt Kézdi-Kovács is a quiet, understated and impressive film that is very different from the stylistic opulence of the same director's earlier *Romanticism*. Lili Monori plays a young, newly married woman whose husband, a merchant seaman, is away from home for ten months of every year. Her sexual and personal loneliness is accentuated by the fact that she has little in common with her mother-in-law, with whom she lives and who occasionally brings a boyfriend from work to spend the night. Bored and frustrated, she drifts into an affair which costs her her job, leads to outright quarrels with her mother-in-law, and leaves her pregnant. She then works for a time as a housemaid for her lover's employer, in a setting whose lavishness contrasts sharply with the cramped, confined flat she shares with the older woman. She loses this job too—ordered to give up her relationship with Laci for the sake of appearances, she retaliates by smashing a good many of the valuables in the house—and shortly afterwards has a miscarriage. This is followed by a temporary reconciliation with her husband's mother, but she deliberately provokes another quarrel which leads to her being thrown out of the house. Once again, things are patched up and the film ends with the two women

waiting at the airport to greet Joseph, but with the implication that this is merely a lull and that the central problem of the marriage—the husband's absence—is one
that has no solution. The film conveys the underlying
tensions of the relationships by means of glances, hints,
implications, pauses and silences, and Lili Monori gives
a fine performance of a woman whose energies and de-
sires can find no fruitful and positive outlet and become
increasingly, and more and more senselessly, self-de-
structive—a working class and female version, perhaps,
of the prince in *Private Vices and Public Virtues*.

János Rózsa and Ferenc Kardos, who began their
career with the jointly-directed *Grimaces* in the early
1960s—an amiable, if derivative, work about school-
children—have each recently produced films satirising
aspects of contemporary society. Rózsa's *Spider Football*
(1976) is set in a newly-opened technical school and
concerns the attempts of the principal to shuffle off the
blame for all the institution's weaknesses and defects onto
his colleagues—who indulge in their own varieties of
spitefulness, back-biting, and self-preservation as well.
Kardos's *The Accent* (1977) begins with an interesting
conception: a young man full of bright ideas and official
notions is sent to work as an "educational activist" in a
hopelessly inefficient small-town factory. Faced with the
lethargy and indifference of those he is expected to inspire with a thirst for culture, he discovers that he can
communicate better with them on a personal, more
intimate level, finding out what their private interests
are and sharing these with them. So far so good; but the
film falls apart towards the end when the young man

discovers a room full of official banners, portraits and productivity slogans from the early 1950s and—most improbably—decides to use these to inspire the workers with a greater sense of social responsibility and self-denial. His scheme goes wrong and he is dismissed, but by that point the film, too, has gone so far astray that it hardly matters.

The Accent contains several scenes of speeded-up slapstick that Kardos had used in a similar form in *Grimaces* and that obviously derive in turn from Louis Malle's *Zazie dans le Métro* (especially in the chase scenes). András Kovács's *Labyrinth* (1976) also inevitably invites comparison with the work of other European directors, especially Truffaut, Wajda, and Fellini in their films about film-making and the problems faced by the director. Kovács's director is in the middle of a film that is not going at all well and is forced to break off shooting for a few days in an attempt to resolve the problems. Everyone is willing to offer him advice, all claiming that what he is doing is "unreal" or "irrelevant" and offering their own versions of how the characters should behave—despite the fact that the film is based on actual events and real people. At first, the director attempts to pay heed to all these suggestions and to adapt his script to accommodate them; finally, he decides that the only person whose judgement he can really trust is his own and prepares to go ahead on that basis. The film has some interesting scenes revealing the process of film-making, and it explores some important questions of artistic and personal integrity, but ultimately is not itself excitingly enough made to hold our attention completely.

Rezső Szörény's *Reflections* (1976) has faint echoes of Bergman's *Persona* in its story of a young girl confined in a mental hospital who at first refuses to speak and resists the attempts of a woman doctor to help her and communicate with her. The complexity of the narrative structure of the film, with its non-chronological flashbacks, contrasts rather strangely with the simplicity of the plot-line, in which it is discovered that Erzsi's problems are the result of a series of personal misfortunes and frustrations, and the film ends with the strong probability that she will soon be cured. Gyula Maár's two most recent films, *Mrs Déry, Where Are You?* (1975) and *Flare and Flicker* (1977), both of them starring his wife Mari Törőcsik, are almost impossible to evaluate, especially the latter, which is such an eclectic mixture of devices borrowed from other directors that it is impossible to discern whether Maár really has a voice of his own or not. Both films deal with the personal and psychological problems of a talented middle-aged woman, but do so in a manner that is unlikely to interest or involve an audience for long. Pál Zolnay's *Shaman* (1977), two years in the making, is equally impossible to assess: Zolnay appears to be intending to make some very large statements about the artist and the nature of art itself, and the film is brilliantly photographed by Elemér Ragályi, but it sinks rapidly under the weight of its own pretensions.

It would be unfair, however, to end a discussion of Hungarian cinema today on such a negative note. In 1977 Hungarian cinema is still healthy, even if it is less inspired than it was a decade ago and even if the very real problem persists that the best films command a relatively small audience within Hungary itself and depend on outside acclaim for most of the prestige that they do achieve. The best film-makers are continuing with their task of assessing and evaluating contemporary Hungarian society, and the work of Mészáros, Kézdi-Kovács, Elek, Dömölky and others contains a healthy and necessary self-criticism in its presentation of a society that, for all its progress towards socialism, still carries an unnecessary dead-weight of baggage in such forms as frustration and neglect of the full potential of women as equal partners in society; the inhibiting effects of outworn traditions and practices, combined with a failure to adapt and breathe new life into the pattern of village existence; the boredom and alienation of too many young people; bureaucratic arrogance and inefficiency; and the continuing existence of social privileges and inequalities. None of these problems, of course, is unique to Hungary, but it is important that film-makers should continue to recognise, identify, and pay attention to them. And as long as they do so, Hungarian cinema will continue to fill an honourable and respected niche in the total pattern of world production.

Bibliography

The following is a selective list of useful works in English and French on the Hungarian cinema.

General works

BUDGEN, Suzanne: "The Festival of the Hungarian Feature Film—Pécs, 1969", *Screen* 11 (1970), 58–63.

HIBBIN, Nina: *Eastern Europe: an Illustrated Guide* (Screen Series, Zwemmer's, London/A.S. Barnes, New York, 1969). A reference handbook, rather than a historical or critical analysis. *Sound* 26 (Winter 1956–57), 124–130.

NEMESKÜRTY, István: *Word and Image: History of the Hungarian Cinema,* Budapest: Corvina Press, 1968 (revised edition, 1975).

ROBINSON, David: "Quite Apart from Miklós Jancsó...", *Sight and Sound* 39 (Spring 1970), 84–89.

VAS, Robert: "Yesterday and Tomorrow: New Hungarian Film", *Sight and Sound* 29 (Winter 1959/60), 31–34.

The following periodicals have produced special Hungarian Film issues:

Cinéma 72, No. 165 (avril 1972): includes articles and an interview with Jancsó; articles on *Love* and an interview with Makk; and a "Dictionnaire du cinéma hongrois contemporain".

Image et Son, No. 217 (mai 1968): includes articles on post-War Hungarian cinema; István Szőts; organization of the Hungarian film industry; Imre Gyöngyössy writing on peasants and film; and an interview with Jancsó.

Image et Son, No. 255 (décembre 1971): includes articles on Kovács; youth in Hungarian films; interviews with Kovács, Elek, Kósa and Szabó.

Hungarofilm Bulletin (published quarterly in Budapest) contains information and credits on all significant Hungarian films as they appear. The issue for 1973/3–4 has useful biographical information on the major directors, plus a filmography of films made between 1948 and early 1973.

The New Hungarian Quarterly (published in English in Budapest) normally reviews important new films in each issue.

On Jancsó:

BACHMANN, Gideon: "Jancsó Plain", *Sight and Sound* 43 (Autumn 1974), 217–221.

BEYLIE, Claude: "Les Maelstroms de la Liberté", *Ecran* 10 (décembre 1972), 10–13.

CRICK, Philip: "Three East European Directors: Makaveyev, Menzel, Jancsó", *Screen* 11 (1970), 64–71.

CZIGANY, Lorant: "Jancsó Country", *Film Quarterly* XXVI (Fall 1972), 44–50.

ELLEY, Derek: Review of *Agnus Dei, Films and Filming* 19 (February 1973), 49 and 52.

ESTEVE, Michel (ed.): *Miklós Jancsó, Etudes Cinématographiques,* No. 104–108 (Paris: Lettres Modernes, 1975). This contains a full bibliography of writings in French on Jancsó up to *Red Psalm.*

HOUSTON, Penelope: "The Horizontal Man", *Sight and Sound* 38 (Summer 1969), 116–120.

——————, reviews of *Agnus Dei* and *La Pacifista, Sight, and Sound* 41 (Winter, 1971/72,) 32–33.

interview in: *Cahiers du Cinéma* 188 (mars 1967). 54–57.

interview in: *Cahiers du Cinéma* 212 (mai 1969), 16–30.

interview in: *Cinéma 67,* No. 113 (février 1967), 88–95.

interview in: *Cinéma 72,* No 171 (décembre 1972), 64–68.

interview in: *Ecran* 10 (décembre 1972), 6–10.

interview in: *Image et Son* 267 (janvier 1973), 93–102.

interview in: *New Hungarian Quarterly* 27 (Autumn, 1962), 96–101.

MARTIN, Michel: "Un 'Rouge' Noir sur Blanc", *Ecran* 10 (décembre 1972), 3–6.

PRICE, James: "Polarities: the Films of Miklós Jancsó", *London Magazine* IX (1969), 189–194.

VAS, Robert "Out of the Plain", *Sight and Sound 35* (Summer 1966), 151–153.

——————————, review of *The Confrontation, Sight and Sound* 39 (Summer 1970), 157–158.

YOUNG, Vernon: "Films From Hungary and Brazil", in his *On Film,* Chicago: Quadrangle Books, 1972, 357–364.

On other directors:

"István Gaál: Hungarian Director", interview in: *Cinéma Canada* 7 (April/May 1973), 24–29.

PETRIE, Graham: "István Gaál and 'The Falcons' ", *Film Quarterly* XXVII (Spring 1974), 20–26.

"Rencontre avec István Gaál", interview in *Cahiers du Cinéma* 178 (mai 1966), 12–13.

"Rencontre avec István Szabó", interview in *Cahiers du Cinéma* 179 (juin 1966), 12–13.

SITTON, Bob: "Hungarian Director Szabó Discusses his Film 'Father' ", *Film Comment* 5 (Fall 1968), 58–63.

YOUNG, Vernon: "Film Chronicle: Natural and Unnatural History", *Hudson Review* 25 (1972–73), pp. 93–100. Includes a review of *The Falcons*.

N.B. Several of the literary works on which the films discussed in this book were based have been translated, in whole or in part, *in The New Hungarian Quarterly*. A translation of Miklós Mészöly's *The Falcons,* for example, can be found in No. 40 (Winter 1970), pp. 83–111.

The script of Kósa's *The Ten Thousand Suns* has been published in French in *L'Avant-Scène Cinéma,* No. 87 (décembre 1968).

Selected Filmography

SPRING SHOWER
Tavaszi zápor (1932)

Directed by Pál Fejős – Screenplay: Ilona Fülöp – Camera: István Eiben, Marley Pawerel – Music: László Angyal, Scotta Vincent – Cast: Annabella (Marie), István Gyergyai, Ilona Dajbukát, Karola Zala, Gyula Gózon, Margit Ladomerszky, Zoltán Makláry, Sándor Pethes, László Kürthy – b/w

PEOPLE ON THE ALPS
Emberek a havason (1942)

Directed by István Szőts – Screenplay: István Szőts – based on the short stories of József Nyirő – Camera: Ferenc Fekete – Music: Ferenc Farkas – Cast: János Görbe (the woodcutter), Alice Szellay (his wife), József Bihari (the old man) – b/w – 2,471 metres; 90 minutes

SOMEWHERE IN EUROPE
Valahol Európában (1947)

Directed by Géza Radványi – Screenplay: Béla Balázs, Géza Radványi, Judit Fejér, Félix Máriássy – Camera: Barnabás Hegyi –Music: Dénes Buday – Cast: Arthur Somlay (Péter Simon, conductor), Miklós Gábor (the tall boy), Zsuzsa Bánki (the girl), Laci Horváth (Kuksi) – b/w – 2,812 metres; 102 minutes

THE SOIL UNDER YOUR FEET
Talpalatnyi föld (1948)

Directed by Frigyes Bán – Screenplay: members of the Hungarian dramaturgists' company, based on the novel by Pál Szabó – Camera: Árpád Makay – Music: Sándor Veress – Cast: Ádám Szirtes (Jóska Góz), Ági Mészáros (Mari Juhos), Viola Orbán (Mrs Góz), Ferike Vidor (Mrs Juhos), Benő Tamás (Mr Juhos), Árpád Lehotay (Mihály Zsiros Tóth) – b/w – 2,270 metres; 84 minutes

ANNA SZABÓ
Szabóné (1949)

Directed by Félix Máriássy – Screenplay: György Szinetár, Péter Bacsó, Tamás Banovich – based on the novel by István Nagy – Camera: György Illés – Music: György Ránki – Cast: Kornélia Sallay (Mrs Szabó), Sándor Pécsi (Hódis), Erzsi Orsolya (Mrs Oravecz), Gábor Mádi Szabó (party secretary), Ádám Szirtes (secretary of the youth organization) – b/w – 2,720 metres; 99 minutes

THE BIRTH OF MENYHÉRT SIMON
Simon Menyhért születése (1954)

Directed by Zoltán Várkonyi – Screenplay: Tibor Déry – Camera: István Pásztor – Music: Ferenc Farkas – Cast: Ádám Szirtes (István Simon), Ági Mészáros (Éva, his wife), Sándor Pécsi (Bonta), Béla Barsi (József Espersit), Bertalan Solti (the doctor) – b/w – 2,700 metres; 98 minutes

LILIOMFI (1954)

Directed by Károly Makk – Screenplay: Dezső Mészöly – based on a play by Ede Szigligeti – Camera: István Pásztor – Music: Ottó Vincze – Cast: Iván Darvas (Liliomfi), Mariann Krencsey (Mariska), Margit Dayka (Camilla), Samu Balázs (Professor Szilvay), Éva Ruttkai (Erzsi), Imre Soós (Gyuri), Sándor Pécsi (Szellemfi) – colour – 3,410 metres; 125 minutes

SPRING COMES TO BUDAPEST
Budapesti tavasz (1955)

Directed by Félix Máriássy – Screenplay: Gábor Thurzó, Ferenc Karinthy – based on a novel by Ferenc Karinthy – Camera: György Illés – Music: Imre Vincze – Cast: Miklós Gábor (Zoltán

Pintér), Tibor Molnár (Bertalan Gozsó), Gábor Rajnay (Turnovszky), Mária Mezey (Mrs Turnovszky), Zsuzsa Gordon (Jutka)
– b/w – 2,680 metres; 97 minutes

A GLASS OF BEER
Egy pikoló világos (1955)
Directed by Félix Máriássy – Screenplay: Judit Máriássy – Cam-
era: István Eiben – Music: Imre Vincze – Cast: Éva Ruttkai
(Juli), Tibor Bitskey (Marci), Elma Bulla (Mrs Cséri), János Görbe
(Kincse), Mária Sulyok (Mrs Kincse) – b/w – 2,420 metres; 88
minutes

MERRY-GO-ROUND
Körhinta (1955)
Directed by Zoltán Fábri – Screenplay: Zoltán Fábri, László Ná-
dasy – based on a short story by Imre Sarkadi – Camera: Barnabás Hegyi – Music: György Ránki – Cast: Béla Barsi (István
Pataki), Manyi Kiss (Mrs Pataki), Mari Törőcsik (Mari, their
daughter), Imre Soós (Máté Bíró), Ádám Szirtes (Sándor Farkas) –
b/w – 2,770 metres; 101 minutes

ABYSS
Szakadék (1956)
Directed by László Ranódy – Screenplay: József Darvas – Cam-
era: István Pásztor – Music: Ferenc Szabó – Cast: Margit Bara
(Klári Böröcz Horváth), Ferenc Bessenyei (Horváth Böröcz),
József Bihary (Uncle Jani), Margit Dayka (Mrs Bakos), Teri
Horváth (Juli) – b/w – 3,070 metres; 113 minutes

PROFESSOR HANNIBAL
Hannibál tanár úr (1956)
Directed by Zoltán Fábri – Screenplay: Zoltán Fábri, István
Gyenes and Péter Szász – Camera: Ferenc Szécsényi – Music:
Zdenkó Tamássy – Cast: Ernő Szabó (Béla Nyul), Manyi Kiss
(Mrs Nyul), Zoltán Makláry (Manzák), Noémi Apor (Lolo),
Mihály Selmeczi (director Ofenthaler), Rudolf Somogyvári (Vid-
rozsil), László Mensáros (Török), Oszkár Ascher (Schwarz), Jó-

zsef Szendrő (Wilhelm), Ödön Bárdi (Danielisz), Béla Barsi (Menyus), Lajos Rajczy (Gébics), László Misoga (Vogelmayer), György Kálmán (journalist), Hilda Gobbi (Mrs Vogelmayer), Zoltán Gregus (Muray), Emmi Buttykay (Mici), Ferenc Bessenyei (Hannibal) – b/w – 2,531 metres; 92 minutes

A SUNDAY ROMANCE
Bakaruhában (1957)

Directed by Imre Fehér – Screenplay: Miklós Hubay – based on a short story of Sándor Hunyady – Camera: János Badal – Music: Tibor Polgár – Cast: Iván Darvas (Sándor), Margit Bara (Vilma), Sándor Pécsi (Bodrogi), Mária Lázár (Mrs Bodrogi), Vali Korompai (Piri), Rózsi Csikós (soubrette), Béla Barsi (Kontra), Samu Balázs (the major), Ádám Szirtes (Jacob), – b/w – 2,710 metres; 98 minutes

THE HOUSE UNDER THE ROCKS
Ház a sziklák alatt (1958)

Directed by Károly Makk – Screenplay: Károly Makk, Sándor Tatay – Camera: György Illés – Music: István Sárközy – Cast: János Görbe (Ferenc Kós), Irén Psota (Tera), Margit Bara (Zsuzsa), József Bihari (Uncle Kós), Viola Orbán (Mrs Kós), Sándor Deák (Firedi), György Bárdi (forester), Ádám Szirtes (Sándor), Béla Barsi (brother-in-law), Mária Sivó (his wife) – b/w – 2.730 metres; 99 minutes

THE BELLS HAVE GONE TO ROME
A harangok Rómába mentek (1958)

Directed by Miklós Jancsó – Screenplay: Lajos Szilvás – Camera: Tamás Somló – Music: Iván Patachich – Cast: Miklós Gábor (Tibor), Ferenc Deák B. (Péter), Vilmos Mendelényi (Jóska), Sándor Pécsi (Uncle Angel), Gabi Magda (Jana), Ferenc Ladányi (Captain Bánfalvy), Antal Farkas (Gregorics), József Fonyó (Center), István Holl (Tüske), János Pásztor (forced labourer), Mari Szemes (maid), János Zách (Gyulaváry), Elemér Ragályi (gipsy), József Madaras (official), Siegfried Brachfeld (German officer) – b/w – 2.450 metres; 89 minutes

FOR WHOM THE LARKS SING
Akiket a pacsirta elkísér (1959)
Directed by László Ranódy – Screenplay: József Darvas – Camera: István Pásztor – Music: Endre Szervánszky – Cast: Éva Pap (Julis), Géza Tordy (Sándor), Klári Tolnay (Mrs Csiszér), Gábor Agárdy (Csiszér), József Bihary (Süle), Erzsi Somogyi (Mrs Süle), Margit Dayka (Mrs Varga), Antal Páger (teacher), László Bánhidy (Táltos), Nusi Somogyi (Mrs Palugyai) – b/w – 2,630 metres; 95 minutes

TWO HALF-TIMES IN HELL
Két félidő a pokolban (1961)
Directed by Zoltán Fábri – Screenplay: Péter Bacsó – Camera: Ferenc Szécsényi – Music: Ferenc Farkas – Cast: Imre Sinkovits (Ónodi), Dezső Garas (Steiner), László Márkus (Pogány), Tibor Molnár (Rácz), János Koltai (Géza), Sándor Suka (Koczina), Zoltán Gera (Sándor Tankó), István Velenczei (Ferenczi), József Horváth (Officer Szabó), Gyula Szilágyi (Sztyepán), Tamás Végvári (Pali Tankó), András Komlós (Balogh), János Rajz (Lipták), János Görbe (Eberhardt), István Egri (Dr. Hollander), Bertalan Solti (Agárdi), László Misoga (Siska), Noémi Apor (Cica), Emil Fenyő (the colonel), Siegfried Brachfeld (Officer Heilig), János Makláry (Sergeant Holup), Antal Farkas (Corporal Csorba) József Szendrő (Sergeant Rápity), Károly Bángyörgyi (Lieutenant Zalán) – b/w – 3,400 metres; 124 minutes

THE FANATICS
Megszállottak (1961)
Directed by Károly Makk – Screenplay: Lajos Galambos, Károly Makk – Camera: György Illés – Music: Szabolcs Fényes – Cast: György Pálos (László Bene), Lajos Básti (István), Ferenc Kállai (Frigyes), Tibor Molnár (general manager), Zoltán Makláry (Uncle Józsi), Éva Pap (Eti), Ádám Szirtes (János Kecskés) – b/w – 2,820 metres; 102 minutes

CANTATA
Oldás és kötés (1962)

Directed by Miklós Jancsó – based on a short story by József Lengyel – Camera: Tamás Somló – Music: Bálint Sárosi – Cast: Zoltán Latinovits (Ambrus), Andor Ajtay (the professor), Béla Barsi (Ambrus's father), Miklós Szakáts (lecturer), Gyula Bodrogi (Gyula Kiss), Edit Domján (Márta, Ambrus's lover), Mária Medgyesi (Eta) – b/w – 2,720 metres; 98 minutes

CURRENT
Sodrásban (1963)

Directed by István Gaál – Screenplay: István Gaál – Camera: Sándor Sára – Music: András Szöllősy – Cast: Marianne Moór (Böbe), Andrea Drahota (Vadóc), Mrs Zsipi (Aunt Anna), Sándor Csikós (Laci), János Harkányi (Gabi), András Kozák (Luja), Tibor Orbán (Zoli), Gyula Szersén (Karesz), Lajos Tóth (Berci), Mária Fogarassy (mother) – b/w – 2,430 metres; 89 minutes

DIFFICULT PEOPLE
Nehéz emberek (1964)

Directed by András Kovács – Screenplay: András Kovács – Camera: Tibor Vagyóczky – b/w – 2,930 metres; 106 minutes

THE AGE OF DAY-DREAMING
Álmodozások kora (1964)

Directed by István Szabó – Screenplay: István Szabó – Camera: Tamás Vámos – Music: Péter Eötvös – Cast: András Bálint (Jancsi), Ilona Béres (Éva), Judit Halász (Habgab), Kati Sólyom (Anni), Cecília Esztergályos (Ági), Béla Asztalos (Laci), Tamás Erőss (Matyi), László Murányi (Gergely), István Dékány (Füsi), János Rajz (Mr Zsoldos), Imre Sinkovits (Harrer), Miklós Gábor (Flesch) – b/w – 2,802 metres; 102 minutes

TWENTY HOURS
Húsz óra (1964)

Directed by Zoltán Fábri – Screenplay: Miklós Köllő – Camera: György Illés – based on a novel by Ferenc Sánta – Cast: Antal

Páger (Jóska), János Görbe (Anti Balogh), Emil Keres (riporter), Ádám Szirtes (Béni Kocsis), Teri Horváth (Ilonka), László György (Sándor Varga), József Bihary (György Czuha), Lajos Őze (Kiskovács), János Makláry (György Venczel), Károly Kovács (the count), Ági Mészáros (Terus), Tibor Molnár (Máthé), Gyula Bodrogi (the doctor) – b/w – 3,230 metres; 118 minutes

MY WAY HOME
Így jöttem (1964)

Directed by Miklós Jancsó – Screenplay: Gyula Hernádi – Camera: Tamás Somló – Music: Zoltán Jeney – Cast: András Kozák (Jóska), Sergei Nikonenko (Kolja), János Görbe (man with cap), Sándor Siménfalvy (the old faced man), László Csurka (man with telescope), Vilmos Izsóf (pilot), Judit Meszléry (girl), József Madaras, Zoltán Gera, Lajos Tándor (prisoners) – b/w – 2,920 metres; 106 minutes

GRIMACE
Gyermekbetegségek (1965)

Directed by Ferenc Kardos and János Rózsa – Camera: Sándor Sára – Music: András Szöllősy – Cast: István Géczy (little boy), Tünde Kassai (Zizi), Emil Keres (father), Judit Halász (teacher), Gábor Lontay (Dagi), Rita Baranyai (Rita), Márta Mamusich (mother), Irma Patkós (grandmother), Dóri Bánfalvi (fashion model), Béla Horváth (uncle) – colour – 2,120 metres; 77 minutes

THE GREEN YEARS
Zöldár (1965)

Directed by István Gaál – Screenplay: Imre Gyöngyössy and István Gaál – Camera: Miklós Herczenik – Music: András Szöllősy – Cast: Benedek Tóth (Marci), Virág Darab (Bori), Gábor Koncz (Laci Ács), Teri Horváth (Margit), Judit Meszléry (Eszter), Mrs Zsipi (grandmother), Sándor Siménfalvy (grandfather), Sári Feleky (tenant), Gyöngyvér Demjén (Anci), Mária Dudás (Jolán Görög), Gyula Szersén (Surányi), István Szilágyi (Jakab Nagy), György Kézdi (Lencse), Béla Barsi (party secretary) – b/w – 3,000 metres; 108 minutes

THE ROUND-UP
Szegénylegények (1965)

Directed by Miklós Jancsó – Screenplay: Gyula Hernádi – Camera: Tamás Somló – Cast: János Görbe (Gajdor), Tibor Molnár (Kabai), András Kozák (his son), Gábor Agárdy (Torma), Zoltán Latinovits (Imre Veszelka) – b/w – 2,589 metres; 94 minutes

COLD DAYS
Hideg napok (1966)

Directed by András Kovács – Screenplay: András Kovács – Camera: Ferenc Szécsényi – based on a novel by Tibor Cseres – Cast: Zoltán Latinovits (Büky), Iván Darvas (Tarpataki), Ádám Szirtes (Szabó), Tibor Szilágyi (Pozdor), Margit Bara (Mrs Büky), Éva Vas (Edit), Mari Szemes (Milena), Irén Psota (Betty) – b/w – 2,770 metres; 101 minutes

FATHER
Apa (1966)

Directed by István Szabó – Screenplay: István Szabó – Camera: Sándor Sára – Music: János Gonda – Cast: Miklós Gábor (father), Dániel Erdélyi (the son as a child), András Bálint (Takó), Zsuzsa Ráthonyi (young mother), Klári Tolnay (mother), Katalin Sólyom (Anni) – b/w – 2,615 metres; 96 minutes

THE TEN THOUSAND SUNS
Tízezer nap (1967)

Directed by Ferenc Kósa – Screenplay: Imre Gyöngyössy, Sándor Csoóri and Ferenc Kósa – Camera: Sándor Sára – Music: András Szöllősy – Cast: Tibor Molnár (István Széles), Gyöngyi Bürös (Juli), András Kozák (jr. Széles), János Koltai (Fülöp Bánó), Ida Siménfalvy (Széles's mother), János Rajz (Balogh), Sándor Siménfalvy (uncle Sándor), János Görbe (József Bócza) – b/w – 2,980 metres; 109 minutes

THE RED AND THE WHITE
Csillagosok, katonák (1967)

Directed by Miklós Jancsó – Screenplay: Gyula Hernádi, Georgi

Mdivani and Miklós Jancsó – Camera: Tamás Somló – Cast: András Kozák (László), Krystyna Mikolajewska (Olga), Jácint Juhász (István), Tatjana Konjuhova (Elizaveta), Mihail Kozakov (Nestor), Viktor Avdiushko (sailor), Bolot Beisenalyev (Tschingiz), Sergei Nyikonyenko (Cossack officer), Anatoli Yabbarov (Tshelpanov), József Madaras (the commander), Tibor Molnár (András) b/w – 2,545 metres; 92 minutes

CLOWNS ON THE WALL
Bohóc a falon (1967)

Directed by Pál Sándor – Screenplay: Pál Sándor and Zsuzsa Tóth – Camera: János Zsombolyai – Music: Zdenkó Tamássy – Cast: Gábor Ferenczi (Kiki), Balázs Tardy (András), Miklós Szurdok (Péter), Vera Venczel (Andrea) – b/w – 2,220 metres; 81 minutes

WALLS
Falak (1967)

Directed by András Kovács – Screenplay: András Kovács – Camera: György Illés – Music: Mikisz Theodorakisz, Ismael – Cast: Zoltán Latinovits (László Ambrus), Miklós Gábor (Béla Benkő), Zsuzsa Bánki (Erzsi), Mari Szemes (Anna), László Mensáros (Ferenczi), Andrea Drahota (Zsuzsa), Imre Rádai (Szamosi), Philippe March (Lendvay), Bernadotte Lafont (Marie) – b/w – 2,580 metres; 94 minutes

THE VALLEY
Völgy (1967)

Directed by Tamás Rényi – Screenplay: Gyula Hernádi – Camera: Ottó Forgács – Music: András Mihály – Cast: Gábor Koncz (Gábor), Magda Kohut (Edit), Mária Sulyok (mother-in-law), János Koltai (Iván), István Avar (Zoltán), György Bárdi (György), Tibor Molnár (Tibor), Irén Psota (leader of women), Mária Medgyesi (Márta), Éva Pap (Ilona) – b/w – 2,073 metres; 76 minutes

THE GIRL
Eltávozott nap (1968)

Directed by Márta Mészáros – Screenplay: Márta Mészáros –

Camera: Tamás Somló – Music: Levente Szörényi – Cast: Kati Kovács (Erzsi Szőnyi), Teri Horváth (Mrs Zsámboki), Ádám Szirtes (Zsámboki), András Kozák (Gábor), Jácint Juhász (the boy from the train), Ilona Gurnik (teacher) – b/w – 2,240 metres; 82 minutes

SILENCE AND CRY
Csend és kiáltás (1968)

Directed by Miklós Jancsó – Screenplay: Gyula Hernádi – Camera: János Kende – Cast: András Kozák (István), Zoltán Latinovits (Kémeri), József Madaras (Károly, the peasant), Mari Törőcsik (Teréz, his wife), Andrea Drahota (Anna, his sister-in-law), István Bujtor (Kányási), Kornélia Sallai (Veron), Ilona Schütz (the fool girl), Mária Gór Nagy (Veron's daughter), János Görbe (the neighbour) – b/w – 2,187 metres; 80 minutes

BAPTISM
Keresztelő (1968)

Directed by István Gaál – Screenplay: István Gaál – Camera: István Hildebrand – Music: Zsolt Durkó – Cast: György Kálmán (György Barta), Mari Törőcsik (Éva Keller), Gyula Bodrogi (Péter Czakó), Antal Páger (Puckner), Zoltán Latinovits (Dr. Bán), Éva Ruttkai (Zizi), Ferenc Kállai (his husband), Margit Makay (Olga Radics), László Inke (chemist), Andrea Drahota (Dóra, his wife) – b/w – 2,476 metres; 90 minutes

CONFRONTATION
Fényes szelek (1968)

Directed by Miklós Jancsó – Screenplay: Gyula Hernádi – Camera: Tamás Somló – Cast: Andrea Drahota (Jutka), Lajos Balázsovits (Laci), Kati Kovács (Teri), András Bálint (András), Balázs Kosztolányi (Balázs), András Kozák (András), József Madaras (priest Kellér), István Uri (Pista), Tibor Orbán (teacher) – colour – 2,207 metres; 80 minutes

THE UPTHROWN STONE
Feldobott kő (1968)

Directed by Sándor Sára – Screenplay: Sándor Sára, Sándor Csoóri and Ferenc Kósa – Camera: Sándor Sára – Music: András Szöllősy – Cast: Lajos Balázsovits (Balázs Pásztor), János Pásztor (his father), Katalin Berek (his mother), József Bihary (his grandfather), Todor Todorov (Iliasz), Nadezsda Kazassian (Irini, his wife), László Bánhidy (Uncle János) – b/w – 2,460 metres; 90 minutes

BINDING SENTIMENTS
Holdudvar (1968)

Directed by Márta Mészáros – Screenplay: Márta Mészáros – Camera: János Kende – Music: Levente Szörényi – Cast: Mari Törőcsik (Edit), Lajos Balázsovits (István), Gáspár Jancsó (Gáspár), Kati Kovács (Kati), Ági Mészáros (Aunt Margit), Mari Szemes (Manci), István Avar (Apor), Gyöngyi Bürös (Bözsi) – b/w – 2,650 metres; 96 minutes

A LADY FROM CONSTANTINOPLE
Sziget a szárazföldön (1969)

Directed by Judit Elek – Screenplay: Iván Mándy – Camera: Elemér Ragályi – Music: Vilmos Körmendy – Cast: Manyi Kiss (the old lady), István Dégi, Ági Margittay (young couple), Gyuri Korga (their son), István Novák (Venczel), Erzsi Pásztor (Mrs Venczel), Éva Schubert (Mrs Troppauer), Mária Sivó (neighbour), Tihamér Vujicsics (pianist) – b/w – 2,090 metres; 76 minutes

PALM SUNDAY
Virágvasárnap (1969)

Directed by Imre Gyöngyössy – Screenplay: Imre Gyöngyössy – Camera: Ferenc Szécsényi – Music: Bálint Sárosi – Cast: Frantisek Velecky (Simon), Benedek Tóth (Urenus), Erzsi Hegedüs (their mother), József Iványi (Priest Kormanik), József Máriáss (vicar), Gábor Koncz (Garai, sailor), Mária Medgyesi (his wife), Gyuri Korga (his son), János Makláry (old Nyári) – b/w – 2,224 metres; 81 minutes

WINTER WIND
Sirokko (1969)

Directed by Miklós Jancsó – Screenplay: Gyula Hernádi–Camera: János Kende – Music: Tihamér Vujicsics – Cast: Jacques Charrier (Marko Lazar), Marina Vlady (Maria), Éva Swan (Ilona), József Madaras (Markovics), István Bujtor (Tarro), György Bánffy (Jive), Pascal Aubier (Tihomir), András Kozák (József Farkas), Philippe March (Hungarian officer) – colour – 2,177 metres, 79 minutes

THE TÓT FAMILY
Isten hozta őrnagy úr (1969)

Directed by Zoltán Fábri – Screenplay: Zoltán Fábri – based on the novel by István Örkény – Camera: György Illés – Music: András Mihály – Cast: Iván Darvas (narrator), Zoltán Latinovits (major), Imre Sinkovits (Lajos Tót), Márta Fónay (Mariska, his wife), Vera Venczel (Ágika, his daughter), István Dégi (Gyuri, the postman) – colour – 2,900 metres; 106 minutes

JUDGEMENT
Ítélet (1969)

Directed by Ferenc Kósa – Screenplay: Sándor Csoóri, Ferenc Kósa – Camera: Sándor Sára – Music: Cornel Taranu – Cast: Ferenc Bessenyei (György Dózsa), János Koltai (priest Lőrinc), Tamás Major (Werbőczy), Gheorghe Motoi (Student), István Török (Gergely Dózsa), Klára Sebők (Teréz) – b/w; – 2,718 metres; 99 minutes

THE FALCONS
Magasiskola (1970)

Directed by István Gaál – based on a short story by Miklós Mészöly – Screenplay: István Gaál – Camera: Elemér Ragályi – Music: András Szöllősy – Cast: Ivan Andonov (the boy), György Bánffy (Lilik), Judit Meszléry (Teréz) – colour – 2,414 metres; 88 minutes

TEMPERATE ZONE
Mérsékelt égöv (1970)

Directed by Zsolt Kézdi-Kovács – Screenplay: Zsolt Kézdi-Kovács – based on the short story of Árpád Ajtony – Camera: János Kende – Music: János Gonda – Cast: Rudolf Somogyvári (Dr. Imre Kalán), Mari Törőcsik (Mari, his wife), András Kozák (András), Péter Benkő (Pista) – b/w – 2,343 metres; 85 minutes

LOVE FILM
Szerelmes film (1970)

Directed by István Szabó – Screenplay: István Szabó – Camera: József Lőrinc – Music: János Gonda – Cast: András Bálint (Jancsi), Judit Halász (Kata) – colour – 3,935 metres; 143 minutes

LOVE
Szerelem (1970)

Directed by Károly Makk – Screenplay: Tibor Déry – Camera: János Tóth – Music: András Mihály – Cast: Lili Darvas (the old lady), Mari Törőcsik (her daugther-in-law), Iván Darvas (her son) b/w – 2,538 metres; 92 minutes

OUTBREAK
Kitörés (1970)

Directed by Péter Bacsó – Screenplay: Péter Bacsó and György Konrád – Camera: János Zsombolyai – Music: György Vukán – Cast: Sándor Oszter (Laci), Edit Lendvai (Anna), József Iványi (Laci's brother), Zsuzsa Hőgye (his wife), László Pataki (Anna's father), Tibor Liska (engineer Pray) – colour – 3,108 metres; 113 minutes

AGNUS DEI
Égi bárány (1970)

Directed by Miklós Jancsó – Screenplay: Gyula Hernádi and Miklós Jancsó – Camera: János Kende – Cast: József Madaras (Father Varga), Márk Zala (the priest), Lajos Balázsovits (the canon), Anna Széles (Maria), Jaroslava Schallerova (Magdalena), Daniel Olbrychsky (Daniel) – colour – 2,514 metres; 91 minutes

HORIZON
Horizont (1970)

Directed by Pál Gábor – Screenplay: Gyula Marosi and Pál Gábor
Camera: János Zsombolyai – Music: János Gonda – Cast: Péter
Fried (Karesz), Lujza Orosz (his mother), Szilvia Marossy (Ágnes),
Zoltán Vadász (Hajdu) – b/w – 2,408 metres; 84 minutes

SARAH, MY DEAR
Sárika, drágám (1970)

Directed by Pál Sándor – Screenplay: Zsuzsa Tóth and Pál Sándor – Camera: Elemér Ragályi – Music: Zdenkó Tamássy, Gábor
Presser – Cast: Irma Patkós (Sárika), András Kern (Péter Bóna),
Erika Bodnár (his wife), Ági Margittai (Mari) – b/w – 2,581
metres; 94 minutes

SINDBAD
Szindbád (1971)

Directed by Zoltán Huszárik – Screenplay: Zoltán Huszárik –
based on novels by Gyula Krúdy – Camera: Sándor Sára – Music: Zoltán Jeney – Cast: Zoltán Latinovits (Sindbad), Margit
Dayka, Éva Ruttkai, Erika Szegedi, Bella Tanay, Ilona Dorián
(the ladies) – colour – 2,695 metres; 98 minutes

PRESENT INDICATIVE
Jelenidő (1971)

Directed by Péter Bacsó – Screenplay: Péter Bacsó and Péter
Zimre – Camera: János Zsombolyai – Music: György Vukán –
Cast: Ágoston Simon (Imre Mózes), Irén Bódis (Irene, his wife),
Zoltán Sárközi (the director), Tibor Liska (Kulcsár), Ádám Raj-
hona (Kárász) – colour – 2,938 metres; 106 minutes

DEAD LANDSCAPE
Holt vidék (1971)

Directed by István Gaál – Screenplay: István Gaál, Péter Nádas –
Camera: János Zsombolyai – Music: András Szöllősy – Cast:
Mari Törőcsik (Juli), István Ferenczi (Anti), Irma Patkós (Aunt
Erzsi) – colour – 2,578 metres; 94 minutes

RED PSALM
Még kér a nép (1971)

Directed by Miklós Jancsó – Screenplay: Gyula Hernádi – Camera: János Kende – Cast: Andrea Drahota, Lajos Balázsovits, András Bálint, Gyöngyi Bürös, József Madaras, Tibor Molnár, Tibor Orbán, Bertalan Solti – colour – 2,443 metres; 88 minutes

LEGEND ABOUT THE DEATH AND RESURRECTION OF TWO YOUNG MEN
Meztelen vagy (1971)

Directed by Imre Gyöngyössy – Screenplay: Imre Gyöngyössy, Barna Kabai – Camera: János Kende – Music: Emil Petrovics – Cast: Sándor Oszter (Gera), István Szegő (Lénárt), Irénke Rácz (Dina) – colour – 2,574 metres; 93 minutes

JOURNEY WITH JACOB
Utazás Jakabbal (1972)

Directed by Pál Gábor – Screenplay: István Császár, Pál Gábor – Camera: János Kende – Music: János Gonda – Cast: Péter Huszti (István), Ion Bog (Jacob), Györgyi Andai (Emese), Erika Bodnár (Eszter), Mariann Moór (Juli), Ildikó Bánsági (Ildikó), Éva Szabó (Kata) – colour – 2,445 metres; 88 minutes

ROMANTICISM
Romantika (1972)

Directed by Zsolt Kézdi-Kovács – Screenplay: Géza Bereményi – Camera: János Kende – Cast: István Szegő (Kálmán Linczényi), Ádám Szirtes (György, his father), József Madaras (gang leader Zsibó), Edit Soós (Barbara), Dezső Garas (Csepele), Mariann Moór (girl in cloak), Michel Delahaye (Zoietta) – colour – 2,387 metres; 87 minutes

PHOTOGRAPHY
Fotográfia (1972)

Directed by Pál Zolnay – Screenplay: Orsolya Székely, Pál Zolnay – Camera: Elemér Ragályi – Music: Ferenc Sebő – Cast: István Iglódi, Márk Zala (the photographers) – b/w – 2,262 metres; 82 minutes

ONE DAY MORE OR LESS
Plusz minusz egy nap (1972)

Directed by Zoltán Fábri – Screenplay: Zoltán Fábri and Péter
Zimre – based on the novels of Ádám Bodor – Camera: György
Illés – Music: Emil Petrovics – Cast: Anatol Constantin (Baradla),
Ferenc Bencze (Obrád), Márton Andrássi (Boócz, the innkeeper),
Ildikó Pécsi (Zsófi's sister), Noémi Apor (Mrs Csutor) – colour –
2,760 metres; 100 minutes

BEYOND TIME
Nincs idő (1972)

Directed by Ferenc Kósa – Screenplay: Sándor Csoóri, Ferenc
Kósa – Camera: Sándor Sára – Music: Zsolt Durkó – Cast:
Lóránd Lohinszky (Udvardy, prison governor), Tibor Szilágyi
(Babella, senior warden), János Konyorisik (István Kallós), László
Bencze, Jácint Juhász, István Szőke (political prisoners), Péter
Haumann (Fóthy, minister of justice) – colour – 2,723 metres;
100 minutes

TECHNIQUE AND RITE (Italy)
Il Tecnico e il Rito (1972)

Directed by Miklós Jancsó – Screenplay: Ginovannà Gagliardo,
Gyula Hernádi, and Miklós Jancsó – Camera: János Kende –
Music: Francesco de Masi – Cast: József Madaras (Attila),
Adalberto Maria Merli (Massimo), Luigi Montini (Philosopher),
Anna Zinneman (Bleda's wife), Sergio Enria (Bleda) – colour –
90 minutes

THE LAST CHANCE
Harmadik nekifutás (1973)

Directed by Péter Bacsó – Screenplay: Péter Bacsó, Péter Zimre –
Camera: János Zsombolyai – Music: György Vukán – Cast: Ist-
ván Avar (Jakus), Ilona Kassai (his wife), Mari Szür (newsgirl),
István Török (Tax, brigade leader), József Madaras, György
Szirmai, Árpád Zsoldos, Jenő Sipos, László Szabó (brigade mem-
bers) – b/w – 2,919 metres; 106 minutes

RIDDANCE
Szabad lélegzet (1973)

Directed by Márta Mészáros – Screenplay: Márta Mészáros – Camera: Lajos Koltai – Music: Levente Szörényi – Cast: Erzsébet Kútvölgyi (Jutka), Gábor Nagy (András), Mariann Moór (Zsuzsa), Ferenc Kállai (Jutka's father), Mari Szemes (Jutka's mother), Lajos Szabó (András's father), Teri Földi (András's mother) – b/w – 2,294 metres; 93 minutes

25 FIREMEN'S STREET
Tűzoltó utca 25. (1973)

Directed by István Szabó – Screenplay: István Szabó – Camera: Sándor Sára – Music: Zdenkó Tamássy – Cast: Rita Békés (Mrs Gaskóy), Lucyna Winniczka (Mária), Péter Müller (János, Mária's husband), András Bálint (Andris), Mari Szemes (Julika), Ági Mészáros (Aranka), Margit Makay (Mária's mother), Károly Kovács (Mária's father) – colour – 2,668 metres; 97 minutes

FOOTBALL OF THE GOOD OLD DAYS
Régi idők focija (1973)

Directed by Pál Sándor – Screenplay: Zsuzsa Tóth – based on the novel by Iván Mándy – Camera: Elemér Ragályi – Music: Zdenkó Tamássy – Cast: Dezső Garas (Minarik), Gizi Péter (his wife), Tamás Major (Mr Kerényi), Hédi Temessy (the woman in the cinema), Cecília Esztergályos (the fur-coated woman), Károly Voigt (Vallay, the wonderful goalkeeper), Gabriella Szabó (Vallay's sweetheart) – colour – 2,346 metres; 85 minutes

AT THE END OF THE ROAD
Végül (1973)

Directed by Gyula Maár – Screenplay: Gyula Maár – Camera: Lajos Koltai – Cast: Josef Kroner (the man), László Szacsvay (his son), Katalin Lázár (the boy's girl-friend), Mari Törőcsik (the girl's mother) – b/w – 2,725 metres; 99 minutes

A HUNGARIAN VILLAGE
Istenmezején (1974)

Directed by Judit Elek – Screenplay: Judit Elek – Camera: Elemér Ragályi – Cast: non-professionals – b/w – 2,221 metres; 81 minutes

SONS OF FIRE
Szarvassá vált fiúk (1974)

Directed by Imre Gyöngyössy – Screenplay: Imre Gyöngyössy, Barna Kabai – Camera: János Kende – Music: Zoltán Jenei – Cast: Mari Törőcsik (pregnant woman), Erzsi Hegedüs (the mother), Sándor Lukács, Todor Todorov, Frantisek Velecky (her sons), András Kozák (revolutionary), István Szőke (revolutionary), Erzsébet Kútvölgyi, Katalin Gyöngyössy, Ilona Bencze, Sarolta Jancsó (prisoners) – colour – 2,357 metres; 87 minutes

SNOWFALL
Hószakadás (1974)

Directed by Ferenc Kósa – Screenplay: Ferenc Kósa, Sándor Csoóri – Camera: Sándor Sára – Music: Zsolt Durkó – Cast: Imre Szabó (Márton Csorba, the soldier), Maria Markovcova (mother), Péter Hauman (gendarme), Pola Raksa (partisan girl) – colour – 2,753 metres; 100 minutes

DREAMING YOUTH
Álmodó ifjúság (1974)

Directed by János Rózsa – Screenplay: János Rózsa, István Kardos – based on a novel by Béla Balázs – Camera: Elemér Ragályi – Music: György Ránki – Cast: Zoltán Csoma (Herbert), Csaba Domenija (his friend), Eva Ras (his mother), Lóránd Lohinszky (his father) – colour – 2,205 metres; 81 minutes

CATSPLAY
Macskajáték (1974)

Directed by Károly Makk – Screenplay: Károly Makk, János Tóth – based on a novel by István Örkény – Camera: János Tóth – Music: Péter Eötvös – Cast: Margit Dayka (Mrs Orbán), Elma

Bulla (Giza, her sister), Margit Makay (Paula), Samu Balázs (Viktor) – colour – 2.997 metres; 109 minutes

UNRULY HEYDUCKS
Hajduk (1974)
Directed by Ferenc Kardos – Screenplay: István Kardos – Camera: János Kende – Music: Levente Szörényi – Cast: Dzoko Rosich (captain), Doyne Bird (preacher), István Avar (Turkish officer), Dragomir Felba, József Madaras, Sándor Oszter, Ferenc Bencze, Ion Bog, György Cserhalmi, Jácint Juhász, Géza Léka, László Marosi, András Mészáros, Todor Todorov, Frantisek Veleczki (heyducks), Lujza Orosz (mother), Lili Monori (her daughter) – colour – 2,214 metres; 80 minutes

THE UNFINISHED SENTENCE
141 perc a befejezetlen mondatból (1974)
Directed by Zoltán Fábri – Screenplay: Zoltán Fábri – based on the novel by Tibor Déry – Camera: György Illés – Music: György Vukán – Cast: András Bálint (Lőrinc Parcen Nagy), Zoltán Latinovits (Professor Vavra), Mari Csomós (Évi), Anikó Sáfár (Desirée), László Mensáros (Lőrinc's father), Mária Bisztray (Lőrinc's mother), Lujza Orosz (Mrs Rózsa), Sándor Lukács (Vidovics), Noémi Apor (Mrs Timmermann), Margit Dayka (Mrs Hubka) – colour – 3,964 metres; 141 minutes

BLINDFOLD
Bekötött szemmel (1974)
Directed by András Kovács – Screenplay: András Kovács – based on a novel by Gábor Thurzó – Camera: Ferenc Szécsényi – Cast: András Kozák (chaplain), József Madaras (Balog), Sándor Horváth (priest), János Koltai (doctor), Imre Szabó (bishop), Lajos Őze (chairman of the magistrates), Erzsébet Kútvölgyi (nun), László Szabó (wounded man), István Avar (Szekeres) – b/w – 2,295 metres; 85 minutes

ELEKTREIA
Szerelmem, Elektra (1974)

Directed by Miklós Jancsó – Screenplay: László Gyurkó and Gyula Hernádi – based on the play by László Gyurkó – Camera: János Kende – Music: Tamás Cseh – Cast: Mari Törőcsik (Electra), József Madaras (Aegisthos), György Cserhalmi (Orestes), Lajos Balázsovits, Mária Bajcsay (the courtiers of Aegisthos), Gabi Jobba (Chrisothemis) – colour – 2,104 metres; 76 minutes

HOLIDAY IN BRITAIN
Jutalomutazás (1974)

Directed by István Dárday – Screenplay: György Szalai and István Dárday – Camera: Lajos Koltai – Cast: Kálmán Tamás (father), Mrs. Tamás (mother), József Borsi (their son), Mária Simai (Anna Forgó) – colour – 2,401 metres; 87 minutes

PHEASANT TOMORROW
Holnap lesz fácán (1974)

Directed by Sándor Sára – Screenplay: Géza Páskándy, Sándor Sára – Camera: Sándor Sára, Péter Jankura – Music: János Gonda – Cast: Lóránd Lohinszky (István), Erika Szegedi (Mari), Gyula Benkő (the professor), Ádám Szirtes (Kozma), Tünde Szabó (the schoolmistress), Anna Nagy (Mrs Mátyás) – colour – 2,280 metres; 83 minutes

ROME WANTS ANOTHER CAESAR (Italy)
Roma Rivuole Caesar (1974)

Directed by Miklós Jancsó – Screenplay: Ginovanna Gagliardo, Miklós Jancsó – Camera: János Kende – Music: Uberta Bertacca – Cast: Daniel Olbrychski (Claudius), Hiram Keller (Ottavius), Lino Troisi (Proconsul), Gino Lavagetto (First Republican), Luigi Montini (Second Republican), Guido Lollobrigida (Blue Tunic), Jose De Vega (Oxyntas), Renato Baldini (Old Senator) – colour – 100 minutes

ADOPTION
Örökbefogadás (1975)

Directed by Márta Mészáros – Screenplay: Márta Mészáros and Gyula Hernádi – Camera: Lajos Koltai – Music: György Kovács – Cast: Kati Berek (Kata), László Szabó (Jóska), Gyöngyvér Vigh (Anna), Árpád Perlaky (doctor) – b/w – 2,462 metres; 89 minutes

MRS DÉRY, WHERE ARE YOU?
Déryné, hol van? (1975)

Directed by Gyula Maár – Screenplay: Gyula Maár – Camera: Lajos Koltai – Cast: Mari Törőcsik (Mrs Déry), Ferenc Kállai (Mr Déry), Mária Sulyok (Déry's mother), Tamás Major (old actor), Imre Ráday (intendant) – colour – 2,790 metres; 102 minutes

EXPECTATION
Várakozók (1975)

Directed by Imre Gyöngyössy – Screenplay: Imre Gyöngyössy, Barna Kabay – Camera: János Kende – Music: Zoltán Jeney – Cast: Mari Törőcsik (Klára), Maya Komorowska (the nanny), Erika Bodnár (Mária), Lajos Balázsovits (István), Juraj Durdiak, Jerzy Zelnik (the twins) – colour – 2,447 metres; 89 minutes

REQUIEM FOR A REVOLUTIONARY
Vörös rekviem (1975)

Directed by Ferenc Grunwalsky – Screenplay: Gyula Hernádi – Camera: Elemér Ragályi – Cast: Péter Andorai (Imre Sallai), Miklós Lantay (Sallai as a boy), László Szacsvay (Sándor Fürst), Ádám Rajhona (village schoolmaster), István Molnár (László Jurányi), Andor Lukács, Károly Ujlaki (the two officers) – b/w – 2,793 metres; 102 minutes

IDENTIFICATION
Azonosítás (1975)

Directed by László Lugossy – Screenplay: István Kardos – Camera: József Lőrinc – Music: Emil Petrovics – Cast: György Cserhalmi (András Ambrus), József Madaras (Mihály Csató, the "commissar"), Lili Monori (his wife), Róbert Koltai (Police Captain Kelemen), Ludovit Gresso (uncle Miska) – colour – 2,514 metres; 91 minutes

A COMMONPLACE STORY
Egyszerű történet (1975)

Directed by Judit Elek – Screenplay: Judit Elek – Camera: Elemér Ragályi – Cast: non-professionals – b/w – 2,762 metres; 101 minutes

NO MAN'S DAUGHTER
Árvácska (1976)

Directed by László Ranódy – Screenplay: Judit Elek, László Ranódy – based on a novel by Zsigmond Móricz – Camera: Sándor Sára – Music: Rudolf Maros – Cast: Zsuzsa Czinkóczy (Csöre), Anna Nagy (foster mother), Sándor Horváth (foster father), József Bihari (the old man), Ádám Szirtes (farmer), Mariann Moór (farmer's wife), Piroska Molnár (young woman) – colour – 2,414 metres; 87 minutes

LABYRINTH
Labirintus (1976)

Directed by András Kovács – Screenplay: András Kovács – Camera: János Kende – Cast: István Avar (the director), Éva Ruttkai (the actress), Ferenc Kállai (the actor), Ilona Bencze (cutter's assistant) – b/w – 2,370 metres; 87 minutes

NINE MONTHS
Kilenc hónap (1976)

Directed by Márta Mészáros – Screenplay: Gyula Hernádi, Ildikó Kórodi, Márta Mészáros – Camera: János Kende – Music: György Kovács – Cast: Lili Monori (Juli), Jan Nowicki (János), Djoko Rosic (Professor) – colour – 2,561 metres; 93 minutes

REFLECTIONS
Tükörképek (1976)

Directed by Rezső Szörény – Screenplay: Rezső Szörény – Camera: Péter Jankura – Cast: Jana Plichtová (Erzsi), Erika Bodnár (Irén) – colour – 2,370 metres; 83 minutes

THE FIFTH SEAL
Az ötödik pecsét (1976)

Directed by Zoltán Fábri – Screenplay: Zoltán Fábri – based on a novel by Ferenc Sánta – Camera: György Illés – Music: György Vukán – Cast: Lajos Őze (watchmaker), Sándor Horváth (joiner), László Márkus (book salesman), Ferenc Bencze (tavern-keeper), István Dégi (one-legged guest), Zoltán Latinovits (fascist commandant) – colour – 3,179 metres; 116 minutes

PRIVATE VICES & PUBLIC VIRTUES (Italy/Yugoslavia) *(1976)*

Directed by Miklós Jancsó – Screenplay: Ginovannà Gagliardo – Camera: Tomislav Pinter – Music: Francesco de Masi – Cast: Lajos Balázsovits (Prince), Pamela Villoresi (Sofia), Franco Branciaroli (Duke), Teresa Ann Savoy (Mary), Laura Betti (Therese), Ivica Pajer (Colonel), Umberto Silva (1st Priest), Zvonimir Črnko (2nd Priest), Demeter Bitenc (Minister) – colour – 104 minutes

ON THE SIDE-LINE
Szépek és bolondok (1976)

Directed by Péter Szász – Screenplay: Péter Szász – Camera: Lajos Koltai – Music: György Vukán, Gábor Presser – Cast: Ferenc Kállai (Ivicz), Gyula Bodrogi (Fedák [Charlie]), Tamás Andor (Gadácsi), Judit Meszléry (the confectioner's shopkeeper), Nóra Tábori (Nelli) – colour – 2,899 metres; 105 minutes

THE SWORD
A kard (1976)

Directed by János Dömölky – Screenplay: István Csurka, János Dömölky – based on a poem by Zoltán Jékely – Camera: János Zsombolyai – Music: Zdenkó Tamássy – Cast: Péter Hauman (Mr Bojti), Mari Szemes (Mrs Bojti) – colour – 2,202 metres; 80 minutes

IMPROPERLY DRESSED
Herkulesfürdői emlék (1976)

Directed by Pál Sándor – Screenplay: Zsuzsa Tóth – Camera: Elemér Ragályi – Music: Zdenkó Tamássy – Cast: Endre Holman (The boy [Sarolta Galambos]), Erzsébet Kútvölgyi (Nurse Zsófi), Ildikó Pécsi (head masseuse), Sándor Szabó (Dr Wallach), Margit Dayka, Irma Patkós, Mária Lázár (old ladies), Hédi Temessy (Miss Ágota), Dezső Garas (itinerant photographer), Carla Romanelli (Italian woman) colour – 2,449 metres; 89 minutes

BUDAPEST TALES
Budapesti mesék (1976)

Directed by István Szabó – Screenplay: István Szabó – Camera: Sándor Sára – Music: Zdenkó Tamássy – Cast: Maya Komorowska, Ági Mészáros, Ildikó Bánsági, András Bálint, Frantiszek Pieczka, Károly Kovács, József Madaras, Simon Surmiel, Zoltán Huszárik, Vilmos Kun, Sándor Halmágyi, Rita Békés, Kati Muharay, Kati Fráter, János Jani, Bertalan Papp, Elemér Szilágyi, Rózsa Gombik, Lehel Óhidy, Szilvia Tóth Szabó, Pál Horváth – colour – 2,496 metres; 91 minutes

SPIDER FOOTBALL
Pókfoci (1976)

Directed by János Rózsa – Screenplay: István Kardos – Camera: Elemér Ragályi – Music: János Bródy – Cast: József Madaras (principal), Judit Halász (Mrs Lengyel), Ádám Rajhona (Mr Lengyel), Hédi Temessy (deputy-principal in charge of general education), Róbert Koltai (physical training instructor), József Mentes (deputy-principal in charge of technical instruction), Péter Balázs (uniformed teacher), Ildikó Pécsi (Mrs Pelikán) – colour – 2,408 metres; 87 minutes

THE ACCENT
Ékezet (1977)

Directed by Ferenc Kardos – Screenplay: István Kardos – Camera: János Kende – Music: Levente Szörényi and the Fonográf Group –

Cast: Sándor Halmágyi (educational activist), Imre Sinkovits (works manager), Éva Ras (Aranka), Ádám Szirtes (steward) – colour – 2,576 metres; 94 minutes

TWO DECISIONS
Két elhatározás (1977)

Directed by Imre Gyöngyössy and Barna Kabay – Camera: Gábor Szabó – b/w – 2,050 metres; 75 minutes

THE PORTRAIT OF A CHAMPION
Küldetés (1977)

Directed by Ferenc Kósa – Camera: János Gulyás and Ferenc Káplár – b/w – 2,637 metres; 96 minutes

FLARE AND FLICKER
Teketória (1977)

Written and directed by Gyula Maár – Camera: Lajos Koltai – Music: György Selmeczi, Tamás Cseh, Géza Bereményi, Vilmos Körmendi and Lajos Boros – Cast: Mari Törőcsik (Teréz), Lenke Lórán (her lady-friend), Stefan Kvietik (works ingenieur), Péter Fried (the boy), Jozef Kroner (man in top-hat), Tamás Major (the pianist) – colour – 2,825 metres; 105 minutes

WHEN JOSEPH RETURNS...
Ha megjön József (1977)

Written and directed by Zsolt Kézdi-Kovács – Camera: János Kende – Cast: Lili Monori (Mária, Joseph's wife), Éva Ruttkai (Ágnes, Joseph's mother), György Pogány (Joseph), Gábor Koncz (the chauffeur), Mária Ronyecz (the chauffeur's boss)

THE TWO OF THEM
Ők ketten (1977)

Directed by Márta Mészáros – Screenplay: Ildikó Kórody, József Balázs, Géza Bereményi – Camera: János Kende – Music: György Kovács – Cast: Marina Vlady (Mari), Lili Monori (Juli), Miklós Tolnay (Feri, Mari's husband), Jan Nowicki (János, Juli's husband), Zsuzsa Czinkóczy (Zsuzsi, Juli's daughter)

Lost Illusions. Notorious in Hungary for his wittily subversive documentaries, director Gyula Gazdag has here created a comic "operetta" with incidental music by The Who. An update of the second part of the famous Balzac novel, transposed to Budapest in the summer of 1968 (after Paris but before Prague), it tells the seriocomic story of an ambitious young writer who comes from the provinces to make a career in the capital. This portrait of literary politics, combined, as in Balzac, with political politics and tangled sexual liaisons), makes this mordant satire consistently entertaining. Part of the joke, of course, is that in Paris or Budapest, 1838 or 1968, things are much the same, and our hero's illusions duly get lost. Hungary, 1982.

Index of Names and Titles

Index of Names and Titles